Design History Beyond the Canon

In memory of our mentor and friend, David Raizman.

Design History Beyond the Canon

Edited by

Jennifer Kaufmann-Buhler, Victoria Rose Pass, and
Christopher S. Wilson

BLOOMSBURY VISUAL ARTS
LONDON • NEW YORK • OXFORD • NEW DELHI • SYDNEY

BLOOMSBURY VISUAL ARTS
Bloomsbury Publishing Plc
50 Bedford Square, London, WC1B 3DP, UK
1385 Broadway, New York, NY 10018, USA
29 Earlsfort Terrace, Dublin 2, Ireland

BLOOMSBURY, BLOOMSBURY VISUAL ARTS and the Diana logo are trademarks of
Bloomsbury Publishing Plc

First published in Great Britain 2019
Paperback edition published 2023

© Editorial content and introductions, Jennifer Kaufmann-Buhler, Victoria Rose Pass,
and Christopher S. Wilson, 2023
© Individual chapters, their authors, 2023

Jennifer Kaufmann-Buhler, Victoria Rose Pass, and Christopher S. Wilson have asserted
their right under the Copyright, Designs and Patents Act, 1988, to be identified
as Editors of this work.

For legal purposes the Acknowledgements on p. xxiv constitute an extension of this
copyright page.

Cover design: Nancy Bernardo

All rights reserved. No part of this publication may be reproduced or transmitted
in any form or by any means, electronic or mechanical, including photocopying,
recording, or any information storage or retrieval system, without prior
permission in writing from the publishers.

Bloomsbury Publishing Plc does not have any control over, or responsibility for, any
third-party websites referred to or in this book. All internet addresses given in this
book were correct at the time of going to press. The author and publisher regret
any inconvenience caused if addresses have changed or sites have ceased to
exist, but can accept no responsibility for any such changes.

A catalogue record for this book is available from the British Library.

A catalog record for this book is available from the Library of Congress.

ISBN: HB: 978-1-3500-5158-4
       PB: 978-1-3503-5347-3
       ePDF: 978-1-3500-5160-7
       ePub: 978-1-3500-5159-1

Typeset by RefineCatch Limited, Bungay, Suffolk

To find out more about our authors and books visit www.bloomsbury.com
and sign up for our newsletters.

Contents

List of figures   vii
Foreword: A pre- and post-history of "Teaching the History of
    Modern Design: The Canon and Beyond"
    Carma Gorman and David Raizman   xii
Acknowledgments   xxiv

Introduction   *Jennifer Kaufmann-Buhler, Victoria Rose Pass,
    and Christopher S. Wilson*   1

Section 1   Users/Consumers
Kul'ttovary: Bringing culture into the Soviet home   *Yelena McLane*   17
Diversionary tactics at work: Making meaning through misuse
    Jennifer Kaufmann-Buhler   35
Everything old is new again: Modernization, historic preservation,
    and the American home, 1920–1966   *Emily Wolf*   49

Section 2   Intermediaries
Representing modern architecture in *The Rockford Files*,
    1974–1980   *Christopher S. Wilson*   71
CLOTHES CLOTHES CLOTHES PUNK PUNK PUNK WOMEN
    WOMEN WOMEN   *Maria Elena Buszek*   87
Using digital tools to work around the canon   *Matthew Bird*   111

Section 3   Designers
Confronting racial stereotypes in graphic design history
    Karen L. Carter   129
The Mangbetu coiffure: A story of cars, hats, branding,
    and appropriation   *Victoria Rose Pass*   145
Adventure play in physical and virtual spaces   *Gayle L. Goudy*   171
The case of William Pahlmann: Challenging the canon of modern
    design   *Marianne Eggler, Erica Morawski, and Sara
    Desvernine Reed*   189

"I was not a woman designer ... I was a designer who happened
 to be a woman" *Russell Flinchum*   209

Epilogue: Beyond the canon—building the case for and cases
 for interdisciplinary design history *Stephanie E. Vasko*   227

Notes on the contributors   235
Index   239

Figures

1.1	National Endowment for the Humanities (NEH) Summer institute small group discussion, 2015	xix
1.2	NEH Summer institute visit to the Philadelphia Museum of Art, 2015	xix
1.3	NEH Summer institute visit to the Fashion Institute of Technology, 2015	xx
1.4	NEH Summer institute visit to the Philadelphia Museum of Art, 2015	xx
2.1	Notebook sketch by Brockett Horne, 2015. Used with permission of the artist	2
2.2	Visual representation of the book by Brockett Horne, 2018. Used with permission of the artist	4
3.1	*Kul'ttovary* store, c. 1960	18
3.2	A loudspeaker and a "*Moskvich*" single-channel radio. Photo by Becki Rutta	23
3.3	Alexey Lavrov's "Buy the *Moskivich*" poster, 1950	24
3.4	Fotokor–1 camera, 1930. Photo by Becki Rutta	26
3.5	Various sports and games equipment. Photo by Becki Rutta	28
3.6	"*Nevalyashka*" roly-poly doll. Photo by Becki Rutta	30
3.7	Alexsandr Laktionov, *Moving to a New Apartment*, 1952. Donetsk Art Museum, Ukraine	31
4.1	Don's Boss Page, 1998. Used with permission from Don Pavlish	41
4.2	"Sabotage" image from *Processed World* 5, 1982. Used with permission from Chris Carlsson	43
5.1	Image from Philip Carey Company trade catalog, "Modern Home Building: Dependable Modern Building Materials," 1939	50
5.2	Page from Weatherbest Stained Shingle Company trade catalog, "Making Old Houses into Charming Homes," c. 1925	53
5.3	Montgomery Ward trade catalog cover, "Complete Catalog of Plumbing, Heating, Building Materials," 1935	55
5.4	Page from Johns-Manville Corporation trade catalog, "101 Practical Suggestions for Home Improvements," 1934	59
5.5	Page from United States Gypsum Company home building and home improvement guide, "Popular Home's Ideas Galore: How to Build, Buy, Modernize and Decorate," 1946	60
5.6	Page from Celotex Corporation trade catalog, "Home Improvement Pictorial," 1961	62
6.1	*The Rockford Files*, Charles R. Runkin Building, Season 2, Episode 14 © Roy Huggins Public Arts Productions/Cherokee Productions/ Universal Television 1974–1980	74

6.2 *The Rockford Files*, Charles R. Runkin Building, Season 2, Episode 14 © Roy Huggins Public Arts Productions/Cherokee Productions/ Universal Television 1974–1980 75
6.3 *The Rockford Files*, Santa Monica County Building, Season 5, Episode 3 © Roy Huggins Public Arts Productions/Cherokee Productions/ Universal Television 1974–1980 76
6.4 *The Rockford Files*, parking lot, Season 5, Episode 3 © Roy Huggins Public Arts Productions/Cherokee Productions/Universal Television 1974–1980 76
6.5 *The Rockford Files*, LAX airport, Season 3, Episode 1 © Roy Huggins Public Arts Productions/Cherokee Productions/Universal Television 1974–1980 77
6.6 *The Rockford Files*, Jim Rockford, Season 2, Episode 1 © Roy Huggins Public Arts Productions/Cherokee Productions/Universal Television 1974–1980 77
6.7 *The Rockford Files*, Los Angeles freeway, opening credits © Roy Huggins Public Arts Productions/Cherokee Productions/Universal Television 1974–1980 79
6.8 *The Rockford Files*, motel in Season 1, Episode 10 © Roy Huggins Public Arts Productions/Cherokee Productions/Universal Television 1974–1980 80
6.9 *The Rockford Files*, fast-food stand in Season 4, Episode 16 © Roy Huggins Public Arts Productions/Cherokee Productions/Universal Television 1974–1980 80
6.10 *The Rockford Files*, concrete parking garage in Season 5, Episode 14 © Roy Huggins Public Arts Productions/Cherokee Productions/Universal Television 1974–1980 81
6.11 *The Rockford Files*, hotel in Season 5, Episode 8 © Roy Huggins Public Arts Productions/Cherokee Productions/Universal Television 1974–1980 82
6.12 *The Rockford Files*, university in Season 4, Episode 13 © Roy Huggins Public Arts Productions/Cherokee Productions/Universal Television 1974–1980 82
6.13 *The Rockford Files*, federal building in Season 2, Episode 15 © Roy Huggins Public Arts Productions/Cherokee Productions/Universal Television 1974–1980 83
6.14 *The Rockford Files*, museum in Season 5, Episode 20 © Roy Huggins Public Arts Productions/Cherokee Productions/Universal Television 1974–1980 83
7.1 Detail of Viv Albertine's "corrected" introductory label, *Punk 1976–78* © British Library Board, 2016. Used with permission. 88
7.2 Photograph of "You're gonna wake up" T-shirt, 1976. Stolper Wilson Collection, London 92
7.3 Photograph of "Tits" T-shirt, 1976. Stolper Wilson Collection, London 95
7.4 Jane England, *Vivienne Westwood and Jordan, Seditionaries, London*, 1977 96

7.5 Photograph of Punks at The Roxy, 1977. Photo by PYMCA/UIG via Getty Images   98
7.6 Photograph of Poly Styrene, 1977. Photo by Daily Mirror/Mirrorpix/ Peter Stone   100
7.7 Photograph of Vivien Goldman and Neneh Cherry, 1970s. Photo by Caroline Coon via Camera Press   101
7.8 Photograph of Alex Michon, 1976. Photo by Alex Michon/Rocco Redondo, courtesy Alex Michon Archives   103
7.9 Photograph of Alex Michon, 1980–1981. Photo by Krystyna Kolowska, courtesy Alex Michon Archives   104
7.10 Photograph of Caroline Coon, 1978. Photo by Daily Mirror/ Mirrorpix/ Mike Maloney   104
7.11 Cover of 1981 *Best* magazine Courtesy of the author   106
8.1 Futurama lipstick case Revlon, collection of the author   115
8.2 Futurama lipstick patent, 1956 Revlon   116
8.3 Futurama lipstick advertisement, 1957 © Photographer commissioned by Revlon   117
8.4 3M DD–1 advertisement, 1947 © 1947 3M Co. Used with permission   118
8.5 3M DD–1 desk tape dispenser. Collection of the author   121
8.6 Edgar Kaufmann, Jr., *What Is Modern Design?*, 1950 Digital image © The Museum of Modern Art/licensed by SCALA/Art Resource, NY   123
9.1 Paul Colin, La Revue Négre, 1925, courtesy of Posters Please, Inc. © 2018 Artists Rights Society (ARS), New York/ADAGP, Paris   135
9.2 Paul Colin, "Josephine Baker, Banana Skirt," 1927, courtesy of Posters Please, Inc. © 2018 Artists Rights Society (ARS), New York/ADAGP, Paris   136
9.3 Emile Lévy (printer), "Ambassadeurs Les Jolly Koon'ess," 1885 © Bibliothèque nationale de France, n.d., Cabinet des Estampes, ENT DN–1 (LEVY, Emile)-FT6, W001101. 138
10.1 Image of Nobosodru, 1925. Manbetu woman Nobosodru, wife of Mangbetu King Touba, Niangra, Belgian Congo [femme d'un chef Mangbetu (Congo Belque)] photograph by Léon Poirier and Georges Specht, 1925, photogravure. Published by La Croisière Noire, *c.* 1926, EEPA postcard collection CG-20-76, Eliot Elisofon Photographic Archives, National Museum of African Art, Smithsonian Institution   146
10.2 Poster for *La Croisière Noire* film, 1926 © Musée du Quai Branly-Jacques Chirac, dist. RMN-Grand Palais/Art Resource, NY   153
10.3 Josephine Baker modeling a hat, 1926   157
10.4 Baron Adolph de Meyer, a hat by Agnés from *Harpers Bazaar*, 1926   159
10.5 Alexandre Iacovleff, image of Madame Agnés from *Vogue*, 1926   160
10.6 Beyoncé in *Lemonade*, 2016. Beyoncé in *Lemonade*, directed by Kahlil Joseph, Beyoncé Knowles Carter, Melina Matsoukas, Todd Tourso, Dikayl Rimmasch, Jonas Åkerlund, and Mark Romanek, 2016. New York, NY: Parkwood Entertainment   163

x *Figures*

10.7 Photograph of Josephine Baker, *c.* 1925. Getty Images/Keystone France/
     Contributor 164
11.1 Bob Cassilly, City Museum. Photo by Rick Kupferer III 173
11.2 Bob Cassilly, City Museum. Photo by Rick Kupferer III 174
11.3 Toshiko Horiuchi MacAdam, "Kaleidoscape," 2013. Photos provided
     by the Children's Museum of Winston-Salem, North Carolina 175
11.4 Toshiko Horiuchi MacAdam, "Takino Rainbow Nest," 2000. Photos by
     Masaki Koizumi provided by NetPlayWorks and Charles MacAdam 176
11.5 Antoni Gaudí's inverted catenary arch model Rüdiger Marmulla/
     Attribution-ShareAlike 3.0. Unported (CC BY-SA 3.0) 177
11.6 Tile work, Shah Mosque, Isfahan, Iran, 1611–1629. Photo by
     Amir Sarabadani 178
11.7 Toshiko Horiuchi MacAdam, "Gothic Arches, Romanesque Church,"
     1976. Courtesy of NetPlayWorks and Charles MacAdam 178
11.8 Nest of the Baya Weaver. Photo by J. M. Garg 180
11.9 *Windosill* computer game, 2009 182
11.10 *Journey* computer game, 2012 183
11.11 *Imagination Playground*, 2011. Photo courtesy of *Imagination
     Playground* 185
12.1 Calvert whiskey's "Man of Distinction" advertisement, 1949. Courtesy
     of Hagley Museum and Library, Series 9, Box 11, Book 4, William
     Pahlmann Papers (Accession 2388), Manuscripts and Archives
     Department, Wilmington, DE 19807 190
12.2 William Pahlmann book plate. Courtesy of Hagley Museum and Library,
     William Pahlmann Papers (Accession 2388), Manuscripts and Archives
     Department, Wilmington, DE 19807 192
12.3 Interior of the Forum of the Twelve Caesars restaurant, 1957. Courtesy
     of Hagley Museum and Library, Hagley ID 2388_09172012_24,
     Series IX, Box OS 7, Folder Public Interiors, Book 16, William Pahlmann
     Papers (Accession 2388), Manuscripts and Archives Department,
     Wilmington, DE 19807 196
12.4 "Pahlmann Peruvian" model room, 1941. Courtesy of Hagley Museum
     and Library, Series 9, Box 1, Book 1, William Pahlmann Papers (Accession
     2388), Manuscripts and Archives Department, Wilmington, DE 19807 199
12.5 Living room designed for Pahlmann Previews, 1954. Courtesy of
     Hagley Museum and Library, Series 9, Box 6, Book 13, William
     Pahlmann Papers (Accession 2388), Manuscripts and Archives
     Department, Wilmington, DE 19807 201
13.1 Publicity photograph of MaryEllen Dohrs, 1951. Collection of
     Russell Flinchum 210
13.2 MaryEllen Dohrs, General Motors, 1950. Courtesy of MaryEllen Dohrs 211
13.3 MaryEllen Dohrs, *Water Wagon*, 1958. Courtesy of MaryEllen Dohrs 212
13.4 Alexander Kostellow at Pratt, 1950. Courtesy of MaryEllen Dohrs 215
13.5 MaryEllen Dohrs, sketch of modular kitchen with female figure.
     Courtesy of MaryEllen Dohrs 216

13.6	MaryEllen Dohrs, Food Mill for Landers, Frary Clark, 1953–1956. Courtesy of MaryEllen Dohrs	217
13.7	Advertisement for "Kid-Size" table and chairs. Courtesy of MaryEllen Dohrs	218
13.8	MaryEllen Dohrs, "Medallion" luggage for Samsonite. Courtesy of MaryEllen Dohrs	219
13.9	Advertisement for Packard Caribbean, 1955. Courtesy of MaryEllen Dohrs	220
13.10	MaryEllen Dohrs, interior scheme for Packard, 1954. Courtesy of MaryEllen Dohrs	221
13.11	MaryEllen Dohrs, jukebox for Seeberg, 1955. Courtesy of MaryEllen Dohrs	222
13.12	MaryEllen Dohrs, sketch of modular kitchen. Courtesy of MaryEllen Dohrs	222
13.13	Harley Earl and MaryEllen Dohrs, 1950. Courtesy of MaryEllen Dohrs	223

Foreword

A pre- and post-history of "Teaching the History of Modern Design: The Canon and Beyond"

Carma Gorman and David Raizman

All of the authors and editors of this book were participants in a four-week National Endowment for the Humanities (NEH) Summer Institute called "Teaching the History of Modern Design: The Canon and Beyond" that we offered at Drexel University in July 2015. These authors and editors might never have met one another, nor we them, had it not been for the month we shared together in Philadelphia. Because this book is ultimately a product of the institute, the editors have kindly invited us to preface it by presenting our goals for the institute and our perceptions of its impact.

Three factors shaped our aims for the institute. The first was our parallel experiences in the 1990s as instructors new to teaching design history, in a country that lacked many of the infrastructures typical of a scholarly discipline. The second was our shared "instrumentalist" bent as instructors, a perspective shaped by our many years of teaching design history to undergraduate design majors, and especially by our recent experiences as faculty appointed to and/or housed in design programs. The third factor was our realization in the early 2010s that many, if not most, of the (still relatively few and mostly survey-level) design history courses being offered in US universities and art schools were being taught by faculty who had trained as designers or art historians, and who had in many cases, like us, had little or no formal instruction in design history themselves.

Although we are sixteen years apart in age, attended different undergraduate and graduate programs, and came to design history from different directions, our journeys were in many respects remarkably parallel. We were both trained as art historians: David as a medievalist, Carma as an Americanist. Though like many people in our respective fields, we both had an interest in material culture, neither of us ever had an opportunity to take a survey of the history of industrial or graphic design—as opposed to a survey of art history or architectural history—during our undergraduate or graduate studies. Nonetheless, after realizing that a survey of design history was listed in Drexel University's College of Design Arts course catalog but was not being regularly offered, David volunteered to teach it, and at the request of the design faculty, began doing so regularly in 1992. This "combined" survey course addressed graphic and industrial design along with the decorative arts. In the mid-1990s, he also began teaching a new required course for graphic design majors entitled "History of 20th-Century Graphic Design and Beyond." Carma, in contrast, was hired in 1998 at

Southern Illinois University Carbondale specifically to teach—as part of an otherwise fairly conventional art historical teaching load—one section per year of the history of industrial design. In 2001, at the request of the communication design faculty, she also began teaching a separate survey of the history of graphic design that until that date had been taught by a member of the design faculty.

Both of us faced very steep learning curves in preparing to teach these courses, not only because we had had no formal training in design history ourselves, but also because the infrastructure of the field of design history was at a very different stage of development in the USA in the 1990s than it was in the UK. In Britain, a number of institutions already offered master's and doctoral degrees in the history of design, which provided even British institutions that lacked design history degree programs of their own with a pipeline of qualified instructors. Moreover, the UK-based Design History Society, established in 1977, sponsored annual conferences that allowed those teaching and doing scholarship in the field to learn from one another, and in 1988 began publishing the peer-reviewed *Journal of Design History* in conjunction with Oxford University Press. In contrast, prior to the establishment of the Bard Graduate Center's master's and doctoral programs in design, decorative arts, and material culture in 1993, the US had no doctoral programs specifically dedicated to design history. A notable MA program in the field was the Winterthur Program in Early American Culture (established by the University of Delaware and the Winterthur Museum in 1952), but like Yale's art history doctoral program, which also offered coursework in the decorative arts, its focus was until recently on the eighteenth and nineteenth centuries (the program did change its name to the "Winterthur Program in American Material Culture" in 2007 to reflect that its emphasis was no longer exclusively on "early" American material culture).

Although it is difficult to estimate the percentage of US universities and art schools that regularly offered design history courses, anecdotal information suggests that at many institutions a member of the design faculty taught at most a one- or two-semester-long survey course tailored to majors in a specific design field such as fashion, interior, or graphic design. Very few American institutions could claim at that time to regularly offer upper-division or graduate-level courses in design history. Moreover, there were no professional organizations dedicated to the history of design in the USA, nor any annual conferences devoted to research or teaching in the field. (Design Forum, an affiliated society of the College Art Association that was established in 1983, had ceased sponsoring conference sessions at the CAA annual conference by the mid-1990s.) In the USA of the late 1990s, there was therefore no ready means by which new entrants to the field could network with established teacher-scholars, nor even any easy way of reviewing syllabi from design history courses at other institutions.

Fortunately, even in those early days of dial-up modem connections to the primarily text-based internet—that is, prior to the existence of what have since become essential design-historical resources, including Google Images (2001), YouTube (2005), Google Patents (2006), Pinterest (2010), and Instagram (2010)—we were not *entirely* lacking in resources. We were both lucky enough to be teaching at research institutions whose libraries owned or were willing to purchase what were then the essential texts in the field, and that also subscribed to *Winterthur Portfolio* (Winterthur Museum/University of Chicago Press, 1964–present), *Design Issues* (MIT press, 1984–present), *Journal of Design History* (Design History Society/Oxford University Press, 1988–present), and *Studies in the Decorative Arts* (now *West 86th Street*, Bard Graduate Center/University of Chicago Press, 1993–present). Even so, Jstor, begun in 1995, did not provide access to even the most prominent journals in art history until at least the year 2000, and did not add major design history journals such as *Design Issues* and *Journal of Design History* until later in the decade. Thus, we both labored mightily to gather clean originals of readings for photocopied course packs and to create (35mm film!) slides that suited the courses and the students we were teaching.

The problem with most of the design historical literature that was available at the time, however, was that it was either too scholarly or not scholarly enough for our teaching needs. Although we found Clive Dilnot's and John Walker's literature reviews (1984 and 1989, respectively) illuminating, and benefited greatly from the meticulously researched essays on specialized topics in *Design Issues* and the *Journal of Design History*, the vast majority of the undergraduate design majors enrolled in our courses could not be compelled to read lengthy, heavily footnoted research articles, many of which were written in what our students deemed to be impenetrable academese.[1] Even students who gave it their best shot seldom had enough prior knowledge of design history to fully follow the journal articles' arguments. Much of the "serious" academic literature that was available at the time was simply too long, too specialized, too poorly illustrated, and/or too theoretical for the needs of most of our design students, who entered our classes with virtually no prior knowledge of design history and only fuzzy recollections of the art history surveys they had taken a year or two earlier.[2]

Conversely, students had less difficulty comprehending the survey texts that were available on the US market in the late 1990s, but many ended their narratives too early in the twentieth century (Giedion, Pevsner, Ferebee, Pulos, Heskett, Forty, Conway, Frank); others focused *only* on the twentieth century (Dormer, Hiesinger and Marcus, Woodham, Fiell); some were too sparsely illustrated to meet the needs of students unfamiliar with the works being discussed (Sparke); and many others focused on a single style or a limited span of time (Duncan, Meikle, Smith, Collins, and most exhibition catalogs). Hollis's and Meggs's graphic design survey texts were among the only affordable books on the market that provided undergraduates who were unfamiliar with the fixtures of the design historical canon with well-illustrated chronological and stylistic narratives of sufficiently broad temporal range to be useful for our needs.[3]

We were of course both well aware of the drawbacks of survey texts, which—by focusing on "greatest hits" and "things well-educated designers are expected to know"—perpetuated a canon favoring museum-quality works of "good design" over "ordinary" and "merely commercial" works, and works by named, individual, white, male, European or American consultant/freelance designers over works designed by women, people of color, in-house designers, design teams, and uncredited/unknown individuals or teams. However, one must start somewhere, and we both started in the early 2000s by publishing the textbooks that we wished had been available when we first began teaching design history: namely, books that covered a wide span of historical time, including the recent past, in what were to us at the time familiar art historical ways. Like most primary-source readers and survey texts in art history, then, our books focused on the West, were organized chronologically, and favored the writings and works of named, white, male designers. Carma's *The Industrial Design Reader* (2003) featured short, chronologically organized selections of canonical writings, most (but not all) of which were written by famous white, male, European or American designers. David's *History of Modern Design* (first edition, 2004) was a chronological introduction to the canonical designers, works, and styles of industrial design, graphic design, and the decorative arts (primarily but not exclusively) in Europe and the USA. Both of these books, like their predecessors, then, were essentially attempts to *define* a canon of works, designers, and styles that we suspected our students' employers and clients would expect them to know, and to provide new instructors of design history courses with a basic road-map to a terrain with which they were likely not entirely familiar.

When the two of us first met in February 2004 at the College Art Association (CAA) annual conference in Seattle, shortly after the publication of our books, enrollment in undergraduate design degree programs had been rising steadily for at least a decade, and the barriers to teaching design history were becoming significantly less daunting. Carma had revived the CAA-affiliated society Design Forum in 2001 and created an email announcement list for the group, and under the new name Design Studies Forum, it began sponsoring one or two sessions and a business meeting each year at the CAA annual conference. Moreover, Berg's (now Bloomsbury's) decision to publish books and journals in the field of design history resulted in a welcome increase in the number of design history textbooks and readers on the market in the early 2000s, which certainly improved matters. In addition, more resources were becoming available on the internet (though fewer than one might at first recall: both of us were still teaching with slide projectors, since only a few of our classrooms at that time were equipped with digital projectors, and because locating high-quality digital images online was still a challenge).

These new developments, though very welcome, were still not sufficient to rectify the underlying structural problem: that American universities still offered few upper-division and graduate courses in design history, and were turning out at most a handful or two of PhD students each year who were well prepared to teach design history to students of design. Although we agree with design historian Kjetil Fallan that design history should not be construed *solely* as a service discipline, we nonetheless share the perhaps unfashionably instrumentalist view that one of design history's most important functions is to help inform the ways in which designers think.[4] From our experiences teaching undergraduate design majors, we had both come to believe that designers-in-training—who will quite literally determine the shape of things to come—need and deserve instruction that presents the past as a useful and actionable repository of insights into contemporary practice.

It is admittedly challenging to teach and write design history in ways that are useful to *both* design historians and designers. However, we shared a conviction that embracing—rather than distancing—design practice and design practitioners was not only key to establishing the field of design history on firmer footing in the USA, but also to developing research methods that are specific to the history of design. The vast majority of design historians have been content to employ the research methods and critical approaches that literary critics, cultural historians, and art historians developed decades ago for use in their own fields. But design has different aims, and operates under fundamentally different assumptions and constraints, from art, literature, film, architecture, and other creative fields. It therefore seems logical to expect that those design historians who are the most knowledgeable about both contemporary and historical design practices—and in particular about the economic, legal, material, and political constraints that have conditioned the activities of most designers and their clients—will also be among the scholars best positioned to develop research methods that are appropriate specifically to the study of design.

By the late 2000s, at a moment when design majors outnumbered art majors in most US schools of art and design, we had both become confident enough in our design historical scholarship and teaching to begin introducing ourselves professionally as design historians rather than art historians. We also became increasingly evangelical. We shared the belief that design majors deserved at very least a one- or two-semester survey of design history, as well as a suite of advanced history/theory/criticism course offerings comparable in scope to those that students of art and architecture had long enjoyed. But we also knew that if design programs continued expanding at their recent pace, the scarcity of doctoral programs in design history in the USA would make staffing the current (scanty) design history course offerings even more challenging than it already was.

In hopes of encouraging US institutions to bolster their design history course offerings, and perhaps to develop master's and doctoral degree programs in design history as well, David proposed and Carma agreed to help organize sessions about the teaching of design history at the National Association of Schools of Art and Design (NASAD) annual meetings in 2010 and 2011 (NASAD then invited us back to run a half-day pre-conference workshop on the same subject in 2012 in Milwaukee). Feedback we received from participants in these very well-attended sessions suggested that the vast majority of people who were teaching design history in US colleges had had little to no training in design history themselves: design history had not been offered when and where they had attended school, just as it had not been when we were in school. Moreover, informal polls conducted at these sessions suggested that roughly fifty to sixty percent of the faculty who were teaching undergraduate design history surveys had been trained as designers. Art and architectural historians constituted the next-largest group at approximately thirty to forty percent, followed by a small minority of instructors (at most, five percent each) who indicated that they had been trained either in the fine arts or in a humanistic or social science field such as history, anthropology, sociology, or communications. Most of these faculty had to pick up what knowledge they had about design history on their own, as best they could. We knew from experience what a stressful way this was to prepare to teach a new course. Admittedly, the internet, digital projectors, and the flurry of new textbooks and readers that had recently appeared on the market made the task far less daunting than it had been even five or six years earlier. Nonetheless, it seemed clear to us that the only way to meet even the current demand for qualified design history instructors was to find ways to make it easier for art historians and design faculty who were interested in teaching design history to do so successfully.

The large numbers of attendees at the NASAD sessions, and their evident interest in learning about design history and in talking about the pleasures and pitfalls of teaching it, sparked David to begin working on a proposal for a 2013 NEH summer institute that would focus—somewhat unusually for the NEH—on college-level *teaching* of, rather than on research into, design history. David invited Carma to participate in the development of the institute, and as co-directors, we submitted our first NEH proposal in early 2012. Although it was among the seventy-five percent of that year's proposals that were not funded, with encouragement from Deborah Hurtt, Senior Program Officer with the NEH's Division of Education Programs, we submitted a revised proposal in February 2014 for a summer 2015 institute, this time with David as project director, and Carma—who had just relocated to UT Austin and was wary of assuming additional responsibilities—as project faculty. Taking into consideration peer reviewers' and NEH staff comments from the 2012 submission, and cognizant of the results of our informal NASAD polls about the backgrounds of the people who were actually teaching design history courses in the USA, our new proposal was for a thematically organized institute of four weeks' duration called "Teaching the History of Design: The Canon and Beyond."

This proposal—one of seventeen funded from a field of forty-six—hinged on the notion that the scholarship and teaching of design history, and in particular the canon promoted by most survey textbooks, depended far too heavily upon art historical paradigms that privileged expensive, rare objects found in museum collections over inexpensive, ubiquitous ones; objects that hewed to modernist notions of "good design" over objects whose appearance was "commercially motivated" or dictated by other priorities; works by named, individual (usually white male), "star" consultant/freelance designers over the works of women, designers of color, in-house designers, design teams, and unknown designers; and works from Europe and the USA over works by people elsewhere in the world. We hoped that by addressing the biases embedded in the design historical canon head-on, we might help participants to envision design history, and design itself, as a field with aims, values, and methods distinct from those of art history and the fine arts. To that end, we chose to dedicate one week of the summer institute to each of three themes—taste and popular culture; women as consumers and producers of design; and political and global interpretations of design after World War II—that we believed were sufficiently flexible to allow us both to acknowledge the canon (for the benefit of participants who were not already wholly familiar with it) *and* to challenge it. We reserved the final (fourth) week for presentations by teams of the Summer Scholars, whom we charged with designing a lesson plan for a single day's class meeting of an undergraduate survey course that would engage with one or more of the institute's three themes and also require students to actively engage with either a local collection or an online archival resource (such as patent drawings and descriptions from PatFT, Google Patents, or Espacenet; scans of manufacturers' catalogs or other primary sources from archive.org, HathiTrust, or Google Books; images of objects and ephemera from eBay, Pinterest, YouTube, etc.).

Our proposal was therefore an atypical one for NEH to fund, not only because it focused more explicitly on teaching than on research, but also because it welcomed participants who held or were working toward degrees other than the PhD, including the MFA, MA, and BFA. With the assistance of external reviewer Daniel Huppatz of Swinburne University of Technology (Melbourne), we ultimately selected from a pool of nearly seventy applicants a mix of twenty-five graphic designers, interior designers, historians of modern art, architectural historians, fashion historians, a historian of Asian art, and a chemist. We prioritized applicants who were already teaching, or who were imminently scheduled to teach, design history, and sought to strike a balance among designers, art historians, and faculty from other fields that approximately echoed the percentages we had observed in our NASAD sessions. Our rationale for this decision was twofold. First, many US institutions of higher learning grant "degree equivalency" to design professionals who can demonstrate professional expertise, experience, and/or renown commensurate with that of terminal degree-holders in their field, but these faculty have typically had even fewer opportunities than most to take courses in the history of design. Second, we reasoned that in a field in which the country's only graduate programs were small and of recent vintage, applicants' demonstrated interest in design history was a far more germane selection criterion than their academic credentials. Anyone convinced enough of the value of design history to undertake teaching it at the college level—even/especially in the absence of any prior training in the field—was *exactly* the kind of person we were most interested in working with, and also the kind of person who seemed likely to derive the greatest benefit from participating.

During the four weeks of the institute, the group heard from a distinguished group of visiting scholars about those themes, including Regina Lee Blaszczyk, University of Leeds; Maria Elena Buszek, University of Denver; Vladimir Kulic, Florida Atlantic University; Catharine Rossi, Kingston University; and Sarah Teasley, Royal College of Art. Professor Blaszczyk, in fact, did not just visit one day but played an ongoing role in the institute. Because she writes from a business-history perspective, and has argued (most notably in her book *Imagining Consumers*) that design historians have overplayed the significance of consultant designers and underestimated the contributions of manufacturers and other intermediaries in shaping style, she was particularly well-suited to contribute to a summer institute that challenged the design historical canon. For example, Blaszczyk led a lively session in which she asked small groups of participants to analyze manufacturers' catalogs and other ephemera she had purchased inexpensively on eBay, demonstrating that even faculty at institutions without significant archival holdings could engage students in primary-source research. In addition, Blaszczyk accompanied the group on its field trip to the Hagley Museum and Library in Delaware, where we viewed archival materials not only from the Raymond Loewy and William Pahlmann collections, but also color cards and ephemera from the Textile Color Card Association (which, as Blaszczyk discusses in her book *The Color Revolution*, guided many early twentieth-century manufacturers' design choices). Blaszczyk also accompanied the group to the Philadelphia Museum of Art, where we spent a considerable amount of time in the American pressed glass collection, discussing the ways in which instructors can make use of local collections of objects that are non-canonical in medium or style to help students understand the criteria of "quality" that undergird the canon. (Namely, the canon tends to reflect the biases of collectors and curators whose art and decorative arts collections favor objects that

Foreword

Figure 1.1 Participants of the "Teaching the History of Modern Design: The Canon and Beyond" NEH Summer Institute responding to a discussion question about intellectual property, Drexel University, Philadelphia, July 2015.

Figure 1.2 Participants of the "Teaching the History of Modern Design: The Canon and Beyond" NEH Summer Institute visit "Northern Lights: Scandinavian Design" at the Philadelphia Museum of Art, July 2015.

Figure 1.3 Participants of the "Teaching the History of Modern Design: The Canon and Beyond" NEH Summer Institute visit the Study Collection at the Museum of the Fashion Institute of Technology, New York, July 2015.

Figure 1.4 Participants of the "Teaching the History of Modern Design: The Canon and Beyond" NEH Summer Institute examining objects in the Costume and Textile Study Room, Philadelphia Museum of Art, July 2015.

were rare and expensive over those that were ordinary and affordable.) Similarly, in introducing architecture, tourism, and fashion initiatives from the former Yugoslavia, Professor Kulic moved "beyond the canon" geographically, challenging the usual monolithic narratives about design from the eastern side of the Iron Curtain. Kulic's presentation spurred fruitful discussions about the ways in which canonical narratives position some regions of the world as "centers" and others as "peripheries."

However one chooses to measure it, the institute's impact exceeded our expectations. First, the institute seems to have spurred many of the participants to begin speaking about and publishing more of their own scholarship in design history. We were pleased to see participants organize and present a session at the 2016 NASAD annual meeting, and show up in force to present papers and chair sessions at the Popular Culture Association/American Culture Association conference in 2016, the Southeastern College Art Conference (SECAC) in 2016, and the College Art Association conferences in 2017 (New York) and 2018 (Los Angeles). Individually and collectively—as the chapters in this book attest—they have been remarkably productive in expanding the canon of modern design by addressing a wide range of subject matter and, in some cases, devising novel research methods.

Second, one of our hopes was that the institute would provide a career boost to those who participated in it, and indeed, many participants have advanced quite rapidly in the profession since mid–2015. Two participants have returned to graduate school to pursue additional advanced degrees; three participants have moved to new full-time positions; those working as part-time and adjunct instructors have in many cases secured more favorable contracts in their current positions; one full-time faculty member has become head of her program; and another has just earned tenure.

Third, many participants are now engaging in significant professional service in the field. One Summer Scholar became the first design/decorative arts reviews editor for CAA; another continues to serve as reviews editor and managing editor of *Design and Culture*, and as a workshop leader for Design Incubation; another was elected president of Design Studies Forum in 2017; and she and another participant also serve as members of the College Art Association's newly formed Committee on Design.

Fourth, David had expressed a hope in one of his initial emails to Carma in 2011 that the institute "could create a network of people that will have had the experience of learning material and then implementing it and perhaps staying in touch, and then building further with more networking at NASAD and elsewhere." That goal, too, has certainly been met. Like most scholarly groups, the "NEHbors" share useful news, announcements, and resources via an email list and Facebook group. But the real power of what one participant colorfully described as our "hive mind" is that it is friendly. Asking research and teaching questions of strangers on larger, more contentious design research lists is not always productive; doing so on the NEHbors list usually is. As one participant observed, "I'm delighted to leave [the institute] with a stronger sense of a DH-oriented intellectual community. My scholarship [will] be better now that I have the perspectives and knowledge of the seminar's members at my fingertips."

Fifth, in the evaluations that participants anonymously submitted to the NEH, a surprising number described the institute's effects on their teaching and/or their scholarship with words such as *transformative* or *life-changing*. We felt the same way. The institute re-energized us professionally, particularly as teachers. We learned a great deal from the teaching methods and experiences of the participants, and in particular from those who were experienced at teaching online and at incorporating social media tools into the classroom. Last but not least, we made a lot of new friends, many of whom have proven to be helpful interlocutors and advisors on our own research and teaching.

In sum, we remain incredibly grateful to the NEH for funding "The Canon and Beyond," which we both consider a high point in our careers. We have been surprised and delighted by its positive impacts, many of which—including this book—we did not anticipate. Although we both remain convinced that in the long term it is important to increase the number of universities in the United States that offer master's and doctoral degrees in design history, the institute reassured us that there are other, arguably more expedient, means of building the nation's design historical teaching and research capacity. We are pleased and proud to see so many of the participants from the institute working together to bring this volume to fruition, and—more broadly—working together to continue building the field of design history in the USA.

Notes

1. Clive Dilnot, "The State of Design History, Part I: Mapping the Field," *Design Issues*, 1(1) (Spring, 1984): 4–23; Clive Dilnot, "The State of Design History, Part II: Problems and Possibilities," *Design Issues*, 1(2) (Autumn, 1984): 3–20; John Walker, *Design History and the History of Design* (London: Pluto Press, 1989).
2. Two of the earliest readers in design history were composed of reprints of articles on design historical topics that had previously been published in *Design Issues*: Victor Margolin, ed., *Design Discourse: History, Theory, Criticism* (Chicago and London: University of Chicago Press, 1989); Dennis Doordan, ed., *Design History: An Anthology* (Cambridge, MA: MIT Press, 1996).
3. The works referred to in this paragraph by authors' last names are, in order of appearance, Siegfried Giedion, *Mechanization Takes Command: A Contribution to Anonymous History* (New York: Oxford University Press, 1948); Nikolaus Pevsner, *Pioneers of Modern Design* (Harmondsworth: Penguin, 1960); Ann Ferebee, *A History of Design from the Victorian Era to the Present: A Survey of the Modern Style in Architecture, Interior Design, Industrial Design, Graphic Design, and Photography* (New York: Van Nostrand Reinhold, 1970); Arthur Pulos, *The American Design Ethic* (Cambridge, MA: MIT Press, 1983) and *The American Design Adventure* (Cambridge, MA: MIT Press, 1990); John Heskett, *Industrial Design* (New York: Oxford University Press, 1980); Adrian Forty, *Objects of Desire: Design and Society since 1750* (London: Thames & Hudson, 1986); Hazel Conway, *Design History: A Student's Handbook* (London: Allen & Unwin, 1987); Isabelle Frank, ed., *The Theory of Decorative Art: An Anthology of European and American Writings 1750–1940* (New Haven and London: Yale University Press, 2000); Peter Dormer, *Design since 1945* (New York and London: Thames & Hudson, 1993); Kathryn Hiesinger and George Marcus, *Landmarks of Twentieth-Century Design: An Illustrated Handbook* (New York: Abbeville Press, 1993); Jonathan M. Woodham, *Twentieth-Century Design* (Oxford and New York: Oxford

University Press, 1997); Charlotte and Peter Fiell, *Design of the 20th Century* (Cologne: Taschen, 2000); Penny Sparke, *An Introduction to Design and Culture in the Twentieth Century* (New York: Abbeville Press, 1988); Alastair Duncan, *Art Deco* (London: Thames & Hudson, 1988); Alastair Duncan, *Art Nouveau* (London: Thames & Hudson, 1994); Jeffrey Meikle, *Twentieth-Century Limited: Industrial Design in America, 1925–1939* (Philadelphia: Temple University Press, 1979; revised 2001); Terry Smith, *Making the Modern: Industry, Art, and Design in America* (Chicago and London: University of Chicago Press, 1993); Michael Collins and Andreas Papadakis, *Post-Modern Design* (New York: Rizzoli, 1989); Richard Hollis, *Graphic Design: A Concise History* (London: Thames & Hudson; revised 2002); Philip Meggs, *History of Graphic Design* (Hoboken, NJ: John Wiley & Sons, 1982; 6th edn. revised 2016 by Alston Purvis).

4 Kjetil Fallan, "De-Tooling Design History: To What Purpose and For Whom Do We Write?" *Design and Culture*, 5(1) (2013): 13–20.

Acknowledgments

The editors of this volume wish to acknowledge all of the scholars and faculty who participated in the NEH Summer Institute "Teaching the History of Modern Design: The Canon and Beyond." The conversations we have sought to capture and continue in this volume were created by this group, and without each voice these discussions would have been far less rich. As you will see in this volume, for many of us who participated in this Summer Institute, the experience altered our perspectives, as only spending a month living in a college dormitory and learning alongside twenty-four other scholars can do. The interdisciplinary nature of this group, evidenced in the scholarly and design work in this volume, helped to shape the points of view of the editors.

For that we are grateful to the support of the National Endowment for the Humanities. Without the support of the NEH, this group would never have been brought together, most of the included essays never written, and many of our teaching practices would not be nearly as rich as they are now. We are also indebted to David Raizman and Carma Gorman who shaped this unlikely community through the planning and facilitation of this institute, with an eye towards developing the field of design history in the US. We are grateful for their generosity and warmth and their continued efforts to help us stay connected. Thanks also to Drexel University for hosting the institute. We, as the editors, also owe our sincere appreciation to our families (and friend families) who have supported us as we have brought this project to fruition.

The NEH Summer Scholars:

Nancy Bernardo
Mark Biddle
Matthew Bird
Karen L. Carter
Marianne Eggler
Mark Fetkewicz
Russell Flinchum
Gayle Goudy
Keith Holz
Brockett Horne
Karla Huebner
Jennifer Kaufmann-Buhler
Kristopher Kersey
Anya Kurennaya

Yelena McLane
Erica Morawski
Sara Reed
Victoria Rose Pass
Kim Sels
Gunnar Swanson
Maggie Taft
Harry Turfle
Stephanie E. Vasko
Christopher S. Wilson
Emily Wolf

The Institute Faculty:

David Raizman, Director
Carma Gorman, Project Faculty
Regina Lee Blaszczyk, Visiting Scholar
Maria Elena Buszek, Visiting Scholar
Catharine Rossi, Visiting Scholar
Vladimir Kulic, Visiting Scholar
Sarah Teasley, Visiting Scholar

We are also indebted to the museums and collections we visited as a part of the Summer Institute and their excellent curators, librarians, archivists, and other staff members (only some of whom are named here):
The Philadelphia Museum of Art, Philadelphia (Elisabeth Agro and Christine Haugland)
The Hagley Museum and Library, Wilmington
The Fox Historic Costume Collection, Drexel University, Philadelphia (Clare Sauro)
The Gladys Marcus Library at the Fashion Institute of Technology: Special Collections and College Archives, New York (Karen Trivette and April Calahan)
The Study Collection at the Museum at FIT, New York
The Museum of Art & Design, New York (Glenn Adamson and Jennifer Scanlan)
Fox and Lewalski Polish Poster Collection at Drexel University, Philadelphia (Mark Willie and Kim Coulter)
Shofuso, Japanese House and Garden, Fairmount Park, Philadelphia

In Memory

In 2021 we lost our dear friend and mentor David Raizman. Without David this book would quite simply not exist. As noted in their preface, he and Carma Gorman brought us together in the summer of 2015. David was an exceptionally generous person and he supported so many of us with his feedback, his encouragement, and his curiosity. Though David was a renowned scholar in design history, he was not a gatekeeper in the field, but rather invited others to join the conversation. He built communities and this book is a document of one of them. David's work was not about finishing a conversation, but rather about starting one, and inviting others to see themselves as having a place in that conversation. We hope this book serves as a testament to David's influence on the field and an invitation to continue to do the work of expanding the objects we study, the voices we hear, and the stories we tell in design history.

Introduction

Jennifer Kaufmann-Buhler, Victoria Rose Pass, and Christopher S. Wilson

This book comes out of a National Endowment of the Humanities Summer Institute, "Teaching the History of Modern Design: The Canon and Beyond," held in July 2015 at Drexel University. As Carma Gorman and David Raizman detail in their Foreword, the institute brought together scholars and designers from a variety of institutions in the United States who are all tasked with teaching the history of design to design students. For those of us who participated in the intensive and immersive experience of the institute, the creation of a network of colleagues teaching the history of design in the United States has been one of the most valuable results.[1] For many of us, it was also a transformative experience in terms of our careers, research interests, and teaching.

During our four weeks at Drexel, our group spent significant time asking questions about the future of the field, the structure of the discipline and the bounds of design. What would an established design history field look like in the US? Do any easily defined boundaries exist between design, art, and craft (illustrated in a page from Brockett Horne's notes, Figure 2.1)? What are the methods of design history? What are the materials of design history? The subjects? The objects? Whose stories are we telling, and who is telling those stories? Is design a profession, or an act, or a material? The discussions that started over the course of those four weeks have continued. We have brought them into our classrooms, we have continued talking via email and social media, and these issues have also found their way into our research. This collection of essays is an effort to invite others into those conversations.

The canon was a spectral presence throughout the institute; it appeared in our discussions of iconic objects housed in museum collections like MoMA and the Philadelphia Museum of Art, famous designers such as Russel Wright and Eero Saarinen, illustrious companies such as Knoll, and landmark events like world exhibitions and the Milan triennials. These are the kinds of topics that are included in standard design historical textbooks like David Raizman's *History of Modern Design*, Carma Gorman's *The Industrial Design Reader*, Philip Meggs's *History of Graphic Design*, Jeffrey Meikle's *Design in the USA*, and Jonathan Woodham's *Twentieth-Century Design* (to name just a few).[2] While these texts provide a valuable overview of the history of design for students, the canonical focus of these various design texts often betrays an underlying bias in favor of famous (overwhelmingly European or American, white, and male) designers, important objects, and so forth. They often neglect lesser

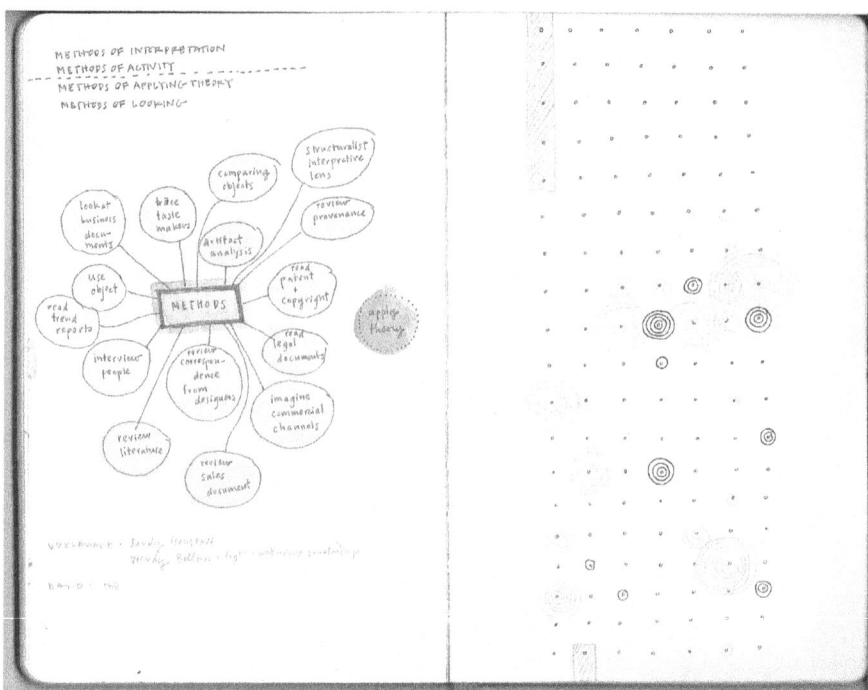

Figure 2.1 A notebook page with a sketch by Brockett Horne, one of the Summer Scholars, made during our discussion about the boundaries between craft and design, 2015.

known designers and objects, sideline users and intermediaries, and only superficially address social and environmental justice issues such as labor, globalization, sustainability, race, and disability. Exhibition catalogs as well as popular coffee-table books have similarly lionized "big-name" designers, often in concert with, or even sponsored by, the very brands that are their subject. More broadly, these kinds of biases against certain classes of objects and certain groups of designers and consumers have canonized notions of "good taste" and "good design," and marginalized alternative narratives and perspectives.

There is already a large body of scholarship that has challenged this canonical approach, expanded the boundaries of the field, and offered new ways to engage in design historical research. This disciplinary turn away from canonical figures and objects began more than three decades ago with the work of Adrian Forty, Penny Sparke, Daniel Miller, Pat Kirkham, Judy Attfield, Thomas Hine, John Heskett, Christopher Breward, and Lou Taylor, among others whose research laid a foundation for transforming the intellectual landscape and legacy of design history.[3] In recent years, many scholars in the field have considered issues around gender and sexuality, sustainability, accessibility, labor, social class and taste, the problems of race, issues of structural inequality, and have also offered a richer and more nuanced exploration of globalization and global interactions.[4] Finding ways of integrating this rich scholarship into the teaching of introductory courses in design history and the development of new upper-level curriculum for design students was one of the critical tasks of the institute, and we continue that effort in this volume. This book builds on this prior research in the field and provides scholarship that is rigorous, but also accessible to the design students whom many US design historians are teaching.

This collection brings together a variety of design disciplines and approaches that reflect the intellectual diversity of the scholars who participated in the Summer Institute. For a number of us, that diversity was both inspiring and challenging; for example, in her Epilogue to this volume, "Building the case for and cases for interdisciplinary design history," Stephanie Vasko describes how the NEH Summer Institute opened up new sets of questions for her research and made her identify more strongly with design history, even though she was formally trained as a chemist. Her essay argues for the productivity of broadening the boundaries of design research and incorporating diverse perspectives, disciplines, and methodologies. By thus continuing to expand the discipline of design history, new voices with different kinds of expertise can be added to the conversation, and new ways of looking at design can open up entirely new sets of questions and new avenues of research as well as new ways of teaching the history of design.

Creating a more diverse design history in the classroom is becoming increasingly important as design becomes a more popular and prominent part of art schools and art departments across the country. Not only are students flocking to design programs in higher education, they are consuming design through television shows (*Antiques Roadshow, American Pickers, Project Runway, HGTV*, etc.) and social media platforms like Instagram. Meanwhile, "Design Thinking" has become a buzzword in everything from business to the self-help industry.[5] Yet the growing interest in design within popular culture only reinforces students' tendency to fetishize design without any analytical criticism.

What is the role of design history in this changing cultural and academic landscape? Most accrediting bodies, such as the National Association of Schools of Art and Design (NASAD), require some amount of design history for design students.[6] As design historians, how do we understand the purpose of this history for our students? In the US context, we are generally not teaching future design historians, but rather teaching future designers. What is it that we are teaching them? Some of our studio colleagues may imagine that we offer our students a parade of chairs and styles, with stacks of flashcards with names and dates to memorize, but the rich literature in the field of design history illustrates how flawed that image is.

Engaging deeply with larger questions is even more critical for teaching diverse cohorts of design students to engage with an increasingly complex and nuanced global landscape. We not only need our students to see themselves (and their diverse identities) in the history of design, but also to look more critically at design as a field, seeing both the possibilities of design and its failures. As these essays reflect, we see our teaching as moving beyond a history of images and styles towards histories of the problems and possibilities of design. By engaging students in a critical questioning of the histories of design, we hope they will see the problems of the past, and recognize how those problems are reflected and often reproduced in the present. We encourage our students to use this criticality to be self-conscious of their role in either maintaining these systems or intervening to challenge them. To accomplish this, engaging students in more active forms of analysis, particularly using diverse primary sources and objects, gives them the tools they need to craft their own understanding of design history and find their place within it.

This collection of essays strives to engage with primary sources, ask critical questions, and situate design in an interdisciplinary way. These case studies not only provide students a model for design historical research, they also serve as interventions into conventional narratives. By organizing this book in terms of people's roles in design, we are foregrounding a kind of social history of design, as opposed to one that might focus on disciplinary categories or materials (Figure 2.2). The book is organized into three main sections: Users/Consumers, Intermediaries, and Designers. Each section features a collection of essays that consider alternative stories, offer unusual approaches, or challenge conventional design-historical narratives. The overall structure of this volume echoes what Grace Lees-Maffei has termed the "production-consumption-mediation paradigm" of design history, which she argues reflects the evolution of research in the field of design history since its formal emergence in the UK in the 1970s.[7] There are also interconnections across these sections that form alternative thematic narratives around

Figure 2.2 A visual representation of the conceptual framework of the book created by Brockett Horne, 2018.

diverse identities, business history as a lens of analysis, and recognizing multiple expressions of modernity.

Users/Consumers

This first section features a group of essays that foreground consumers and users of design. All three essays explore the role of design in the everyday and examine the relationship between people and things. Numerous scholars have examined design through the lens of consumerism and consumer culture. For example, Adrian Forty, Regina Lee Blaszczyk, Ann Smart Martin, Judy Attfield, and Penny Sparke have highlighted the roles of consumers in their research.[8] Much of this research has relied on trade literature, catalogs, advertisements, and other media and commercial spaces that were originally produced to speak to consumers. It is much harder to find the voices of consumers themselves. Furthermore, users, who are often distinct from consumers, are even more difficult to locate in an historical context. Design historians must be creative in cobbling together evidence for understanding users from a variety of sources, and in many cases, it is primarily anecdotal evidence that helps to reveal the story of the uses and lives of designs in the everyday context. The story of your grandmother's coffee table or a hand-me-down dress might tell us just as much as the official history of a company or their publicly available advertisements. While anecdotes are often marginalized within historical narratives, their very granularity, in fact, can offer a specificity that is lacking when we treat users and consumers as an undifferentiated mass.

Users are thus a challenge to study in the history of design, but while the evidence of use is sometimes elusive and incomplete, foregrounding users opens up new questions, new avenues of research, and new ways of looking at design. For example, in Yelena McLane's essay, "*Kul'ttovary*: Bringing culture into the Soviet home," users are evoked through a close analysis of the objects that serve as a gateway into the everyday lives of Soviet people. McLane reveals the complex meanings of these cultural goods that reflected the ideal Soviet citizen as imagined by the Soviet state, but also a potential means of challenging that ideal for users. In Emily Wolf's essay, "Everything old is new again: Modernization, historic preservation, and the American home, 1920–1966," the author uses Federal Housing Administration data alongside trade catalogs to reveal the efforts of homeowners to modernize and update their older houses during the early to mid-twentieth century. Wolf argues that pieces of domestic architecture are not static, unchanging spaces, but rather that they are sites of continuous change and reinvention in response to changing needs, ideals, and expectations of homeowners. Wolf's essay illustrates the long life of designed spaces and objects means that there may be many generations of users whose needs, preferences, and uses are different and even contradictory. Finally, Jennifer Kaufmann-Buhler's "Diversionary tactics at work: Making meaning through misuse" considers the covert behaviors of office workers using the spaces and objects of the office as a means of escape. Kaufmann-Buhler's research demonstrates how evidence of use and misuse often hides in the margins and edges of other kinds of research.

Intermediaries

The second section of this book looks at the role of intermediaries in design. Regina Lee Blaszczyk, in her book *Imagining Consumers*, argues for a centering of design history on what she calls "fashion intermediaries" as a way of capturing a more complex story that looks beyond the narrative of heroic designers to understand design as a system populated by a variety of different people, businesses, and institutions.[9] Blaszczyk identifies everyone from shopkeepers and salesmen to advertising experts and home economists within the category of fashion intermediaries. For Blaszczyk, these intermediaries are part of a system of fashion predicting consumer taste and therefore forecasting future trends through the careful study of consumers. Here, we are borrowing and expanding the term "intermediary" to capture the ways in which a diverse array of people (critics, curators, engineers, advertisers), media (magazines, newspapers, film, television), and institutions (museums, businesses, governments) construct meaning through design.

Looking beyond the fashion system to think about the production of meaning expands the concept of the "intermediary" and reveals the limits of the designer and the ways in which meaning is made within a network. Each of the essays in this section demonstrates how unconventional archives can be used to explore the ways in which design was produced and given meaning. These archives—oral histories, personal photographic archives, a popular television show, and online search engines and marketplaces—allow design historians to trace alternative narratives about well-trodden historical moments, uncovering the work of previously unknown figures or other kinds of readings of familiar designed objects. These very different essays show the importance of looking at intermediaries not only as a source of style, but also a source of insight into the design process.

Maria Elena Buszek's chapter, "CLOTHES CLOTHES CLOTHES PUNK PUNK PUNK WOMEN WOMEN WOMEN," draws out the role of intermediaries in Punk fashion, showing how the entire subculture was significantly shaped by figures who are often considered marginal to its canonical history. Using the story of Vivien Westwood and Malcolm McLaren's famous Punk boutique, Sex, and foregrounding the role of shopworker Jordan, Buszek reveals the complex circulation of style from the street to the shop, and from the shop to the bands and back again, which produced a chaotic network of taste and countercultural style. Most revealingly, Buszek proposes and proves that Punk Fashion begat Punk Music—not the other way around, as is customarily thought and taught.

In Christopher S. Wilson's chapter, "Representing modern architecture in *The Rockford Files*, 1974–1980," a television show about the escapades of a private detective becomes a window into the "vernacular modern" aesthetics of Los Angeles. Shot almost entirely on location in various places around the city, *The Rockford Files* constructs an idealized vision of a modern city as compared to contemporaneous representations of modern architecture as inhuman, cold or brutal. For Wilson, this particular television show is a media intermediary promoting a more quotidian experience of modern design and architecture, exposing the topic on a weekly basis to far more people than any book or museum exhibition could.

Matthew Bird's "Using digital tools to work around the canon" showcases the role of publicly accessible online archives to uncover information about little-known figures and objects in design history. Using sources such as ebay, Google Patents, auction house websites, and personal blogs, Bird's digital sleuthing illustrates how unconventional and obscure designers, unknown intermediary figures, and unidentified objects can actually be found, and therefore exposed. His creative appropriation of commercial tools for academic research reveals the ways in which these digital repositories can provide alternative narratives and literally expand the canon of design history.

Designers

The third section of the book highlights designers and the design process. In conventional design-historical narratives, designers are often at the center of analysis. Pioneers in the field such as Nikolaus Pevsner, Philip Meggs, Reyner Banham, and Jeffrey Meikle have relied on an art-historical model of research that focused on a biographical understanding of a single named designer.[10] These studies often position a designer within a network of influences that shaped their own development, as well as examining the influence of the designer's work on their students and other successors. However, there are limits to this approach: this focus on individual designers tends to overlook figures whose work, personality, or identities place them outside of conventional narratives. It also overlooks designers whose lives and work are less well documented and also ignore the collaborative nature of design. The chapters in this section explore alternative models for examining designers and the labor of design.

Victoria Rose Pass subverts this conventional designer narrative by tracing the source, use, and reuse of an iconic image of a Mangbetu woman taken in 1924 on the *Croisière Noire*. "The Mangbetu coiffure: A story of cars, hats, branding, and appropriation" examines the use of this single image by multiple designers through various contexts, uses, and time periods. Pass offers a critical analysis of the appropriation and stereotypical representation of this iconic silhouette in 1920s and 1930s design practice.

In their chapter "The case of William Pahlmann: Challenging the canon of modern design," Marianne Eggler, Erica Morawski, and Sara Reed use the story of interior designer William Pahlmann to reveal how a stylistic outlier such as Pahlmann is often left out of conventional designer narratives. In the case of Pahlmann, his eclectic taste and his commercial popularity meant that he was not taken seriously as a designer, and instead has been historically maligned by conventional design narratives as an "interior decorator." In a similar fashion, Russell Flinchum's essay, "'I was not a woman designer ... I was a designer who happened to be a woman,'" uncovers the story of MaryEllen Dohrs, an industrial designer who worked for General Motors and Sundberg-Ferar in the post-World War II period. Though a highly successful designer, Dohrs's is story animates the structural elements of sexism in the workplace that created barriers to entry and advancement in the industrial design field that excluded all but the most talented and tenacious female designers.

Gayle L. Goudy's chapter, "Adventure play in physical and virtual spaces," recasts the nature of design labor through an exploration of real and virtual spaces for recreation. Drawing together design, craft, architecture, and gaming software, Goudy's chapter examines the ways in which users can be empowered to explore and experiment through play. The designers and artists she highlights allow the users of their real—as well as virtual—playgrounds to have a hand in their design and use.

In addition to telling the story of lesser-known designers, the work of canonical designers can also be critically re-examined. This is precisely how Karen L. Carter approaches Art Deco graphic designer Paul Colin in her chapter, "Confronting racial stereotypes in graphic design history." Using a pedagogical case study of Colin's posters of the *Revue nègre*, featuring Josephine Baker and her entourage, Carter examines how these images reproduced racist stereotypes of the time. By shifting the focus from designer to subject—Baker—Carter argues for a re-contextualizing of these images as part of a wider system of racist representations in visual culture. For Carter, using representations of Josephine Baker as an example is part of a broader effort to engage her students in a discussion about racist representations in design practice, not only historically but also in present-day advertising.

Thematic re-readings

Looking across the various sections of this collection, there are also broader thematic links that highlight important questions and problems in the study of design history: social identity and its construction; business as a lens of research and analysis; and recognizing diverse expressions of modernity. These themes represent critical interventions into the history of design, and the essays presented here offer new ways of integrating these issues into the design history classroom.

For designers, consumers, and users, design often plays an important role in the construction and performance of identity. The example of interior designer William Pahlmann in Eggler, Morawski, and Reed's chapter demonstrates the ways in which designers had to produce a public persona that conformed to expected social norms of gender and sexuality. Design as a field also structurally excludes certain categories of people both from roles of designers and consumers. In Russell Flinchum's chapter, the story of a female industrial designer in the postwar period reveals the ways in which women have been systematically excluded from the field of industrial design. As a consequence, certain voices are left out of the conversation and design is yet another space in which privilege and the inequity are reproduced. Yet, individuals can also consume and use design in ways that transgress the boundaries imagined by the designers and producers. For example, Maria Elena Buszek's chapter shows how people can use design to subvert normative gendered assumptions. By its very quotidian nature, design is ripe for being used, repurposed, and recycled in order to challenge those norms.

These designed objects and spaces also carry within them the identities, biases, and cultural assumptions of the designers and other figures who produced them. For instance, as Karen L. Carter's chapter shows, celebrated images of Josephine Baker by designer Paul Colin reproduced racial stereotypes. Her pedagogical examples demonstrate how a design history course can be a setting in which students can critically interrogate stereotypes of the past and—more importantly—find ways of undermining them in the present. One conventional strategy for achieving inclusion in design history has been to foreground producers and users of color. While this is a step in the right direction, it proves inadequate to fully address the role of race in design history. As vernacular architectural scholar Dianne Harris has shown, this tendency to treat racial identity as "othered" normalizes and obscures whiteness.[11] Every subject is racialized and design too is never neutral; it must also be considered through the lens of race. Further, racial identities are inherently fluid and complex, and design plays a crucial role in their continuous construction, reproduction, and transgression. In this collection, Pass's essay captures these tensions and contradictions through her analysis of the Mangbetu coiffure, an African woman's hairstyle which she argues became a cipher for a number of different ideas and expressions including modernity, technology, and sexuality. Pass illustrates how this iconic image of black beauty was used to construct white femininity through the early twentieth century, and how the same hairstyle has been reclaimed in contemporary culture by women in the African Diaspora as a symbol of black beauty and power.

These essays provide only a partial view of the ways in which identity can be understood through design history. It is vital to draw attention to issues of identity in order for design students to look more critically at their own assumptions about identity and how their own identities and privileges may be reproduced in their design work. Using the past as a laboratory for exploring issues of gender, race, class, sexuality, ability, and other kinds of identity allows design students to understand the ways in which design can be oppressive, expressive, and even transgressive.

Another common theme throughout this book is the role of business in shaping design practice, as well as the role of design in crafting corporate images and identities. Regina Lee Blaszczyk's role as a visiting scholar in the NEH Institute animated the value of business history in the study of design as well as the potential of trade literature as an archive for research. If we think in terms of designers, we often push the companies they worked for to the background, but if we foreground these companies, we can understand their agency in shaping the kinds of products that are produced and how those products are made and sold. In fact, businesses act as a constellation of objects, branding, materials, designers, intermediaries, manufacturers, and consumers; reading through the lens of business reveals the intersections and interactions of diverse categories of designers, intermediaries, and objects. The Hagley Library and Archives in Wilmington, Delaware, is an example of the richness of business archives. Their collection features not only the papers of individual corporations like RCA and DuPont, but also of individual designers such as William Pahlmann, Raymond Loewy, Marc Harrison, and Thomas Lamb, as well as intermediary organizations such as the Color Association of the United States.[12] Documents such as those in the collection of the Hagley shed light on the network of players in the business of design. Furthermore, as Matthew Bird reveals in his chapter, a digital network of evidence tied to the commodification of design from the patent stage (GooglePatents) to resale (ebay) can be accessed and used by anyone with an internet connection.

Several essays in this collection also animate the role of business in design. Stories about Citroën, General Motors, 3M, and the Soviet Union demonstrate what can be gained by highlighting the role of corporations and government organizations. As complex entities with layers of competing interests, goals, and ideals, reading organizations as actors complicates our understanding of how designed things are produced. The needs, values, and ideals of organizations structure, contain, and restrict design practice in ways that are lost when we focus exclusively on designers. In addition, designers play a role in materializing the values, ideals, and expectations of the companies for which they work. In Jennifer Kaufmann-Buhler's chapter, architects and designers reproduced organizational power not only by deliberately producing organizational hierarchy through office design, but also through the design process itself, which typically afforded greater weight to the goals of management over the preferences of workers.

Finally, Modernism emerges as a central problem in design history. While Modernism in design has been canonized through the heroic narratives of white European and American men, the aesthetics, ideals, and ideologies of Modern design have overshadowed the complexity of taste and created a hierarchical mode that enshrines Modern design as "good" design. These were ideas brought to the fore by Visiting Scholars at the NEH Institute, Sarah Teasley, Vladamir Kulić, and Catherine Rossi, who all pointed out the need for a more geographically de-centered study of Modernism. Teasley used MoMA New York's exhibition of a 1954–1955 Japanese house based on historical architectural forms to illustrate the ways that Modernists often found their aesthetics in other cultures, and yet persisted in framing these cultures as traditional, outside of history, and unchanging. Vladamir Kulić and Catherine Rossi used case studies of Eastern Bloc and Italian design, respectively, to unpack the political meanings of Modernism.

Building on these themes, this book explores some of these alternative stories and multiple expressions of modernity. In recent years, Modernism has been critically re-examined and recast by design historians and other scholars as not one single narrative or aesthetic but understood as multiple expressions of modernity.[13] The mining of design inspiration from other cultures is a cornerstone of Modernism, as revealed in the chapters on William Pahlmann and the Mangbetu coiffure. These narratives highlight the ways in which Modernism constructed Europe and America as progressive, evolving cultures, while reducing all other cultures to unchanging and uncivilized pattern books of inspiration. In addition, chapters by Yelena McLane, Christopher S. Wilson, and Emily Wolf examine the vernacular experience of Modernism. These ordinary expressions of Modernism reveal the ways in which conventional design-historical narratives ignore the complex and divergent textures, aesthetics, and nuances of Modernism. Rather than seeing Modernism only in the work of "starchitects" and utopian avant-garde projects, these essays reveal the ways in which Modernist aesthetics and values have been embedded in everyday life. Rather than reinforcing an illusion of an all-encompassing Modernism, these stories, and others like them, help students to explore and analyze diverse tastes and aesthetics.

Creating histories of design

All of these themes point to the importance of using diverse perspectives, narratives, objects, taste cultures, and methodologies in the teaching of design history. Although our courses are often framed as "The History of Design," they could be more accurately framed as "The *Histories* of Design." As noted in this book's Foreword, design history does not have a well-established institutional home or identity in the United States. In fact, most of the participants in the NEH Institute did not "start out" as design historians, instead originating from art history or a design discipline such as graphic design, industrial design, fashion design, or architecture. However, there are a number of disciplines with a long history of studying objects to understand the world, including, but not limited to: archeology, anthropology, geography, architectural history, decorative arts, and art history. The expansion of the US academy to include a large number of interdisciplinary fields has further expanded the study of physical objects: material culture studies, visual culture studies, area studies such as American Studies and East Asian studies, history of technology, gender studies, and disability studies, just to name a few. Design history might serve to connect the stories told about objects in all of these disciplines. One of the powers of making explicit the study of design history is that design can refer to the object, the process of its making, and even an idea not yet fully realized. In this way, design history can draw together multiple points of view, conflicting meanings, and complex narratives that reflect both macro-level studies of systems and micro-level stories of individuals.

Yet, while the term "design" seems to be an inclusive one, theoretically encompassing a wide array of activities, objects, and disciplines, it is often used in ways that police and maintain disciplinary boundaries among the various types of design practice. For example, commonly used design history textbooks and readers rarely include fashion in a substantive way. In the introduction to their new book *The Story of Design*, Charlotte and Peter Fiell define the history of design "as the story of how all man-made things came into being," but they choose to "not discuss fashion design which has its own history."[14] While this statement acknowledges the existence of rich scholarship in the field of fashion history, the deliberate exclusion of that history from the narrative of "how all man-made things came into being" illustrates how, outside of the blockbuster design shows at major museums like the V&A, it is rather rare to encounter scholarship that puts fashion into meaningful dialogue with other kinds of design.[15] This tendency to exclude fashion from discussions of design has a long history; Lou Taylor, for example, has documented the historic exclusion of fashion from "Industrial Art" collections in the nineteenth century, explaining that it was "an exclusion that was mired within an undercurrent of gendered prejudice."[16]

In design programs in the United States, it is not uncommon for the histories of industrial design, graphic design, interior design, and fashion design to be taught as entirely distinct and separate disciplines and narratives. While this is useful in allowing students to receive very targeted historical content that is directly related to their own focus, this tendency to silo the various design disciplines from each other ignores the ways in which design students cross disciplinary boundaries all the time in their studio classes. Industrial design students are regularly asked to design fashion items such as sneakers; interior designers are sometimes encouraged to create graphic materials like signage; and graphic design students are periodically tasked with designing three-dimensional environments. A more integrated approach to teaching an interdisciplinary history of design gives students the background they need to not just dabble in other areas of design, but to work with a depth and understanding as a practicing designer.

The essays in this volume demonstrate what a more integrated approach to a history of design might look like. They suggest the ways in which various design disciplines can speak to one another, and how research and teaching can be enriched by examining design across the disciplines. In continuing to build a design history field in the United States, we would be wise to learn from the example of dynamically interdisciplinary designers such as Mariano Fortuny, Alphonse Mucha, Dorothy Leibes, Lucienne and Robin Day, or Frieda Diamond. The diversity of their work makes a strong case for developing design history curricula that draw together various design disciplines and consider them holistically, perhaps through more thematic questions.

The very open nature of the act and study of design and design history is in fact a potential strength. Design history's fluidity means that we can refuse to draw boundaries that would inherently and structurally exclude the work and experience of women, people of color, LGBTQ people, people with disabilities, and other marginalized groups. In addition, we should be cautious about privileging professional design activities while marginalizing more informal or everyday acts of design: the home-sewn dress, the selection and arrangement of furniture by non-professionals, hacking IKEA furniture, or even organizing a desk drawer or computer desktop. Recognizing design as an ordinary activity helps us resist re-inscribing structural hierarchies in our research and our teaching. Thus, rather than discipline the field, working between disciplines can allow us to constantly question the definition of design, what might count as design, and also the methods we can use to interrogate it.

This collection of essays offers a series of questions and provocations about the possibilities and potentials of the study and teaching of design history. Our larger pedagogical goal is to give our students the tools and curiosity to learn more—not the illusion that they or we know everything. We must construct a diverse community of design historians and create a rich and ongoing conversation about the multiple histories of design. We need diversity not only in the disciplines from which we hail, and the disciplines that we engage with, but also in the experiences and identities we bring with us. By not attempting to tell a continuous story of the history of design, and not attempting to silo the various kinds of design from one another, we free ourselves up to ask more complicated questions and tell more nuanced stories.

Notes

1 The history of design is a well-established field in the UK and Europe, where there are numerous dedicated degree programs, a prominent journal, and a professional organization that has celebrated its fortieth anniversary. The field is much smaller and less well established in the US.
2 David Raizman, *History of Modern Design*, 2nd edition (Upper Saddle River: Pearson Prentice Hall, [2004] 2011). Carma Gorman, *The Industrial Design Reader* (New York: Allworth Press, 2003). Philip Meggs and Alston W. Purvis, *Meggs' History of Graphic Design* (Hoboken: John Wiley & Sons, [1983] 2016). Jeffrey Meikle, *Design in the USA* (New York: Oxford University Press, 2005). Jonathan Woodham, *Twentieth Century Design* (New York: Oxford University Press, 1997).
3 Adrian Forty, *Objects of Desire: Design and Society from Wedgwood to IBM* (New York: Pantheon Books, 1986). Penny Sparke, *An Introduction to Design and Culture in the Twentieth Century* (New York: Harper and Row, 1986). Daniel Miller, *Why Some Things*

Matter (London: Routledge, 1997). Pat Kirkham, *Women Designers in the USA, 1900–2000: Diversity and Difference* (New Haven: Yale University Press, 2000). Judy Attfield, *Wild Things: The Material Culture of Everyday Life* (Oxford: Berg, 2000). Thomas Hine, *Populuxe* (New York: Alfred Knopf, 1986). John Heskett, *Toothpicks and Logos: Design in Everyday Life* (Oxford: Oxford University Press, 2002). Christopher Breward, *The Hidden Consumer: Masculinities, Fashion and City Life 1860–1914* (Manchester: Manchester University Press, 1999). Lou Taylor, *The Study of Dress History* (Manchester: Manchester University Press, 2002).

4 For issues of taste, social class, and gender, see, for example, Penny Sparke, *As Long as It's Pink: The Sexual Politics of Taste* (Halifax: The Press of Nova Scotia College of Art and Design, 2010); Kristina Wilson, *Livable Modernism: Interior Decorating and Design during the Great Depression* (New Haven: Yale University Press, 2004); Monica Penick, *Tastemaker: Elizabeth Gordon, House Beautiful, and the Postwar American Home* (New Haven: Yale University Press, 2017). For labor issues, see, for example: David Brody, *Housekeeping by Design: Hotels and Labor* (Chicago: Chicago University Press, 2016); Allison Mathews David, *Fashion Victims: The Dangers of Dress Past and Present* (New York: Bloomsbury, 2015). For disability and accessibility, see, for example: Elizabeth Guffy, *Designing Disability: Symbols, Space and Society* (London: Bloomsbury, 2018); Bess Williamson, *Accessible America: A History of Disability and Design* (New York: New York University Press, 2019); Amie Hamraie, *Building Access: Universal Design and the Politics of Accessibility* (Minneapolis: University of Minnesota Press, 2017). For issues of sexuality and queer theory, see, for example: John Potvin, *Bachelors of a Different Sort: Queer Aesthetics, Material Culture and the Modern Interior in Britain* (Manchester: Manchester University Press, 2014). For issues related to globalization, see, for example: Arjun Appadurai, *The Social Life of Things: Commodities in Cultural Perspective* (Cambridge: Cambridge University Press, 1996); Victor Margolin, *World History of Design* (London: Bloomsbury, 2015); Glenn Adamson, Giorgio Riello, and Sarah Teasley, *Global Design History* (New York: Routledge, 2011); Kjetil Fallan and Grace Lees-Maffei, *Designing Worlds: National Design Histories in the Age of Globalization* (New York: Berghahn, 2018). On sustainability and design, see, for example: Jennifer Farley Gordon and Colleen Hill, *Sustainable Fashion: Past, Present, and Future* (London: Bloomsbury, 2015); Tony Fry and Anne-Marie Willis, *Steel: A Design, Cultural, and Ecological History* (London: Bloomsbury, 2014); Jeffrey L. Meikle, *American Plastic: A Cultural History* (New Brunswick: Rutgers University Press, 1995). On race, see Tanisha Ford, *Liberated Threads: Black Women, Style, and the Global Politics of Soul* (Chapel Hill: University of North Carolina Press, 2015); Elizabeth Guffy, "Knowing their Space: Signs of Jim Crow in the Segregated South," *Design Issues*, 28(2) (2012): 41–60.

5 Lee Vinsel, "Design Thinking is Kind of Like Syphilis: Its Contagious and Rots Your Brain," *Medium*, December 6, 2017, https://medium.com/@sts_news/design-thinking-is-kind-of-like-syphilis-its-contagious-and-rots-your-brains-842ed078af29 accessed on July 11, 2018.

6 NASAD Handbook, 2017–2018 https://nasad.arts-accredit.org/wp-content/uploads/sites/3/2017/12/AD-Handbook-2017–2018.pdf

7 Grace Lees-Maffei, "The Production—Consumption—Mediation Paradigm," *Journal of Design History*, 22(4) (2009): 351–76.

8 Adrian Forty, *Objects of Desire: Design and Society from Wedgwood to IBM* (New York: Pantheon Books, 1986); Regina Lee Blaszczyk, *Imagining Consumers: Design and Innovation from Wedgewood to Corning* (Baltimore: Johns Hopkins Press, 2000);

Ann Smart Martin, "Makers, Buyers, and Users: Consumerism as a Material Culture Framework," *Winterthur Portfolio*, 28(2) (1993): 141–57; Judy Attfield, *Wild Things: The Material Culture of Everyday Life* (Oxford: Berg, 2000); Penny Sparke, *As Long as It's Pink: The Sexual Politics of Taste* (Halifax: The Press of Nova Scotia College of Art and Design, 2010).

9 Regina Lee Blaszczyk, *Imagining Consumers: Design and Innovation from Wedgewood to Corning* (Baltimore: Johns Hopkins Press, 2000), p. 12.

10 Nikolaus Pevsner, *Pioneers of Modern Design: From William Morris to Walter Gropius* (New Haven: Yale University Press, [1936] 2005); Philip Meggs and Alston W. Purvis, *Meggs' History of Graphic Design* (Hoboken: John Wiley & Sons, [1983] 2016); Reyner Banham, *Theory and Design in the First Machine Age*, 2nd edition (Cambridge: MIT Press, [1960] 1980); Jeffrey Meikle, *Twentieth Century Limited: Industrial Design in America 1925–1939* (Philadelphia: Temple University Press, 1979).

11 Dianne Harris, *Little White Houses: How the Postwar Home Constructed Race in America* (Minneapolis: University of Minnesota Press, 2013).

12 Eggler, Morawski, and Reed make extensive use of the "William Pahlmann papers" at the Hagley Museum and Library in their chapter.

13 For example: Wilson, *Livable Modernism*; Wendy Kaplan, *Design in California and Mexico, 1915–1985: Found in Translation* (New York: Prestel, 2017); Wendy Kaplan, *California Design, 1930–1965* (Cambridge, MA: MIT Press, 2011); Pat Kirkham, "Humanizing Modernism: The Crafts, 'Functioning Decoration' and the Eameses," *Journal of Design History*, 11(1) (1998): 15–29.

14 Charlotte and Peter Fiell, *The Story of Design: From the Paleolithic to the Present* (New York: The Monacelli Press, 2016), p. 7.

15 For just a few examples of recent fashion histories that go beyond designer-focused books, or books focused on high fashion, see: Daniel James Cole and Nancy Deihl, *The History of Modern Fashion* (London: Lawrence King, 2015); Shaun Cole, *Don We Now Our Gay Apparel: Gay Men's Dress in the Twentieth Century* (London: Berg, 2000); Djurdja Bartlett's *Fashion East: The Spectre that Haunted Socialism* (Cambridge, MA: MIT Press, 2010); Carol Tulloch, *The Birth of Cool: Style Narratives of the African Diaspora* (London: Bloomsbury, 2016); Gordon and Hill, *Sustainable Fashion*; Deirdre Clemente, *Dress Casual: How College Students Redefined American Style* (Chapel Hill: The University of North Carolina Press, 2014). Excellent cross-disciplinary V&A catalogs include: Glenn Adamson and Jane Pavitt, *Postmodernism: Style and Subversion, 1970–1990* (London: V&A Publications, 2011); Charlotte Benton, Tim Benton, and Ghislaine Wood, eds., *Art Deco: 1910–1939* (London: V&A Publications, 2003); Stephen Calloway and Lynn Federle Orr, eds., *The Cult of Beauty: The Aesthetic Movement 1860–1900* (London: V&A Publishing, 2011).

16 Taylor also documents that the "the large part of those involved seriously in the study of artefacts of dress from the late nineteenth century were and are women, whether based in theater wardrobe departments, museums, schools, universities, or collecting privately." Lou Taylor, *Establishing Dress History* (Manchester: Manchester University Press, 2004), p. 2.

Section 1

Users/Consumers

Kul'ttovary: Bringing culture into the Soviet home

Yelena McLane

The Russian term *kul'ttovary* translates roughly as "cultural goods." The concept of cultural goods was well known in the Soviet Union, and, for decades, each city, town, or village had at least one store called "*Kul'ttovary*." The premise behind the concept, and associated consumer goods, was that specified items, broadly available for purchase at affordable prices, would bring culture into workers' and collective farmers' homes. The range of "cultural goods" visible in Figure 3.1—musical instruments, radios, televisions, record players, decorative clocks, drawing and photography supplies, and reproductions of works of art—was typical for these state-owned retailers. The *kul'ttovary* phenomenon was widespread in Russia from the late 1920s into the 1960s, at which point the previously ubiquitous *Kul'ttovary* stores yielded to shops with narrower specializations, consistent with broader changes in the Soviet retail industry.

Soviet product design, along with accompanying commercial propaganda specifically in the context of *kul'ttovary*, is a topic that is virtually unexplored outside of Russia. The marketing and retail strategies for these products were component to a much broader undercurrent of state-sanctioned "consumerism" as a means of implementing the government's political, social, and cultural policies.[1] This story runs counter to the prevailing narrative of the Soviet Union as a country at odds with the more materialist impulses of the capitalist West.[2] Recent scholarship reiterates the true, but incomplete notion that consumer-oriented manufacture addressed material necessities and, to a lesser extent, individual tastes and habits for personal effects like clothing and accessories.[3] *Kul'ttovary* objects are, of course, only a small part of Soviet design history, but the details of how and why and for whom these products were made, how they were used, and how these uses contributed to the formation of a common Soviet national identity illustrate a range of socialist ideologies aimed at promoting culture—literary, musical, and physical—planning for a cultured citizenry, and effectively distributing material goods within the USSR.

Aside from the now canonical experiments of revolution-era avant-gardists, Moscow Metro decoration, and the apotheosis of Art Deco under Stalin (the latter termed "Soviet Classicism"), Soviet design has, by and large, been supposed in contemporary scholarship as of little import—inferior replicas and pallid adaptations of Western styles.[4] Soviet-era "two-balls" sneakers mimicked the more fashionable brand with the "three stripes," and "*Tonika*" electric guitars (Russia's answer to the Fender Stratocaster) were notoriously un-tuneable. It is, nonetheless, worth observing

Figure 3.1 An attendant assists customers shopping for accordions in a *Kul'ttovary* store in the town of Balakovo, Saratov Region, *circa* 1960.

(albeit briefly) the origins of Soviet consumer product design, the political and socioeconomic contexts that shaped its development, and the stories of a few representative examples of *kul'ttovary*, if only to test that supposition. What emerges is a teleological counterpoint to the established, style-driven account of twentieth-century design history, worthy of inclusion in the canon as an alternative milieu for exploring the purpose (rather than the function or the aesthetic) of designed goods.

Creating the "cultured man"

From the early 1920s, the Bolshevik government recognized the importance of literacy and culture in building the new Soviet state. Vladimir Lenin emphasized that an increased "cultural level of the masses" was integral to the task of reorganizing society. Involving the population in artistic and cultural activities would inspire volunteerism, swell the ranks of local government offices and agencies that managed the new Soviet economy, and teach accountability among the legions of state workers needed to manage the wholesale transformation of society.[5] The range of individual pursuits provided for through *kul'ttovary* would offer each citizen a means by which to embrace and enjoy the fruits of the October Revolution.

The realities of life—"*byt*"—were changing rapidly. The concept of a private, domestic life spent amongst family and friends, surrounded by an assortment of personal possessions signifying one's status in society, was at first dismissed by revolutionaries as archaic, dying echoes of the petty bourgeois lifestyle. The new socialist "*byt*" would be marked by communal living, egalitarian workplaces where men and women labored side by side, and group recreation (gymnasiums), sanitation (bathhouses), education (reading rooms), and consumption (cafeterias). Comradery, not family in the traditional sense, was the socialist future, culminating on that eventual bright day in the harmonious reconciliation of the public–private dichotomy. In the words of the revolutionary-era writer, journalist, and period historian Marietta Shaginyan: "This does not mean to 'get rid of the individual,' but to develop a new, restless, richness of individuality (yet undiscovered by art) in the sphere of public service."[6] In short, for a person to be enculturated into a life of collaboration, the person must, through education, overcome the impulse to self-centeredness through engagement with outward-looking arts, sports, and recreation. Party leaders, artists, writers, architects, and musicians strove through their speeches, essays, paintings, and compositions to exemplify this ideal. The reality of implementing this vision for the future was, of course, quite different from the soaring ideals described by leaders, far less pretty than imagined by artists and writers, and far more complicated to enact.

Through the 1920s, tens of millions of peasants moved from rural villages into cities to be conscripted into vast crews at the sites of new urban and industrial building projects. These were "peasants by origin and workers by occupation."[7] Much of this workforce lived in barracks and dormitories. As traditional mechanisms for social control, such as the church and patriarchal family and village structures, fell away under the new socialist regime, epidemics of violence, vandalism, rape, alcoholism, and hooliganism spread.[8] Corporal punishment or imprisonment against numberless restless youths could not be implemented on a mass scale, and such measures were unlikely to be effective as long-term solutions. Instead, the Soviet government opted to adopt (at least officially) an array of positive, non-violent methods to restore discipline and order. The people were to be "civilized" and "cultured."[9]

In 1927, the Communist Party's first five-year plan set forth the twin goals of increasing the "cultural level" of urban and rural populations and connecting "cultural construction" ("*kul'turnoye stroitelstvo*") with industrialization as mutually dependent foundations upon which to build the socialist state and create a new "cultured man" ("*kul'turniy chelovek*").[10] Again, in the interest of squaring the aspirational with the harsh reality of Soviet statism, it must be said, as Vadim Volkov emphasized in his 2000 essay, that as loftily as the rhetoric soared, the cultured man was, "disappointedly, nothing new and nothing more than a Stalinist variation on the theme of the individual, a modern 'society man' externally civilized but internally committed to that society's values."[11] In short, the cultured man's protean precursor (or unfledged counterpart) was a society man, a man who exists to serve the state, and the first step to a culture of cultured men was a society of society men: "neat and accurately dressed" with "good moral character," "hard working," who "spoke without swearing" and had "mastered the government's Marxist-Leninist doctrines that embody Bolshevik consciousness."[12]

First among the priorities in creating this cultural transformation were two key public health issues: personal hygiene, and clean and considerate housing. Posters detailed the proper methods of washing one's hair and body. Sleek advertisements for razor blades reflected the state's campaign against old-believer-style beards. Curtains and partitions were promoted to provide for individual and family privacy in communal settings. Learning initiatives followed, with the goal of universal adult literacy in the Soviet Union by 1930.[13] But being able to read, keep clean, and maintain sanitary living conditions would not be enough to emerge from the post-revolutionary tumult and transform oneself. In 1929, Anatoliy Lunacharskiy, the first People's Commissar of Education and Culture, wrote:

> We must build a new "*byt.*" This new "*byt*" presupposes new material surroundings. These material surroundings—even if purely utilitarian—in human and cultural environments strives to identify aesthetic forms that bring joy to man. It is especially important in material environments that man creates for himself, which, in essence, must be both rational and joyous.[14]

But what exactly were the rational and joyous habits that would affix this culturedness into one's sense of self? Which material things did the cultured person need in order to maintain this culturedness? Consensus formed around a rather urbane lifestyle far removed from the country folkways, sheltered domesticity, and general illiteracy of the peasant stock from which cultured man was meant to emerge.[15] The cultured man read edifying books. He went to theaters and cinemas. He took up hobbies that engaged the mind, like chess, watercolor painting, and photography. He listened to music and played at least one musical instrument. He participated in sports and exercised with his peers at gymnasiums and in parks. For each of these pursuits, the cultured man would need cultural supplies—the right assortment of personal possessions—and with such supplies, his life would be beautiful. As Anton Chekhov wrote, "In a man everything should be beautiful: his face, his clothes, his spirit, and his thoughts" (*Uncle Vanya*, Act II). *Kul'ttovary* would be the means of developing and cultivating this beauty of thought and body, and their distribution was widespread through catalogs and through the specialized, soon to be ubiquitous, stores marked with signs that read only "*Kul'ttovary.*"

Kul'ttovary and "design" in the Soviet Union

Kul'ttovary first appeared in the mid-1930s, and the word itself is a product of its time. After the October Revolution, the renunciation of the old world manifested not only in social and cultural structures, but in the way the Russian language was spoken. An explosion of complex abbreviated words became, according to linguist Lev Scherba, "symbols of the revolution."[16] *Kul'ttovary* is a portmanteau of *kultur* (culture) and *tovary* (products or goods). According to Soviet-era guidelines for retail industry managers, *kul'ttovary* was a group of goods that "primarily satisfies the cultural needs of the population."[17] These were office supplies, art and drawing supplies, radios and televisions, records and record players, musical instruments, sports equipment, cameras and photography equipment, and toys. Each of these products would need to be designed, manufactured, marketed, and delivered to stores in quantities sufficient to meet the growing demand for self-edification through *kul'ttovary*.

The idea of design as we know it today did not exist in the Soviet Union. The word *dizain* (design) did not appear in official documents or publications until the late 1960s. As Vladimir Paperny noted in 1978, "nowadays many of us know what design is ... However, in 1964... nobody could properly explain what it was, though this foreign word was alluring."[18] There were, however, two rather cumbersome word combinations that expressed the idea of design: *tekhnicheskaia estetika* (technical aesthetics) and *hudozhestvennoe konstrutirovanie* (artistic form rendering). These workman-like terms reflect the length of the shadow that mechanical engineering as a visionary vocation cast over art practice during the 1920s at both avant-garde centers like *Vkhutemas* (Higher Art and Technical Studios) and the more traditional Moscow Institute for the Decorative and Applied Arts and Moscow Architectural Institute, at which students' portfolios swelled with geometric abstraction, machine drawings, and elevations of unbuildable structures.[19] By the 1930s, however, Soviet design as state-sanctioned experiment had effectively ended. To the extent that designers continued to design in the Western sense, they were isolated enthusiasts working in scattered polytechnic institutions on unrealized "paper" projects.

At present, post-avant-garde Soviet light industry and product design practices await serious scholarly investigation. From the 1930s through the 1960s, most mass-produced products were copied from the West. Early designers, who staffed plants and factories under centralized management structures and with very limited material resources, were unable to work on anything beyond basic products to meet consumers' basic needs—cookware, electric lights, plumbing fixtures.[20] During the Second World War, virtually all industrial lines were either destroyed or adapted for war. In the aftermath, the equipment that survived was outdated. Postwar designers were tasked with building new industrial manufacturing lines and not with enhancing quality. The goals were inexpensiveness and ease of manufacture.[21]

It is difficult to trace the authors of most products; the socialist system did not recognize the role of an individual designer. Rather, they were members of a larger engineering or technical department within a factory who performed their assigned roles: detailing material components, drafting schematics, and specifying the substances needed to make a product. The Soviet patent system was rudimentary at best, and in any case commenced only in 1965. Interestingly, but hardly representative of the Soviet patent system as a whole, the first eight patents were issued for a suite of lamps designed in Latvia. Very few designers or designer groups were willing to go through the cumbersome paperwork necessary to get a patent. Moreover, the premise that a designer (held in virtually no esteem) should get more social recognition than an engineer (held in the highest esteem) was unthinkable.[22] It naturally followed that the earliest examples of mass-produced *kul'ttovary* were the plainest and most serviceable iterations imaginable: bare pads of drawing paper, undecorated snow skis, boxy radios with a single knob pre-set to a state channel, each stamped only with the name of the manufacturing plant and the price in rubles or kopeks. Although these *kul'ttovary* objects would seldom evidence the sort of originality of purpose or style that we commonly associate with "great design," each of the seven broad categories reflected deliberate ideological, cultural, and design perspectives consistent with their educative *raisons d'être*.

Radios

Foremost among *kul'ttovary* were consumer-scale radios, which were available in primitive kit-forms in limited quantities as early as the 1920s, and mass-manufactured and marketed to everyday people under various Soviet brand names beginning in the 1950s. The Soviet government had long recognized radio as a powerful propaganda and educational tool. Vladimir Lenin called it "a newspaper without the paper."[23] The centrality of radio to the bright technological future promised to the new Soviet citizenry cannot be overstated.

The first Soviet radio station, the largest in the world at the time, opened in Moscow in 1922. From a news bulletin prepared by TASS (Telegraph News Agency of USSR) in 1932, we read that radio "on collective farms, on socialist farms, on manufacturing plants, and at railroad junctures" should serve to increase the cultural development of the masses and be a propagandist and organizer of socialist life. Radio was a "distant teacher;" a means of systematically dispersing information and professional development opportunities to hundreds of thousands of people scattered over the vast territory of the USSR. Prior to World War II, listening was, above all, "a collective activity"[24] that "made a lack of other comforts easier to bear."[25] It occurred "in village reading rooms in workers' clubs, in army barracks, or in city streets and squares."[26] Workers spoke of radio's role in introducing them to literature and classical music, and as an "educational accompaniment to household chores."[27] Television was predicted eventually to play a supporting role in this effort by offering visual illustrations to accompany distance learning through the transmission of plans, construction drawings, schematics, and diagrams.[28]

Pre-recorded music and news made up the majority of the programming, although weekends featured special "children's hours" and live broadcasts of operas and theatrical performances. For rural audiences, radio was an auditory window to the city, with its soundtrack of classical music and announcers whose measured speech differed markedly from country dialects. Perhaps most tellingly, the urbanity and "civilizing" impulse of radio was reflected in the "morning gymnastics" program, which emphasized the importance of physical movement to a presumed audience of otherwise sedentary office workers, ignoring the many millions of Soviet citizens who spent their days toiling in the fields.

The aesthetics of radios as appliances also changed with the times. In the 1920s, it was prestigious to have a receiver that showcased its technical function through exposed lamps, levers, tubes, and hand-spun wiring. By the 1930s, the radio set was an attractive piece designed to be in harmony with room furnishings and ready for use right out of the box.[29] Polished wood and bakelite were common case materials, in streamlined styles that echoed the Art Deco classicism popular through the 1950s. As shown in Figure 3.2, basic "loudspeaker" models were pre-tuned to the primary local broadcaster (users could only adjust the volume), while more deluxe models like the "*Moskvich*" (designed and first produced at the *Moskovsky Radiozavod* [Moscow Radio Plant] in 1949, and the subject of an impressive advertising campaign [Figure 3.3]) offered a range of frequencies, enabling users to choose between music, news, or sports, at various times of day.

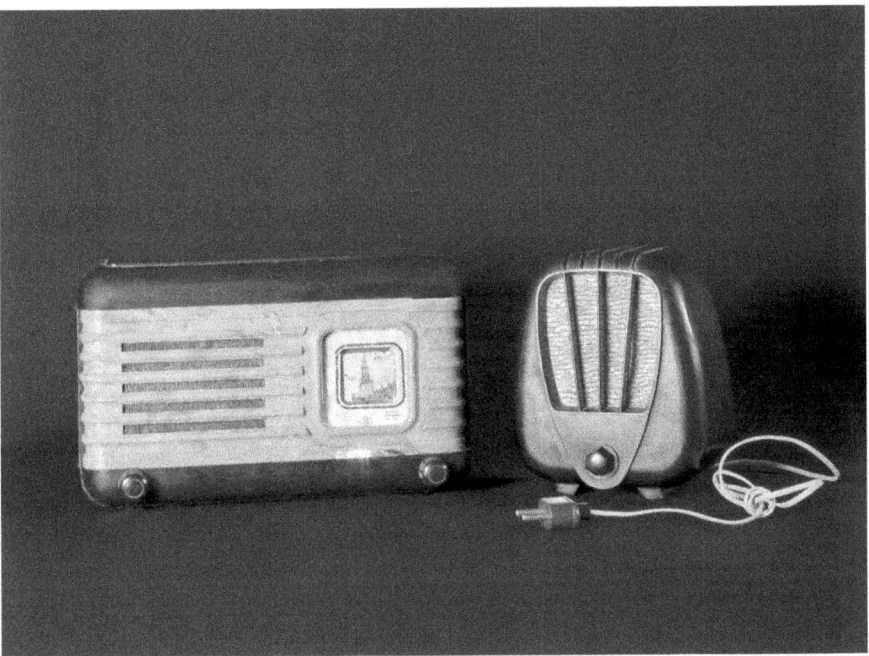

Figure 3.2 A single-channel hard-wired *gromkogovoritel* (loudspeaker) (1959) [right] and a "*Moskvich*" radio (1949) [left].

In her 1958 essay on the Brussels World's Fair, Marietta Shaginyan wrote:

> There is in our simple and dear reality one hybrid word. This word is *kul'ttovary*. It is often seen on store signs. And this not very elegant word includes radio receivers—attributes of culture in an apartment, a means of connection with the country, with the humanity; a peaceful opportunity to listen to music, and to await to the latest news. Our plants are trying to improve this *kul'ttovar*, to make it sturdier, cheaper, better, improve its sound, soften its noises. I am not sure about you, but my heart trembles with tenderness towards our hybrid Soviet word and our simple and unpretentious radio receiver. It has so many markings of our Soviet culture: to be available to everyone, to be accessible to everyone, to become mass-produced, to bring culture to the masses.[30]

Record players

Second perhaps only to the radio, with the range of news, musical, and cultural programming that it brought into the home, gramophones and record players were among the most sought after recreational appliances. Designs for these units tracked

Figure 3.3 Alexey Lavrov's "Buy the *Moskvich* Three-Tube Radio" lithograph poster (1950) instructs that the "*Moskvich*" may be purchased for 212 rubles at all GLAVELECTROSVYAZBYT (Main Domestic Electric Communication) factory stores, department stores, and *kul'ttovary* stores.

prevailing Western tastes (portable player boxes with chromed locking latches and swivel corner drawers for spare needles, "suitcase"-style electric models in teal vinyl with white piping), but with some years of lag time; the hand-cranked portable model remained in mass production at Leningrad's *Molot* (Hammer) factory well into the 1960s.

In contrast to programming on the radio which was strictly regulated, record players subverted government control by affording people access to records whose message and aesthetics were in opposition to socialist ideology. Although there was consensus that record players were worthy *kul'ttovary*, the sorts of records brought to market could be contentious. In a resolution from June 26, 1958, addressing the content of musical records, the Central Committee emphasized the importance of "records use in the ideological and artistic upbringing and cultural development of the Soviet people."[31] Criticism was directed at the questionable artistic quality of musical compositions, and, even worse, some recordings were found to be sympathetic to "alien ideas." There were "too few recordings of USSR's ethnic and folk music, revolutionary songs, symphonic, opera and ballet music, and the best songs of Soviet composers and composers from abroad."[32] Even in the Soviet Union, customers wanted what they wanted. Despite the more traditional leanings of the music pedants nominally in charge of selecting the tracks that would be pressed into vinyl, factories followed the market and minted records of popular songs by the thousands. As official missives advised purchase agents and managers of *Kul'ttovary* stores to "stop chasing profits" and "stop distributing vast numbers of records that satisfy only lowbrow tastes," pop record sales grew year upon year.[33]

Photography

Photography was also recognized early on as a powerful propaganda tool, and was featured prominently in posters and newspapers. The party supported the manufacture and mass distribution of photographic equipment as a means of documenting the revolution. By a special decree of the People's Commissariat for Education (*Narkompros*) in 1919, photography studios and development labs were elevated to a status equal to painting studios, which protected these locations from being transformed into living spaces. Trained photographers were exempt from mandatory labor, an extraordinary privilege in times of civil war and worker shortages.[34]

By the late 1920s, demand for photography equipment and severe trade inequities between the Soviet Union and Western technology manufacturers led to the establishment of an independent Soviet photo industry with the goal of mass production of modern cameras, photo development chemicals, and darkroom supplies. In July 1930, the State Optical and Mechanical Plant (*Gosularstvennyi Optiko-Mekhanicheskii Zavod*, or *GOMZ*) in Leningrad released the first hundred Soviet-made cameras (the "Fotokor–1") just in time for the opening of the 15th Congress of the All-Union Communist Party (Figure 3.4). The Fotokor–1 imitated the standard folding bed-plate cameras manufactured in Europe by such well-known firms as Busch, Voightlander, and Zeiss-Ikon since the late 1800s. For the Soviet market, newness was

Figure 3.4 The Fotokor-1 (1930) *Gosudarstvennyi Optiko-Mekhanicheskii Zavod* (State Optical and Mechanical Plant).

subordinate to standardization, interchangeable parts, and the prospect of making lots of them. With fewer available models, instruction materials were universal and geared towards amateurs. By 1941, more than one million Fotokor-1s were in circulation.

Photography as an extracurricular pastime was widespread. Magazines like *Sovetskoye Foto* (*Soviet Photo*) were brisk sellers, as were books like Nedzvesky and Chibisov's *General Course of Photography* (1930), "a most comprehensive photography manual in three volumes." Historian Yuri Slezkine has described photography as the "most popular form of home entertainment" for men in the 1930s.[35] Technical journals specified the steps needed to convert (temporarily) communal bath spaces into darkrooms. Through "featured artists" and photo competitions, periodicals touted the state of amateur photography among factory workers and collective farmers, emphasizing how photography could (and should) be used to document and highlight developing industries and the organization of "productive labor" (*udarnichestkogo truda*) on a national scale.[36]

Musical instruments

The centrality of music and musicianship in the Soviet Union prompted countless writers to employ surprisingly sincere language to describe the national culture that grew out of the proliferation of this class of *kul'ttovary*. There were pianos, violins, accordions, balalaikas, mandolins, xylophones, and brass instruments in numbers sufficient to blanket the world in the sonorous stylings of Prokofiev, Dunayevsky, or Listov. Accounts of the import of these *kul'ttovary* are hard to read without a dose of irony, but, setting aside the ideological undertones, there is a certain beauty to the intended message:

> The Soviet Union is the country with the most developed musical culture. Music no longer belongs to loners (*dostoyaniye odinochek*). It has entered the daily lives of ordinary people for good. Our Party and the Soviet State have created conditions for studying and listening to music for millions of Soviet people. Radio broadcasts, concerts, and lectures give people opportunities to familiarize themselves with classical and Soviet music. In our country, there is a large group of talented composers and performers. The mass character of Soviet musical culture tasks our industry to produce musical instruments in huge quantities, with ever growing demand. In the Soviet Union, where music belongs to the people, and material well-being of the population is increasing every year, a musical instrument becomes a necessity in every household, and for every family.[37]

Opportunities for musical education were prevalent throughout the Soviet Union: in grade schools, in special music schools, and in extracurricular music programs hosted by the regional "Pioneer Palaces." Trade unions across many industrial sectors sponsored "music circles" in the local high schools—where students received more rigorous training in ensemble and symphonic techniques—and associated bands often performed on holidays and at community events.[38] The goal was not, however, concert-level ability for everyone. As recounted by Russian composer Dmitry Kabalevsky, the mother of a seven-year-old girl once asked her music teacher whether it was worthwhile instructing the little girl in music when she had shown no talent for it. The teacher asked if the mother had questioned the physics, geography, or history teachers about her daughter's ability to assimilate those disciplines. "It does not seem to surprise you," the teacher said, "that she will study all that at school even though she may very well never become a historian, a geographer, or a physicist."[39]

Sports equipment

The *kul'ttovary* phenomenon also encompassed physical culture through mass production and marketing of individual and group sports equipment and games. As detailed in James Riordan's comprehensive *Sport in Soviet Society*, sport was for "achieving better health and physical fitness; character formation, as part of general education in producing a harmonious personality; military training, the identification of individuals with groups (the party, the regional Soviets, trade unions) and their encouragement to be active socially and politically."[40] Youth and athleticism were revered by Stalin and other party leaders who were manifestly (and pathologically) frightened of their own deaths, and who perpetuated through propaganda the vision of a Soviet Union in perpetual springtime, nearly (but never quite fully) achieved.[41] From the outset, sports were an

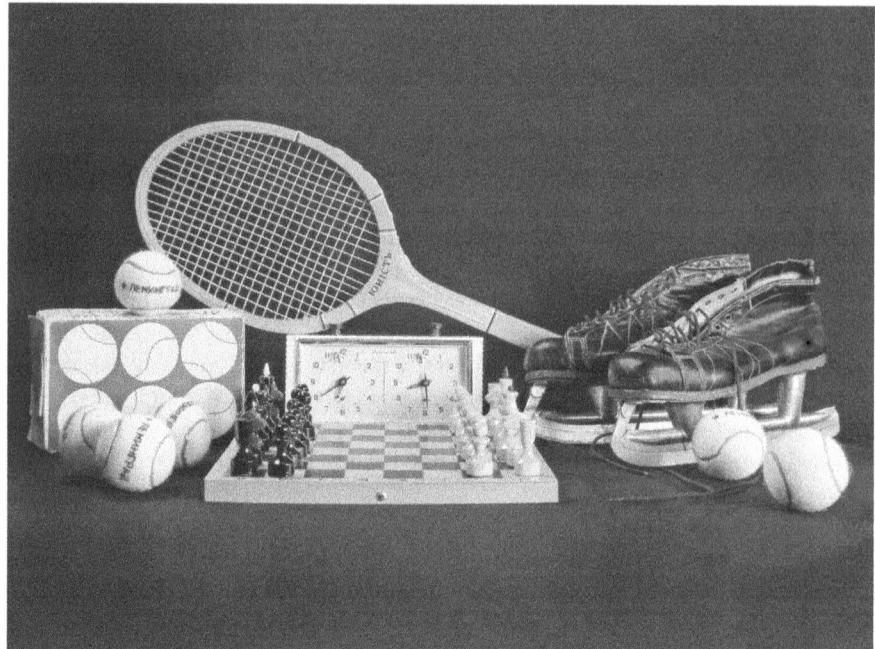

Figure 3.5 An assortment of sports *kul'ttovary*, including an archetypal folding chess set, "*Yantar*" (Amber) analogue tournament chess clock, hockey skates, a "*Yunost*" (Youth) tennis racket, and a box of "Leningrad" brand tennis balls.

integral part of the Soviet social curriculum, and schools, clubs, and unions managed vast inventories of standardized soccer and volleyballs, skates, hockey sticks, rackets, shuttlecocks and portable badminton nets—for fitness of body—together with innumerable chess boards and pieces—for honing the tactical mind (Figure 3.5).

In 1951, T. S. Ostanovsky authored a comprehensive treatment of the *kul'ttovary* industry and market aimed at retail professionals in the Soviet Union, which was issued in several editions over more than a decade with ever expanding inventory from year to year. On the matter of sport, he wrote, "The development of physical culture and sport leads to the need for large amounts and varieties of sports equipment across a range of standards, requirements and regulations. The equipment is manufactured in state-run factories and plants, including in the factories of the Committee on Physical Culture and Sport under the Council of Ministers of the USSR, by cooperative manufacturers, and others."[42] The sports equipment could be classified based on the area of sport it is intended for: sports games (including soccer, basketball, volleyball, water polo, tennis, croquet, chess, and checkers), track and field, weightlifting, boxing, fencing, winter sports, and gymnastics equipment, including fishing and hunting goods. At the time, the Soviet Union rightly viewed itself as a powerhouse in a broad range of competitive sports at which Russia had historically excelled, and a committed aspirant in those to which great powers excelled, and sports *kul'ttovary* tracked closely the specifications common to international regulatory bodies. The Soviet Union made its first appearance in the Olympic Games in 1952, and topped the medal count in six of the eight Summer Olympics in which it competed, a testament, in some part, to the impact of sports *kul'ttovary*.

Toys

Toys were also considered *kul'ttovary*. In 1958, state officials proudly announced that mass production would render these once rare prestige items as affordable as another former luxury reserved only for privileged tables: "We need toys so inexpensive that they cost no more than a good candy."[43] Traditional Russian toys were made of wood and hand painted. Such methods could not get close to satisfying the demand of millions of customers. Beginning in the 1950s, developments in the state chemical industry enabled for the first time the domestic mass manufacture of toys from plastics and synthetics. Quantities went up, and prices came down, but this did not address another key concern: what should the toys be about? In the past, toys had, for the most part, reflected agrarian domestic life—animal carvings and rag dolls.

In the Soviet Union, most children spent time in daycares, kindergartens, pioneer camps, or after-school programs, and there arose a need for different kinds of toys, toys that supported social development, formation of friendship, and, most importantly, the idea of shared property.[44] With demand for toys greatly outstripping supply, kindergartens received delivery of new or replacement toys before stores, and educational administrators prioritized toys with didactic value, like blocks and puzzles. At its best, Soviet toy development and design were driven by the idea of gaining knowledge: "a child develops and learns not only by sitting at the school desk, but through play. Often it is in the process of play that his interests and capabilities get revealed, and often his future profession (*opredelena*) is chosen."[45] Maxim Gorky wrote that toys should be entertaining and they should engage and surprise; because the road to knowledge starts with surprise.[46]

Notwithstanding these lofty goals, there is ample room for criticism. At the retail level, most Soviet toys were quasi-realistic, artistically dull, and not particularly entertaining: unarticulated rubbery figurines, and extruded plastic cars and trucks. Contemporary Soviet scholarship focuses exclusively on the limited educational value that these "commercial" toys provided, and addresses neither the significance of play nor the role of imagination. The now iconic "*Nevalyashka*" (Untopplely) doll (Figure 3.6)—geometrically satisfying, cheerful, and surprising in its smooth bottom-weighted motion and hidden chime—marked the high point of Soviet style and ingenuity in toy design, but other stimulating, hands-on toys (like play kitchens, doll houses, and erector sets) were hard to find. Their assorted parts made them difficult to produce on existing equipment without costly adjustments or re-engineering, and many required complex assembly, discouraging to purchasers who were conditioned to expect that key elements would be missing from the package. Simply put, technical disincentives and lack of consumer discernment (i.e., with material shortages, most toys sold out regardless of their inferiority) led most manufacturers not to bother producing more elaborate toys.

Figure 3.6 Exemplary among Soviet toys is the "*Nevalyashka*" roly-poly doll.

School supplies

Last among the categories of *kul'ttovary* were school supplies—pencils, pens, rulers, and paper. Simple sheet pads (plain, ruled, or graph) were "cultural goods" central to the state's mission of fostering an educated body politic. According to Ostanovsky, "in our country illiteracy has been eradicated in its entirety."[47] Students enrolled in elementary, middle, high schools, and technical centers numbered above 37 million in 1957, with another 1.2 million in institutions of higher learning. In this context, paper acquired a special importance. As one journalist poetically phrased it, "Paper is a non-rusting metal, on which great books live. Paper is the finest instrument for shaping our souls. Out of paper the Soviet people make peace bombs with which to open walls in our enemies' fortresses, and virgin land is turned over to make way for the beneficent sprouts of communism."[48]

The end(s) of *kul'ttovary*

Over time, however, even as the availability of cultural goods proliferated, the word *kul'ttovary* became a stand-in for hackneyed cultural conventions and petit bourgeois ambition, appearing in jokes about out-of-step party leaders with no sense of the era in which they were living: "What is *kul'ttovary*?—An exhibition of presents to Stalin from 1949" (the occasion of his seventieth birthday).[49]

Figure 3.7 Aleksandr Laktionov, *Moving to a New Apartment*, oil on canvas, 1952.

Aleksandr Laktionov's 1952 painting *Moving to a New Apartment* (Figure 3.7) could serve as an illustration for this joke. As Oliver Johnson detailed in his 2008 article "*Kul'turnost* or Kitsch," it is a problematic painting for several reasons, but it is a veritable inventory of *kul'ttovary*—bringing culture into the Soviet home—under Stalin's watchful eye.[50] The state has granted this war widow a luxurious apartment, and she imagines the good times that she and her family will have there. They have toys to play with, an instrument to make music with, books and a globe to learn about the world with, a bicycle to ride, and a handsome radio (nearly identical to the radios on display in the *Kul'ttovary* store in Balakovo). These are Stalin's presents back to his devoted people, the objects that signified the state's purported investment in the future, but which, as reflected in period responses to Laktionov's painting, seep with nostalgia.

The instrument is a Ukrainian mandolin, a folk instrument known only by a people whose survivors were just emerging from twin decades of starvation and war. The collected writings of the Soviet revolutionary poet Mayakovsky is among the books stacked on the floor; he had been dead by suicide since 1930.

We, the Western audience, look at these *kul'ttovary*, these "Soviet antiques," not, however, through a lens of nostalgia for what they once represented, but as objects as far out of time as obsolete goods from a deceased civilization. The chronotopically adjacent but ideologically remote Soviet Union made these objects—designed and produced in volumes that implicate widespread use by people who seem to have lived in a mildly distorted mirror of our world. We recognize the radio, but marvel that it was pre-tuned to a single broadcaster. The tennis balls and racket are, at a distance, indistinguishable from our own, but with strangely unsubtle "branding": "Leningrad" (the "City of Lenin"), "Youth."

Scholarly treatments of well-known brands and styles too often reiterate the canon, with its twin cults of origination and progress. The Soviet Union did not invent the radio, the photo camera, or tennis balls, and in most cases the quality of manufacture was regressive (i.e., behind its Western counterparts). Whether the conceptual end of *kul'ttovary*—a nation of fit, literate, artistically talented, citizen musicians—was achieved *en masse* is debatable. But by inviting the audience to probe the distinctive "technical aesthetic" of Soviet cultural goods, highly durable, quasi-functional, irredeemably authorless, they re-encounter the fundamentals of form and purpose. These ordinary objects take on a qualitatively different life as case studies in design practice and the conveyance of meaning through design. It is design as social history rather than through novelty or aesthetics. The objects are treated not as sources of information on technical innovation, fashion trends, and individual designers' résumés, but as means and tools for shaping the identity of *kul'turniy chelovek*, as weft and weave of the fabric of the material culture of Soviet society—ubiquitous and unnoticed as things, yet important as bearers of twin political purposes: culturedness and enculturation.

Notes

1 Amy Randall, *The Soviet Dream World of Retail Trade and Consumption in the 1930s* (Basingstoke, England, and New York, NY: Palgrave Macmillan, 2008).
2 See, for example, Nicholas Timasheff, *The Great Retreat: The Growth and Decline of Communism in Russia* (New York, NY: E. P. Dutton, 1972), and Vera Dunham, *In Stalin's Time: Middleclass Values in Soviet Fiction* (Durham and London: Duke University Press, 1990).
3 See Julie Hessler, *A Social History of Soviet Trade: Trade Policy, Retail Practices, and Consumption, 1917–1953* (Princeton, NJ: Princeton University Press, 2004).
4 See, for example, Aleksandr Lavrentiev and Yuri Nasarov, *Russian Design: Traditions and Experiment, 1920–1990* (London: Academy Editions, 1995), pp. 50, 54–73; Vladimir Runge, *Istoriya dizayna, nauki i tekhniki*, vol. 1 (Moskva: Architectura-C, 2006), pp. 300, 336; Victor Margolin, *World History of Design*, vol. 2 (London and New York, NY: Bloomsbury Academic, 2015), p. 348.

5 Ludmila Bulavka, "Sovetskaya Kul'tura kak Ideal'noye SSSR," in *Kul'tura. Vlast'. Sotsialism. Lunacharskiy i ne tol'ko*, ed. Ludmila Alekseyevna Bulavka (Moskva: LENAND, 2013), p. 106.
6 Marietta Shaginyan, *Noviy byt i iskusstvo* (Tiflis, 1926), p. 51.
7 Vadim Volkov, "The Concept of 'Kul'turnost': Notes on the Stalinist Civilizing Process," in *Stalinism: New Directions*, ed. Sheila Fitzpatrick (London: Routledge, 2000), p. 214.
8 Natalia B. Lebina, "Teneviye storony zhizni sovetskogo goroda 20–30-kh godov," *Voprosy istorii*, 2 (1994): 30–42.
9 Volkov, "The Concept of 'Kul'turnost'," p. 215.
10 *KPSS o Kul'ture, Prosveschenii i Nauke* (Moskva: Izdatel'stvo Politicheskoy Literatury, 1963), p. 31.
11 Volkov, "The Concept of 'Kul'turnost'," p. 216.
12 Ibid., 225.
13 Charles E. Clark, *Uprooting Otherness: The Literacy Campaign in NEP-Era Russia* (Selinsgrove, PA: Susquehanna University Press, 2000).
14 Anatoliy Lunacharskiy, *Sobraniye Sochineniy*, vol. 7 (Moskva), quoted in Anatoly I. Mazayev, *Iskusstvo i Bolshevism* (Moskva: KomKniga, 2007), p. 123.
15 Moshe Lewin, "Society, State, and Ideology during the First Five-Year Plan," in *Cultural Revolution in Russia, 1928–1931*, ed. Sheila Fitzpatrick (Bloomington, IN: Indiana University Press, 1978).
16 Lev Scherba, quoted in Galina M. Pospelova, "Moskovskiye vyveski v poslerevolyutsionnoye vremya," *Russkaya Rech*, 5 (2013): 92.
17 M. Veisman and M. Yermolayeva, *Organizatsiya I Tehnika Roznichnoy Torgovli Kul'ttovarami* [Organization and Techiques for Trading *Kul'ttovary*] (Moscow: Zaochniy Institut Sovetskoy Torgovli Soyuztranstorgpita NKPS, 1937), p. 8.
18 Vladimir Paperniy, "How I was a designer," *Iunost* [Youth] (January 1978): 100.
19 Ibid., 101.
20 Yuri Soloviev, "Design na sluzhbe obschestva," in Design i Gosudarstvennaya Politika (Moskva: VNIITE, 1975), pp. 1–2.
21 Alena Sokolnikova, "Soviet Design: Crowdsourcing and Anticopyright in the USSR," *Polit.ru.*, December 15, 2012, http://polit.ru/article/2012/12/15/soviet-design-museum/ (accessed March 4, 2018).
22 Ibid.
23 T. S. Ostanovsky, *Tovarovedeniye Kul'ttovarov* (Moskva: Gostorgizdat, 1951), p. 245.
24 Stephen Lovell, *Russia in the Microphone Age: A History of Soviet Radio, 1919–1970* (Oxford: Oxford University Press, 2015), p. 51.
25 Aleksandr Lavrentiev and Yuri Nasarov, *Russian Design*, pp. 54–5.
26 Stephen Lovell, *Russia in the Microphone Age*, pp. 51–2.
27 Ibid., p. 52.
28 Felix Kon, "Sovetskoye Radio – Moschnoye Orudiye Kul'turniy Revolyutsii" Kul'tura I Byt (Moskva: Telegraph News Agency of the USSR, April 14, 1932), p. 1.
29 V. Legar, "Komfort radiopriyemnogo ustroystva," *Radiofront*, 17–18 (1940): 17–18.
30 Marietta Shaginyan, "Lestnitsa Vremeni," Oktyabr', September 1958, p. 118.
31 *KPSS o Kul'ture, Prosveschenii i Nauke*, Moskva: Izdatel'stvo Politicheskoy Literatury, 1963, p. 250.
32 Ibid.
33 Ibid.
34 Vladimir Runge, *Istoriya dizayna, nauki i techniki*, p. 300.

35 Yuri Slezkine, *The House of Government* (Princeton, Woodstock: Princeton University Press, 2017), p. 510.
36 "Otpusknikam v derevne i praktikantam na predpriyatiyah," editorial, *Sovetskoye Foto*, 12 (1930): 353–5.
37 Ostanovsky, *Tovarovedeniye Kul'ttovarov*, 156.
38 Abraham Schwadron, "Music in Soviet Education," *Music Educators Journal*, 53(8) (1967): 86–93; Maya Pritzker, "The Music Education System in the USSR," *American Music Teacher*, 41 (August–September 1991): 18–20, 62–4.
39 Dmitri Kabalevsky, "Soviet Music Education as Seen by a Soviet Composer," *Music Educators Journal*, 60(1) (1973): 45–6.
40 James Riordan, *Sport in Soviet Society* (Cambridge, London, New York, Melbourne: Cambridge University Press, 1977), p. 106.
41 Aleksandr I. Morozov, *Konets Utopii* (Moskva: Galart, 1995), p. 74.
42 Ostanovsky, *Tovarovedeniye Kul'ttovarov*, p. 58.
43 S. Michalkov and B. Brodsky, "Igrushka – Delo Seryoznoye," *Dekoativnoye Iskusstvo SSSR*, 10 (1958): 2.
44 Ibid., 4.
45 Ibid., 4–5.
46 Maxim Gorky, *Pravda*, January 1, 1949, quoted in S. Michalkov and B. Brodsky, "Igrushka – Delo Seryoznoye," p. 5.
47 Ostanovsky, *Tovarovedeniye Kul'ttovarov*, p. 9.
48 Leonid Leonov, *Literaturnaya Gazeta*, January 29, 1949, quoted in T. S. Ostanovsky. *Tovarovedeniye Kul'ttovarov*, p. 9.
49 *Russian National Corpus*, Collection of Anecdotes, "Stalin" (1956–1991).
50 Oliver Johnson, "Kul'turnost' or Kitsch? Varnishing Reality in the Art of Aleksandr Laktionov," *Studies in Slavic Cultures*, VI, (2007): 82–106.

Diversionary tactics at work: Making meaning through misuse

Jennifer Kaufmann-Buhler

In the opening sequence of King Vidor's 1928 film *The Crowd*, the camera pans over a large office with rows and rows of identical desks, each with a worker appearing hard at work. As the camera lands on the protagonist, a single clerical worker within a sea of clerical workers, it soon becomes apparent that he is not actually working at all, but rather jotting down slogans on a piece of scrap paper for a newspaper contest to name a motor fuel. Though the sweeping overhead view implies management's total surveillance of the work and the workers, the main character's non-work is hiding in plain sight. In contemporary organizational behavior literature, this kind of non-work is considered "time theft" because the worker is siphoning time and energy away from their job to engage in non-productive activities.[1] This practice has a long history in all kinds of workplaces, and it is just one of a range of counter-productive behaviors that are characterized in management literature as "organizational misbehavior."[2] Although organizations often invest enormous resources in attempting to prevent such misbehavior, workers in diverse industries, job types, and workplaces have found ways to undermine those efforts through small and large acts of subversion.[3]

Using a case study of late twentieth-century American offices, this chapter examines how organizational culture, power, and prescribed use were encoded into the spaces and objects of the office through design, and how office workers historically repurposed those same technologies and spaces of the office for personal use. The late twentieth-century period is particularly interesting because of the transformation of office space from a conventional design to the new open plan at that time along with the widespread adoption of new office technologies, particularly personal computers in the 1980s and 1990s. Together, these changes altered the interior arrangement of offices and the structure of office work, and simultaneously created new modes of escape for workers.

While organizations of this period would typically consider these types of non-work behaviors that are described in this chapter as a form of "misuse" of time and corporate resources, I argue that these covert activities are politically charged actions that inscribe new meanings into the objects and spaces of work. By reading for misuse, this research illustrates the need for a more inclusive understanding of the office that gives greater weight to the experiences, intentions, and meanings constructed by workers rather than focusing exclusively on the intentions of designers or the organizations that employ them. More broadly, drawing on the concept of affordances, I argue that users of all types have the power to encode new meanings and new uses into the things and spaces they use every day. Rather than analyzing designed objects and spaces exclusively through the lens of intended use, this project proposes a history of design as told through the lens of misuse.

Designing the organization

There is significant research on the ways in which spaces and technologies can reproduce systems of power in the workplace. Scholars in numerous fields, including architectural history, design history, labor history, history of technology, sociology, and management, have examined the ways in which organizations have intentionally leveraged the material objects, technologies, and spaces of work to support the goals of management.[4] This diverse research has demonstrated how managers in many different industries and workplaces throughout the nineteenth and twentieth centuries implemented material, spatial, and technological change intended to increase productivity and efficiency, organize the work process, and control worker behavior.

From the early twentieth century through the postwar period, for example, offices were explicitly designed to facilitate and enable managerial control over the work process; management books from the early twentieth century through the postwar period championed these kinds of spatial solutions for problems of efficiency, often with an emphasis on paper-flow, ensuring that desks were arranged to support the circulation of paper through the office.[5] The design of American offices through this period was not only a means of ordering the workspace and the work process, it was also a means of surveillance. By arranging workers in the open, supervisors could maintain continuous watch over them and ensure that they remained productive.[6] The objects and spaces of the workplace are thus not neutral bystanders of organizational power; they are a means of ensuring organizational control over the process and structure of work. Further, the spaces, technologies, and objects of the office are deliberate reflections of the priorities, values, and goals of the organization; reading the material and spatial aspects of the office is thus a means of reading the organization itself.

Throughout the latter part of the twentieth century, architects and designers played a vital role in crafting this spatial index of the organization. In the postwar period, that manifested in a fixation on organizational hierarchy; architects and designers working in that era sought to create a highly rationalized and standardized office that optimally expressed organizational status from the top leadership to the lowest-level staff.[7] In the 1970s, as the open plan office concept became popular, office design increasingly became a process of reflecting and reproducing organizational culture by using office design to spatially and materially embody organizational values and goals. In his 1978 book on office planning, designer John Pile describes how the office facility should ideally "express the character of the organization," and described a detailed process for understanding the culture and priorities of the organization in order to arrive at a suitable design.[8] Pile thus characterized the designer as a kind of corporate ethnographer, whose primary responsibility was to observe the culture of the organization and faithfully and honestly translate that culture into office space. This appeared in material form through the careful selection of appropriate furniture and finishes, the allocation and design of amenities in the office, and the overall layout of the space itself.

In addition to this cultural translation of the organization into finishes and furniture, architects and designers were also responsible for ensuring that material and spatial needs of each position in the organization were met. To accomplish this, architects and designers surveyed the needs of the various departments and their staff, and translated those various needs into a suitable office design. Among architects and designers who championed the open plan from the late 1960s through the early 1980s, a central priority in the planning process was achieving optimum functionality. The goal was to design a workplace that met the functional needs of workers as expressed through their particular jobs, responsibilities, and tasks. In the design process, architects and designers collected an exhaustive array of data by way of surveys and interviews, documenting workers' communication networks, technologies, and tasks.[9] This data was then translated into an optimum combination of desks, chairs, storage elements, and partitions. While a very practical approach, this process effectively prioritized workers' functional roles in the organization over their human or personal needs.

Further, in determining the needs of different positions, architects and designers did not treat all information equally. Through this process of reading organizations and designing a suitable workspace to support the organization and its workers, architects and designers were effectively reproducing the power structure of the organization. In addition to inscribing organizational status in office space, architects and designers also internalized power structures in their design process by giving greater weight to the preferences of leadership over those of lower-level workers. In this way, architects and designers accepted organizational power as an intrinsic aspect of decision-making, and made choices in their designs regarding the needs of workers through the prism of organizational power and authority.[10] John Pile, for example, describes how it is "inevitable that managers' views should carry weight in rough proportion to their rank in an organization."[11]

Through the process of collecting data, architects and designers were thus assessing the relevance of information received from different individuals within the organization and reproducing the organizational power structure accordingly, ranking the opinions and preferences of those in leadership over the perspectives of lower-level workers. In fact, lower-level workers were rarely consulted at all in the design process. For example, in his work for Union Carbide architect Kevin Roche and his team interviewed more than fifty people across the organization as part of the planning process for their corporate office in the late 1970s. Yet, even as they took several days to conduct interviews, the majority of the people interviewed were executives and managers; only a handful of support staff (secretaries and clerical workers) were included.[12] In their 1978 study on office design for office furniture manufacturer Steelcase, opinion research firm Louis Harris and Associates found that office planning in the United States was largely handled by top executives, supervisors, or administrators, with only nineteen percent of lower-level employees indicating some involvement in the planning process.[13]

Lower-level workers in large organizations were often treated as "interchangeable units" by architects and designers; low-level administrative and clerical staff were thus not people so much as components within the organizational machinery.[14] By prioritizing the views of management over the preferences of workers, architects and designers treated the workspace as a tool of management to optimize productivity and efficiency; each worker only needed the space, technologies, and objects to perform their assigned role in the organization as defined by management. According to environmental psychologist Franklin Becker, the desire of management to create "rules, procedures and environmental supports that emphasize punishment for transgressions" often created an office environment that served as "a symbol of efficiency and an instrument of power."[15] Further, by internalizing this ideal of efficiency and managerial authority, architects and designers created offices in which workers were discouraged from engaging in "discretionary activities."[16] In other words, the workspace was optimized to support work and restrict, prevent, or limit any acts of non-work, which were treated as a misuse of time and space. By letting the requirements of the organization drive the process of allocating space and furniture, architects and designers presumed that the organization knew what workers needed for their jobs better than the workers themselves, and further treated workers as controllable widgets whose behavior could be predicted, constrained, and ultimately redirected towards productivity.[17]

Office design is just one facet of the power dynamic between management and workers that was embedded in nearly all aspects of office work in the late twentieth century. For example, office technologies of that time, including word processors and computers, were frequently designed in ways that prioritized technical requirements, productivity, and cost over the safety, comfort, or general well-being of users.[18] These new office technologies organized the work process, managed workers' time, and attempted to restrict workers' behavior by tracking workers' efficiency, monitoring their activity, and even actively enforcing certain levels of productivity.[19]

Reading office space and office technologies through a lens of embedded functionality reproduces this structural power imbalance and assumes that the task or activity prescribed by a particular kind of workspace or technology is in fact how that workspace or technology was used. In other words, a typewriter sitting on a desk suggests that the person seated at that desk used the typewriter to type, and further that the typing the worker did on that typewriter was naturally productive. Thus, the typewriter, by its very existence, implies the productive labor it ostensibly prescribes. But, what if the worker at that desk did not type at all? Or if the typist, sitting at that typewriter, was actually writing a novel instead of doing their assigned work? While the specification of a typewriter for a particular workstation implies an intended use on the part of management, it does not determine how that typewriter was actually used nor what that typewriter meant in real terms to the worker who used it.

Diversionary tactics

In fact, the same objects and spaces of the office that formalized power could also become a mode of escape for workers. Through deliberate misuse, workers could effectively transform these technologies and spaces into a means of diversion, and even subversion, of the power structure. Looking at the objects and spaces of work through the lens of non-work thus tells an alternative story of office work that challenges these systems of power that were built into office spaces and technologies. Although these types of transgressive behaviors are common in nearly all workplaces, they are difficult to see because they deliberately fly below the radar of observation and detection.[20] Drawing on research from diverse disciplines and sources, including organizational behavior, psychology, motivational research, industrial systems engineering, sociology, business, folklore, popular media, and government reports, I collected stories and other references to workers misusing, abusing, or otherwise repurposing the spaces and objects of the office. Individually, these various examples are anecdotal, referenced in the margins of other seemingly unrelated research, but stitched together they offer a small glimpse into the ways in which workers regularly repurposed the objects and spaces of the office to subvert or challenge the organization or the work process.

Historically, workers have hidden non-productive labor in plain sight by using the space of the office as a stage set, and the objects of the office as props to create an illusion of productivity. In fact, the objects and spaces of office work not only disguise non-work, they also become a means of engaging in transgressive behaviors. For example, in 1981 *The New York Times* reported that employees at the United States General Services Administration were spending so much time ringing up services such as "dial-a-joke" at the office that the Federal Government had as much as $3,000 in fees on their phone bill.[21] The enormous phone bill reveals the lack of supervision over telephone communications and illustrates how this kind of subterfuge works. These workers looked as though they were on business phone calls but were in fact using their workstation telephone as a means of escape from their work day. In this way, workers were repurposing a familiar workplace artifact, the telephone, for personal entertainment. Because the object was associated with an appropriate workplace activity, the use of the phone was an easy act of subterfuge even in a completely open office where one could conceivably be seen at any moment by a passing colleague or manager. The telephone represents a tool of the office and a signifier of productivity while also serving as a means of escape.

Typewriters and photocopiers could also be used as technological disguises and decoys for engaging in non-productive work. There is significant research in folklore on the creation and circulation of subversive corporate humor in the form of print artifacts. In their 1975 book on the subject, folklorists Alan Dundes and Carl Pagter attempt to categorize these types of humorous and satirical stories and objects that were commonly produced and circulated in American offices.[22] Dundes and Pagter offer a truly astounding collection of these print objects that they spent many years collecting, including chain letters, cartoons, satirical office memos, and parody office forms. Building on their work, folklorist Danielle Roemer analyzes the common practice of "photocopy lore," in which workers use the technology of the office to produce these subversive print objects that are circulated through the organization.[23] These subversive objects offer material evidence of counter-productive behaviors at work. Like the workers using their workstation telephone for calls to dial-a-joke, workers' production and circulation of these photocopied objects relies on the repurposing of office spaces and technologies to engage in acts of non-work. The number of examples of fake or satirical memos and forms produced by workers is particularly significant in that it suggests the ways in which workers could utilize office objects like typewriters and photocopiers to appear busy with real work (typing or copying an office memo or form) when they were in fact engaged in a creative act of subterfuge (producing a parody of a memo or form).

The increasing presence of personal computers in workstations starting in the late 1970s and early 1980s created new opportunities for disguising non-work as work. In fact, early personal computers, which pre-dated the widespread use of GUI (graphical user interface), easily masked non-work through their code-like display. Because the computer itself was a work-related artifact, just sitting in front of a computer typing or reading could signify work to a casual observer, even if the text on the screen was not work-related at all. Although word-processing and data-processing systems often featured electronic monitoring in which workers' activity was tracked and reported to ensure productivity, new personal computers, which were used by a much wider array of office workers (including managers, executives, professional, technical, and clerical workers), rarely had any kind of monitoring in place.[24]

In the mid-1980s, the development and spread of Microsoft Windows created another mechanism for disguising non-work behavior. Workers could quickly minimize inappropriate images, games, or other programs, or simply switch to an appropriate (or at least innocuous) window with the click of a mouse or a stroke of the keyboard. Microsoft Windows included some simple games and creative programs (Solitaire, Minesweeper, Paintbrush) that workers could use on their computers. The covert usage of these built-in programs at work was sufficiently problematic that some organizations (Ford, Boeing, and Sears) deleted those time-wasting programs from all company computers in the mid-1990s.[25] Other software, like those produced by FriendlySoft, actually included a "boss key" feature which allowed workers to quickly exit out of a game to avoid detection at work.[26] In 1989, *PC Mag* reported that game manufacturer Broderbund similarly had a "boss key" function that would generate a spreadsheet that was itself a diversion (with user-controllable features creating a game within the game).[27] The presence of a built-in "boss key" in these kinds of software suggests that some gaming companies anticipated a market of players who were covertly playing games on their workplace computers.

In contemporary organizational behavior literature, personal use of the internet at work is called "cyberloafing," and has been an organizational concern since internet access first became common on office computers in the 1990s.[28] Early office internet was rarely monitored, and so the main challenge for office workers was to avoid being seen by a supervisor who might catch a glimpse of personal internet usage on a computer monitor. In 1995, Don Pavlish, then a student at New York University, launched his "Don's Boss Page" website which was dedicated to supporting the unique needs of illicit office web surfers. Similar to the Broderbund software, the website featured a decoy excel spreadsheet on the top half of the screen, allowing workers to quickly disguise their recreational browsing (Figure 4.1). The site later also included a so-called "personal protector" that would launch in a separate window, providing workers a quick exit from any unsanctioned browsing. Fans of Don's Boss Page even shared their own strategies of digital escape on the site, for example using alt-tab to quickly shift from non-work-related activities to work applications, hiding the task bar so that open applications were not visible to passers-by, and using the company website as a foil for non-work-related internet browsing.[29] To this day, mimicking office software to disguise recreational internet usage remains a common tactic. Since 2006, the NCAA (National Collegiate Athlete Association) has included a similar feature on their website for the annual "March Madness" college basketball season, and the website Reddit has a "skin" that allows readers to disguise the site to look like Microsoft Outlook, a commonly used office email program.[30]

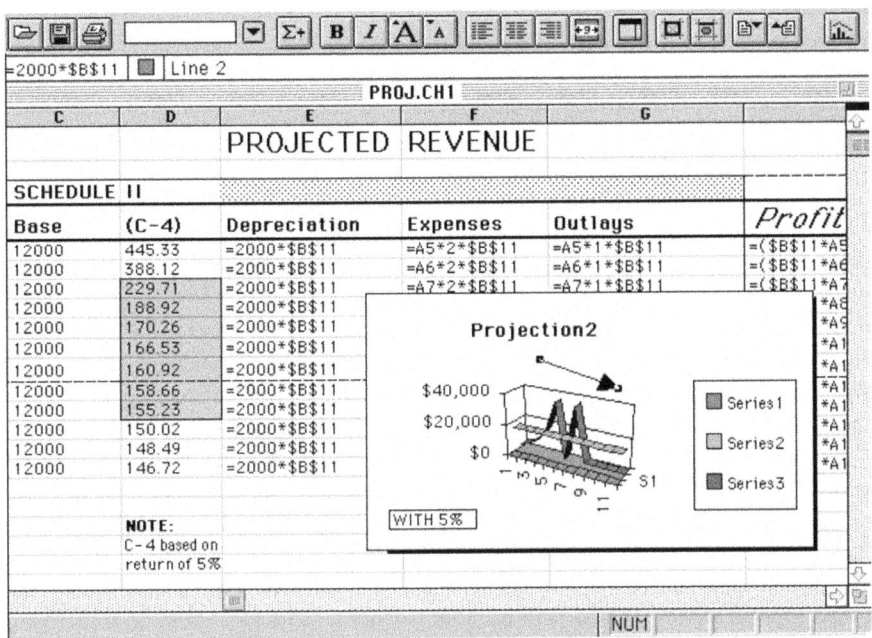

Congratulations! You've discovered the only web site designed to protect those surfing the net from their workplaces or classrooms. With Don's Boss Page, all it takes is a quick click of the mouse to turn any Internet-addicted employee into a hard-working, productive member of society.

Bookmark me now!   Wednesday, February 04, 1998

Figure 4.1 A screenshot of Don's Boss Page showing the fake spreadsheet and the real front page of the website below, as seen on February 4, 1998 from the Wayback Machine on the Internet Archive.

The vast majority of such web browsing in the 1990s was likely fairly innocuous in terms of content (shopping, news, sports, etc.), but some workers used their workplace computer for viewing sexually explicit images and websites. An article in *The New York Times* from 1996 reported that pornography usage at work had become a significant problem when workers at a number of major companies, including IBM, Apple, Hewlett Packard, AT&T, NASA, and Compaq, had been found visiting websites like *Penthouse* and other sexually explicit internet sites on their office computers.[31] *Newsweek* similarly reported in 1999 that Xerox had fired forty employees for spending entire working days viewing pornography using the Xerox network. Indeed, in some cases, the downloading of pornographic images and video was so hefty that it actually disrupted the network, slowing down all other activity.[32] In the late 1990s, some offices began implementing early internet-monitoring software so that management could catch their workers using their office computer for these kinds of salacious activities. In 1998, one hundred companies in the US tested software that tracked workers' activities online, and allowed managers to catch workers viewing pornography in real time. Yet this type of software was not used unilaterally on all workers in the office; according to *The New York Times*, there was often some reluctance to put top-level executives and administrators in jeopardy by using such monitoring software on their computers.[33] This illustrates how workers of different classes and positions within the same office could have vastly different opportunities for these types of activities, and those opportunities were not just tied to their access to technology, but rather were a reflection of their position within the organization as whole.

Other covert activities could take a more destructive turn, sometimes in the form of retaliation against the organization for mistreatment or for dehumanizing working conditions. In organizational behavior literature, such deliberate actions against the organization were often characterized as "sabotage."[34] In 1981, a group of writers, artists, and labor activists in San Francisco began producing an underground zine called *Processed World*. Filled with humorous stories, satirical art, and an underlying political message, *Processed World* gave voice to the frustrations and challenges of many American office workers in low-level clerical, temporary, and other computer-based jobs. Sabotage was a recurring theme throughout the history of the zine (Figure 4.2). In an article from their sixth issue titled "Ten Ways to Wreck a Digital Video Terminal," users were encouraged to pour salted coffee on the keyboard, unplug and re-plug the circuit board with the power on, reverse ribbon cables, damage ribbon cables with cuticle scissors, dump small objects like paperclips directly into the machine through cooling slots, blow cigarette smoke into the machine, remove microchips and put them in backwards, use a magnet around a disc, and deploy a bulk tape eraser.[35] Another article in issue eleven of *Processed World* even provided users specific lines of code that they could use to disrupt computer systems by making information invisible or causing deliberate glitches in the hardware.[36]

Though often treated in the zine in a satirical manner, this kind of sabotage was not just a worker fantasy; a study conducted in 1993 found that managers had seen a number of deliberately destructive behaviors in their offices, including clipped word-processing machine cables; deliberate efforts to crash computer and office systems; and deleted, altered, or otherwise destroyed data on computers.[37] These actions turned misuse into a form of political subversion and directly challenged the dominance of

Figure 4.2 "Sabotage" image from *Processed World* 5 (1982), p. 25. Scanned edition from the Prelinger Library on the Internet Archive.

the organization. By abusing the technologies, objects, and spaces of the office, workers could express their frustration and reassert their own individuality and autonomy within the organizational system.

In the field of organizational behavior, all of these examples are considered organizational misbehavior. By violating formal and informal rules and norms through small and large acts of subversion, these workers were deliberately undermining the organization and disrupting the working process. According to sociologist Jan Karlsson, such behaviors reflect the underlying power dynamics embedded in all types of industries in which management seeks ways of controlling, ordering, and structuring work, while workers seek opportunities to reclaim their autonomy, independence, and dignity from within the work process.[38] Yet, the opportunity to engage in any of these activities is by necessity defined by the organizational and social context. Indeed, an activity that is against the official policies in one workplace may be standard practice in another. For example, in some workplaces, leaving one's workspace during the day for a coffee, smoking, or bathroom break is not contentious at all, and in others, such escapes from work might be closely monitored and sharply limited.[39] The opportunities workers have are also tied to an individual's organizational status—those in higher positions are rarely as restricted as lower-level workers whose jobs are often carefully controlled and monitored in ways that make any deviation from work a challenge. Further, individuals within the organization charged with creating systems that are intended to control or restrict the behavior of workers (for example, managers) are equally capable of engaging in behaviors that subvert those same rules and policies, the main difference being that those in higher positions, who make organizational decisions, typically have greater latitude for such behaviors than those in lower positions who are often subject to higher levels of control and scrutiny.

The meanings of use and misuse

As organizations construct and reinforce their power through the spaces and objects of the workplace, workers challenge that power through deliberate misuse. The objects and spaces of the office thus carry both sets of meanings and uses; they simultaneously enable organizational authority and worker transgression. Yet, in design history we often privilege the intended uses of things and spaces as defined by designers, manufacturers, and organizations over the informal uses, or "misuses," deployed by workers and other classes of users. When design historians read objects and spaces through the lens of function and prescribed use, we are reading for the intentions of designers rather than reading for the experiences of users. As a type of "script analysis," this form of examination empowers designers to inscribe use into the objects and spaces they create, but sometimes treats users as mere actors fulfilling their assigned role by correctly using the object.[40] This way of thinking structurally prioritizes the intentions of architects and designers (and the people who employ them) over the real behavior of users, and naturalizes the systems of power embedded in designed objects.

There are other ways of conceptualizing this gap between use and misuse. In their 2010 article "Affording Meaning," design researcher Julka Almquist and literature scholar Julia Lupton challenge the present culture of design practice in which designers treat users as variables within a human–design interaction. They argue that prescribed use, as embedded in the design of a given object or space, represents a form of control that attempts to order and restrict users. In this model of design practice, users' actions can be predicted, contained, and controlled through the deployment of visual and tactile cues for correct usage.[41] Drawing on the concept of "affordances," Almquist and Lupton argue that objects and spaces often have "latent" functions and meanings that might transgress or subvert the original intended uses. The concept of affordances was first developed by psychologist J. J. Gibson in 1977 to describe the inherent properties of a given material and was later popularized in design discourse by design theorist Donald Norman, who appropriated the idea of "affordances" to describe the ways in which objects could be encoded with cues for action. According to Almquist and Lupton, Norman's interpretation of affordances has tended to emphasize the prescription of use by a designer rather than the possibilities of use created by a user. They argue for a more dynamic concept of "affordances" in which users can repurpose, adapt, and transform both the meaning and use of particular objects in ways that subvert, challenge, or resist the meanings and uses prescribed by designers. In this way, an object is not defined by use as intended by a designer or a manufacturer, but rather constructed through the diverse uses and meanings deployed by users.[42] For Almquist and Lupton, these alternative uses (and re-uses) are as much a part of the designed object or space as those intended by a designer or the organization that employs the designer. "Misuse" is thus no longer misuse at all, but merely an alternative usage.

Looking at objects and spaces of the office through this broader definition of "affordances" as proposed by Almquist and Lupton not only challenges the standard narratives of design that too often privilege a designer's intentions over users' experiences, but also helps address the ways in which designers' intentions may be directly undermined, challenged, or subverted by the organizations and companies who produce or use their designs. For example, in developing Herman Miller's Action Office furniture in the 1960s, designer Robert Propst wanted workers to use the inner walls of their workstations to post personal and work-related materials, but in practice some organizations purchasing this new kind of furniture, designed to allow display, instituted strict rules preventing workers from posting such things to the furniture partitions.[43] Thus, organizations are also users who deploy these designed objects and spaces in ways that may be entirely separate from, and even antithetical to, those intentions of the designer or the manufacturer. The concept of affordances creates a structure for disambiguating these conflicting layers of intention, meaning, and use.

In addition, this way of thinking about the multiple and conflicting uses of things and spaces also gives design historians a means of thinking more intentionally about the various meanings and uses over time. Instead of fixing the object in a single moment tied to its inception by a designer, its first production by a manufacturer, or its first purchase by a consumer, the concept of affordances engages in the life of the object or space through various historical contexts and users. Scholars in fields like vernacular architecture, material culture, and history of technology have developed robust methodologies to explore this issue of change over time, recognizing that spaces, technologies, and things do not stay the same but rather evolve and change through usage.[44] Bringing this idea to office design, for example, instead of fixing a particular piece of furniture in the moment when it was specified by an architect or designer, or installed for its very first user, we should recognize that after installation a desk might serve as a workspace for decades to come, and over that time would likely be used for very different kinds of work, by very different types of workers. The initial user is not more important than all of the subsequent users, and we need to find ways to think about that life of the object through its use. Building on this way of thinking about the life of things and spaces, the concept of affordances creates the opportunity to acknowledge a longer and more complex life in which the object's use and meaning may change significantly over time and through multiple generations of users.

Finally, the concept of affordances is also useful in that it creates a pathway for thinking about diverse users who may inscribe vastly different meanings and uses in the same object or space. In the context of the office, workers in different organizational positions might have entirely different relationships to the spaces of that office: one worker might see a bright, supportive, and attractive workspace, and another might view the same office space as a dimly lit, dreary, prison-like environment. Similarly, an office technology that symbolizes freedom and escape for one class of workers may be an oppressive mechanism of control and surveillance for another class. Further, these types of differences in perspective are not mere matters of preference; they can reflect underlying structural divisions between different classes of workers. Recognizing that context and identity can inform uses and meanings, instead of treating users as an undifferentiated mass of people, design historians need to continue to think about the ways in which identity, context, and experience can inform how users might encounter and relate to a designed object or space. Reading designed things and spaces for these multifarious meanings and uses offers design historians the opportunity to build a more nuanced, complex, and inclusive understanding, not only of design itself, but also of diverse communities of users.

Notes

1 Christine A. Henle, Charlie L. Reeve, and Virginia E. Pitts, "Stealing Time at Work: Attitudes, Social Pressure, and Perceived Control as Predictors of Time Theft," *Journal of Business Ethics*, 94(1) (2010).
2 Stephen Ackroyd and Paul Thompson, *Organizational Misbehavior* (Thousand Oaks, CA: Sage, 1999).
3 Jan Karlsson, *Organizational Misbehaviour in the Workplace* (New York: Palgrave MacMillan, 2012), pp. 15–18.
4 Anna Andrzejewski, *Building Power: Architecture and Surveillance in Victorian America* (Knoxville: University of Tennessee Press, 2008). Shoshana Zuboff, *In the Age of the Smart Machine* (New York: Basic Books, 1988); Thomas Haigh, "Remembering the Origins of Word Processing and Office Automation," *IEEE Annals of the History of Computing*, 28(4) (2006). Oliver Zunz, *Making America Corporate, 1870–1920* (Chicago: University of Chicago Press, 1990). Angel Kwolek-Folland, *Engendering Business: Men and Women in the Corporate Office, 1870–1930* (Baltimore: The Johns Hopkins University Press, 1994). Venus Green, *Race on the Line: Gender, Labor, and Technology in the Bell System, 1880–1980* (Durham: Duke University Press, 2001). Lindy Biggs, *The Rational Factory: Architecture, Technology and Work in America's Age of Mass Production* (Baltimore: Johns Hopkins Press, 1996); David Nye, *America's Assembly Line* (Cambridge, MA: MIT Press, 2013); David F. Noble, *Forces of Production: A Social History of Industrial Automation* (New York: Alfred A. Knopf, 1984). Alfred Chandler, *The Visible Hand: The Managerial Revolution in American Business* (Cambridge, MA: Harvard University Press, 1977). Harry Braverman, *Labor and Monopoly Capital: The Degradation of Work in the Twentieth Century* (New York: Monthly Review Press, 1974).
5 George Terry, *Office Management and Control* (Homewood, IL: R. D. Irwin, 1958), pp. 348–50; Carl Parsons, *Office Organization and Management* (Chicago: La Salle Extension University, 1921), pp. 18–22; *How to Plan Your Office Layout* (Washington, DC: National Stationary and Office Equipment Association, 1953).
6 Andrzejewski, pp. 72–4.
7 Vance Packard, *The Status Seekers* (New York: David McKay, 1959), pp. 114–18. Fred Steele, *Physical Settings and Organization Development* (Reading, MA: Addison-Wesley, 1973), p. 48.
8 John F. Pile, *Open Office Planning: A Handbook for Interior Designers and Architects* (New York: Whitney Library of Design, 1978), pp. 54–5.
9 Ibid., pp. 72–95. Lila Shoshkes, *Space Planning: Designing the Office Environment* (New York: Architectural Record Books, 1976), pp. 43–60. In the Kevin Roche and John Dinkeloo Associates (KRJD) records at Yale University, multiple projects for corporate headquarters included detailed space planning information to determine workspace size, enclosure, technology needs, and adjacencies.

10 Franklin D. Becker, *Workspace: Creating Environments in Organizations* (New York, NY: Praeger, 1981), p. 58.
11 Pile, p. 64.
12 Interview Schedule for Union Carbide Corporation, October 18, 1976, KRJD MS 1884, Box 426, folder "Program," Yale University.
13 Louis Harris and Associates, *Office Environments: Do They Work?* (Grand Rapids, MI: Steelcase, 1978), p. 90.
14 Pile, p. 58.
15 Becker, pp. 72–3.
16 Ibid., p. 68.
17 Alan Lipman et al., "Power, a Neglected Concept in Office Design," *Journal of Architectural Research*, 6(3) (1978): 30.
18 Karen Nussbaum and Judith Gregory, "Race against Time: Automation of the Office— An Analysis of the Trends in Office Automation and the Impact on the Office Workforce," *Office Technology and People*, 1(2/3) (1982): 226.
19 Ibid., pp. 203–6.
20 Michel de Certeau, *The Practice of Everyday Life* (Berkeley: University of California Press, 1988), pp. 36–8.
21 William Schmidt, "For Employers, Dialing a Joke Isn't So Funny," *The New York Times*, March 14, 1981.
22 Alan Dundes and Carl Pagter, *Work Hard and You Shall Be Rewarded: Urban Folklore from the Paperwork Empire* (Detroit: Wayne State University, 1992).
23 Danielle Roemer, "Photocopy Lore and the Naturalization of the Corporate Body," *The Journal of American Folklore*, 107(423) (1994).
24 Office of Technology Assessment, *The Electronic Supervisor: New Technology, New Tensions* (Washington, DC: US Government Printing Office, 1987), pp. 28–9.
25 Mitch Betts, "Drop that Mouse: The Boss Is Coming," *Computerworld*, January 23, 1995, p. 12.
26 FriendlySoft advertisement, *PC Mag*, September 1983, pp. 404–5.
27 John C. Dvorak, "Inside Track," *PC Mag*, June 13, 1989, p. 73.
28 Christine Henle, Gary Kohut, and Rosemary Booth, "Designing Electronic Use Policies to Enhance Employee Perception and to Reduce Cyberloafing: An Empirical Test of Justice Theory," *Computers in Human Behavior*, 25 (2009): 997.
29 "Don's Boss Page," Internet Archive Wayback Machine, February 4, 1998: https://web.archive.org/web/19980204204901/http://www.donsbosspage.com:80/ (accessed on July 11, 2017).
30 Adam Epstein, "This Year's 'Boss Button' for the NCAA March Madness Livestream is the Best Yet," *Quartz*, March 2015. Jennifer Calfas, "The NCAA's March Madness Life Site has an Emergency 'Boss Button,'" *Time*, March 17, 2017. Nina Golgowski, "Fake Outlook Skin Lets Users Discreetly Browse Reddit at Work," *Huffpost*, November 23, 2015.
31 Trip Gabriel, "New Issue at Work: On-Line Sex Sites," *New York Times*, June 27, 1996.
32 "CyberSlacking: The Internet Has Brought Distractions into Cubicles, and Now Corporate America is Fighting Back," *Newsweek*, November 29, 1999, p. 62.
33 Denise Grady, "Keeping Track of Employees On-Line Voyeurism," *New York Times*, May 7, 1998.
34 Ron DiBattista, "Forecasting Sabotage Events in the Workplace," *Public Personnel Management*, 25(1) (1996); John Brehm and Scott Gates, *Working, Shirking, and*

Sabotage: Bureaucratic Response to a Democratic Public (Ann Arbor: University of Michigan Press, 1997).
35 Digital Dogshit, "Ten Ways to Wreck a Digital Video Terminal," 1982, *Processed World*, 6: 28–9.
36 Power to the Processor Igor, "Sabotage," 1984, *Processed World*, 11: 37–8.
37 DiBattista, 50.
38 Karlsson, pp. 174–87.
39 Marc Lindner and Ingrid Nygaard, *Void Where Prohibited: Rest Breaks and the Right to Urinate on Company Time* (Ithaca, NY: ILR Press, 1998), p. 2.
40 Kjetil Fallan, *Design History: Understanding Theory and Method* (New York: Berg, 2010), pp. 78–84. Madeleine Akrich, "The De-Scription of Technical Objects," in *Shaping Technology/Building Society Studies in Sociotechnical Change*, ed. Wiebe Bijker and John Law (Cambridge, MA: MIT Press, 1992).
41 Julka Almquist and Julia Lupton, "Affording Meaning: Design-Oriented Research from the Humanities and Social Sciences," *Design Issues*, 26(1) (2010): 7–8.
42 Ibid., 9–14.
43 Robert Propst, *The Office: A Facility Based on Change* (Elmhurst, IL: The Business Press, 1968), p. 48; "Process Aesthetic: Some Thoughts on the Thinking Process," *Progressive Architecture* (1974); Geri Brin, "Office Decorations: Shipshape Space vs Sinking Employee Morale," *Chicago Tribune*, January 25, 1981.
44 Gabrielle M. Lanier and Bernard L. Herman, *Everyday Architecture of the Mid-Atlantic: Looking at Buildings and Landscapes* (Baltimore: Johns Hopkins University Press, 1997); James Deetz, *In Small Things Forgotten: An Archaeology of Early American Life* (New York: Anchor, 1996); David Edgerton, *The Shock of the Old: Technology and Global History since 1900* (Oxford and New York: Oxford University Press, 2007).

Everything old is new again: Modernization, historic preservation, and the American home, 1920–1966

Emily Wolf

In the February 1952 issue of *House Beautiful*, the magazine's then-architectural editor James Marston Fitch introduced a thirty-page spread with a promise for owners of older houses. Using the physical evolution of George Washington's Mount Vernon as an example, he assured homeowners that the feature would demonstrate "how to merge what you've got (the past) with what you want (the future)."[1] Fitch, an architect and leader in the American preservation movement who would go on to co-found the nation's first graduate program in historic preservation at Columbia University in 1964, positioned the tensions between past, present, and future as ones that had plagued homeowners from time immemorial, concluding "the first thing you can learn from American history is this: Contemporary problems always demand contemporary solutions. If your solutions are as sound for your day as Washington's were for his, you'll have no difficulty integrating your possessions. Good design is ageless."[2]

With its emphasis on contemporary, professionally conceived but consumer-driven design solutions, the feature followed a pattern established by numerous promotional materials and mass-circulation publications during the interwar and postwar periods that addressed the modernization of the older or historic single-family home, a building type at the center of American socio-cultural identity. Put forth by magazines, retailers, government agencies, and manufacturers of home improvement products as diverse as *House Beautiful, Popular Science, Ladies' Home Journal*, Armstrong Cork, Benjamin Moore, DuPont, Montgomery Ward, the Federal Housing Administration (FHA), and Sears, Roebuck and Company, such articles, trade publications, advertisements, films, and prescriptive literature defined domestic modernity in terms of superior building materials, open interiors, clean lines, and labor-saving and life-improving technologies.[3]

The plans and actions recommended by this body of literature required varying degrees of creative input on the part of the homeowner, blurring the boundary between designer and consumer.[4] Rather than foregrounding the designers of the proposed interventions, homeowners were instead given prominence as directors of their own aesthetic choices. Even when consuming designs produced and marketed by others, the homeowner was in control. As Armstrong World Industries' chief interior designer Hazel Dell Brown wrote in *Ideas for Old Rooms and New*, published in 1944, "Whatever you do, use your own ideas. Don't be afraid of them ... a bit of imagination, a good knowledge of your own family and its needs, and your own good taste are just about the only requirements."[5] Whereas Richard S. Tedlow positions the corporate advertiser or publisher as taking the active role in such design transactions, arguing "the customer disposes. But the company proposes," this ignores much of the homeowner's agency.[6] While the manufacturer or publication proposed design interventions, it was the consumer, in the end, who exercised the most control by selecting and effecting the design.

These publications and promotional materials frequently presented homeowners with a choice: march forward, or slip back into the past.[7] The ideological or aesthetic superiority of modern design was rarely debated, in contrast to highbrow and professional architectural publications of the period (with the notable exception of Elizabeth Gordon's vehemently anti-modern *The Threat to the Next America*).[8] Instead, modernization was broadly defined as an individualistic act that maintained aging, outdated housing stock by bringing it into the luminous present. Even when the remodeled houses presented to the public retained an overall historic appearance in terms of style or form, especially at their exteriors, they were described as modern and up to date (Figure 5.1). Nor were the recommended interventions framed as acts of canonical historic preservation, in which the careful retention of older or historic building fabric was a stated goal. They were more often encouraged as a means of maintaining "old-fashioned charm," safeguarding property value, or improving a house's appearance.[9] Although the modernization strategies often altered historic fabric for the sake of modern comfort and ease of maintenance, they ultimately resulted in the retention and continued use of historic buildings.

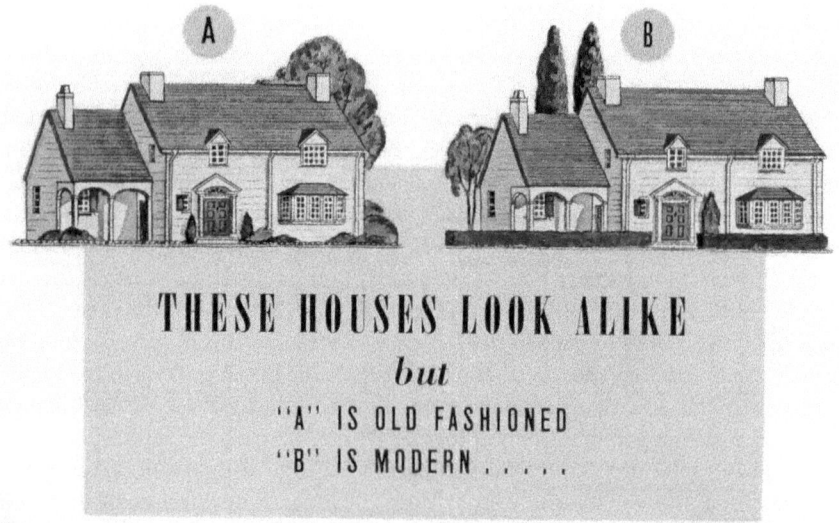

Figure 5.1 Domestic modernity was largely defined in terms of ease, comfort, and modern building materials, as opposed to architectural style or form.

It is not surprising that the recommended design interventions were not framed within the context of historic preservation, given the narrow historic, aesthetic, and class-based focus of the nascent historic preservation movement, which was largely led by educated elites and centered on the architectural and cultural achievements of well-known early Americans. I argue that the strategies for modernizing older and historic houses presented in advertising, promotional materials, and mass-circulation publications between the close of World War I and the passage of the National Historic Preservation Act in 1966 can be reinterpreted as hybrid, mediated acts of both historic preservation and modern design, in which homeowners were active participants as opposed to passive consumers. Given the lack of comprehensive documentation of actual homeowner choices and house remodels, and the changeable nature of the home itself (modernization completed during this period may never have been formally documented with a building permit, and is likely to have been altered in successive remodeling campaigns), this research relies on Federal Housing Administration data for non-farm residential buildings, trade literature, and other primary source materials as a proxy for the actions individual homeowners were undertaking in their own homes.

Positioning the actions recommended by these promotional materials and publications as hybrid, user-driven acts of preservation and modern design requires several essential paradigm shifts. Definitions of Modernism and preservation must be broadened to include mediated styles, materials, and intents. The construct of the designer must be expanded to recognize homeowners and other users as legitimate participants in a complex cycle of design. Buildings must be understood as locations of inherent change as opposed to static entities, an idea the contemporary preservation movement is beginning to embrace. Historic preservation interventions must be recognized as valid acts *of* design, rather than something that is only done *to* design. Modernized houses must be accepted as simultaneous embodiments of modernization and preservation, forces that are often perceived as oppositional.

Limited attention has been paid to the role of mass-circulation publications and advertising in promoting the modernization of the existing American home, from either an historic preservation or design history lens. A robust body of research has addressed the histories of domestic architecture, intersections between Modernism and historicism, historic preservation, and the do-it-yourself (DIY) movement, but there has been little study of the manner in which these elements came together during the interwar and postwar periods to influence the remodeling of older or historic housing stock.[10] While analysis of FHA records, advertisements, corporate literature, and mass-circulation publications has been undertaken, especially in relation to DIY, these materials have not typically been considered with respect to their recommended treatment of the older or historic home.

New homes from old houses

The push to modernize older houses is closely tied to fluctuations in the American homeownership rate and home-building industry. In 1900, just under half of all households (46.5 percent) owned their own home.[11] Whereas homeownership had previously been an important goal for blue-collar workers and immigrants, it was not a priority for middle-class workers and white-collar professionals until the economically robust 1920s.[12] Expanded systems of consumer distribution (such as mail-order catalogs), mass advertising, and hardware stores emerged during this period, making it possible for homeowners to obtain the tools and materials necessary to undertake their own home repair and remodeling projects.[13] Corporations and publications saw older and historic houses as an untapped market, and created modernization materials aimed specifically at this subset of homeowners.[14] Entities that had previously advertised exclusively to the building professional now communicated directly with the homeowner, recommending modernization measures that ran the gamut from essential home maintenance to ambitious improvement projects.[15]

The Better Homes in America campaign, unveiled in women's magazine *The Delineator* in 1922, sought to create responsible consumers and citizens by encouraging homeownership and home improvement through local committees and demonstration weeks.[16] Manufacturers of building supplies joined together to form the Home Modernization Bureau in 1928.[17] Regional offices of the bureau advertised in local newspapers, with aim of inspiring the modernization of three-fifths of existing American houses; these twelve million households represented a potential market of $24 billion.[18] Often conversational in tone and designed to guide the homeowner through the remodeling process, many of the advertising materials produced during the 1920s, such as National Steel Fabric's "New Homes from Old Houses," Weatherbest Stained Shingle Company's "Making Old Houses into Charming Homes," and Barrett Company's "Better Homes from Old Houses: How to Make Your Old House More Comfortable, More Attractive and Worth More Money," continued the "before and after" trope seen in architectural pattern books and decorating and women's magazines since the nineteenth century (Figure 5.2).[19]

These materials presented "before" houses as "sadly in need of repairs" and "with poor exterior design" yet retaining some redeeming qualities in terms of size, location, or sound construction; old houses were "too good to tear down, yet not attractive enough for a home."[20] The modernized "after" houses were generally light and bright, with new exterior cladding materials, and often made more spacious via an addition or the removal of interior partition walls. Typical "after" improvements included "an entrance changed; a broad inviting porch added, or the old one transformed into a cosy sun parlor; the roof lines enhanced by the addition of appropriate dormers or, in some cases, the old ones replaced by a low sweeping roof," all of which allowed "the old home to take its place among those of modern-day design."[21]

The Great Depression caused homeownership rates to drop to 43.6 percent in 1940, the lowest rate of the twentieth century, and stalled residential construction almost completely, with new housing starts falling 95 percent between 1928 and 1933.[22] Although home repair expenditures also fell during the Depression, the lack of new construction created a market, albeit a more limited one, for existing home repair and remodeling that was promoted in many of the era's leading shelter magazines.[23] *Better Homes & Gardens* magazine's 1933 "Better Homes Contest" received 18,706 reader-submitted entries from forty-two states, including the District of Columbia,

Figure 5.2 Many materials produced during the 1920s continued the "before and after" trope seen in pattern books and mass circulation publications since the nineteenth century, with modernized houses typically retaining an overall historic appearance.

all vying for $3,000 in prize money.[24] Seventy percent of entrants modernized the exterior of their homes, with 78 percent adding or altering a porch, building a dormer, or modifying gable details. Thirty-eight percent of entrants altered interior plans by removing room partitions, and 29 percent intended to install new heating systems. Seventy-three percent of entrants installed new wallpaper, paint, or both, and 26 percent refinished their basements, often incorporating up-to-date laundry rooms.[25] Held annually, the competition drew 150,000 entries over its first five years.[26] *House Beautiful* hosted a similar competition with larger prizes, conceived to entice its upper-middle-class readership to hire architects to design more substantial remodels.[27] Such contests demonstrate the continued enthusiasm for home improvement, even during the Depression.

Recognizing that many older houses were in need of "repairing and modernizing to bring them up to the standard of the times," as President Franklin Delano Roosevelt observed in 1934, the federal government initiated a number of programs to stimulate the building and remodeling industries, increase homeownership rates, and improve the quality of American housing stock.[28] The passage of the National Housing Act in 1934 created the Federal Housing Administration, which supported both home buying and home modernization with government loan-guaranty programs. New, federally guaranteed bank mortgages lowered necessary down-payments and made homeownership feasible for a larger sector of the population. The National Housing Act also mandated federally guaranteed home improvement loans of up to $2,000 for "repairs, alterations, or improvements" to existing single-family residences.[29]

These modernization loans were promoted by the FHA's Better Housing Program, which advertised through newsreels (*Better Housing News Flashes*, produced by Pathé News and Movietone), radio programs, pamphlets, and posters. It was estimated that over twenty-seven million Americans saw some form of FHA advertisement in 1934, and by 1936 over forty million Americans had viewed the nine *Better Housing News Flashes* at 150,000 screenings.[30] Between 1934 and 1937, 1.5 million American homeowners (one in eight) had an FHA home improvement loan.[31] Homeowners borrowed approximately $400 on average in 1939, with funds most often used to install new plumbing and heating equipment, refinish exteriors and interiors, replace roofing materials, or make additions or structural alterations.[32] Nearly 50 percent of loans ranged from $100 to $300 (average household income was $1,368), indicating that many homeowners were undertaking thrifty yet substantive updates.[33] Funds were loaned to homeowners in all forty-eight states, the District of Columbia, Alaska, and Hawaii, but the number of loans varied significantly from state to state, with nearly one-third of all loans allocated to homeowners in New York and California.[34] Even when accounting for population distribution by state, these figures suggest that homeowners in more populous regions were more likely to modernize.

Modernization was widely encouraged by shelter magazines, building products companies, retailers, banks, and individual tradesmen, since it increased the consumer market for their goods and services. Promotional materials, such as Bird & Sons, Inc.'s "Are You Going to Build or Repair," Eljer Plumbing Fixtures's "Modern as Tomorrow," Weyerhaeuser Sales Co.'s "Good Homes Never Grow Old," and Montgomery Ward's "Complete Catalog of Plumbing, Heating, Building Materials," underscored the ease, affordability, and desirability of modernization.[35] Leading retailer Sears, Roebuck and Company marketed itself as "the store for home modernizing," while Montgomery Ward declared, "it costs so little at Ward's to modernize your home inside and out" (Figure 5.3).[36] Homeowners with limited modernization budgets typically concentrated

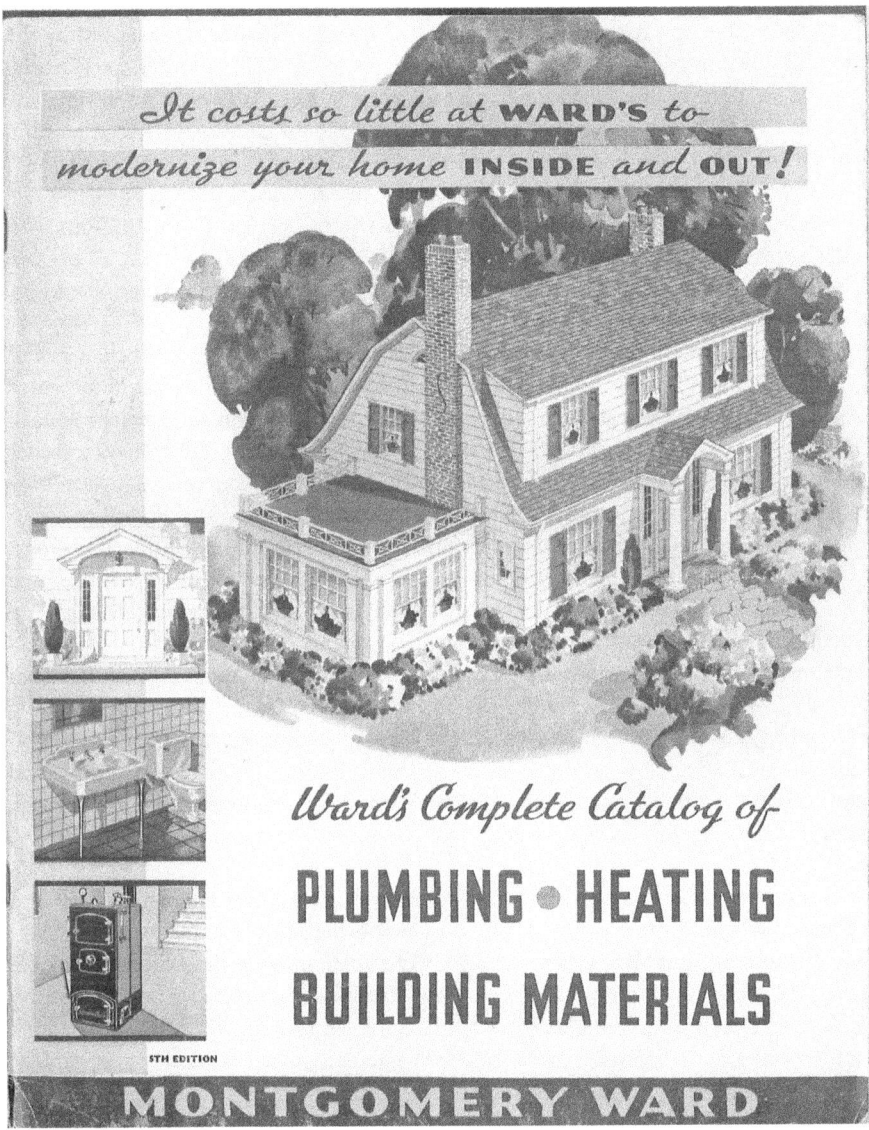

Figure 5.3 During the 1930s, modernization was widely encouraged by the FHA, shelter magazines, building products companies, retailers, banks, and individual tradesmen. Promotional materials underscored the ease, affordability, and desirability of modernization.

on the kitchen and bathroom (a focus shared by retailers), installing mass-produced porcelain and ceramic bathroom fixtures and new appliances, built-in cabinets, and counters of uniform height.[37] Sears, for example, sold a Coldspot refrigerator for $149.50 and a matched steel "ultra-modern" kitchen unit for $28.95 in 1940, meaning a kitchen could be substantially modernized for under $200, well in line with a typical FHA loan of the period.[38]

Homeownership rates did not rebound until after World War II, advanced by the booming economy, favorable financing and tax laws, and benefits afforded to returning veterans as part of the Servicemen's Readjustment Act of 1944.[39] An immediate need for five million new homes to house the growing number of American families spurred the rapid rate of suburban growth that characterized the postwar period.[40] Approximately 114,000 single-family houses were under construction in 1944; in 1950, the number of houses under construction had grown exponentially, to 1.7 million, with "little boxes" rising in new subdivisions across the United States.[41] By 1950, 55 percent of American households owned their own home; 73 percent of these were detached, single-family houses.[42]

Even during this period of expansive new construction, however, more than half of the US population lived in housing stock that was twenty years old or older and which lacked "the utility and livability made possible by postwar technical developments."[43] Only in suburban areas did sales of new houses outnumber older ones; in cities and towns of fewer than 50,000, the ratio of old to new houses sold between 1949 and 1950 was almost two to one.[44] Owners of these older houses were well aware of the new houses under construction across the country and desired similarly modern building materials, floor plans, and technologies in their own homes. Postwar home improvement manuals addressed the specific needs of these homeowners, providing practical advice on how to make old houses "livable in our modern sense."[45] To aid these owners, the federal government's Housing and Home Finance Agency declared 1956 as "National Home Improvement Year." The program, supported by building material dealers, contractors, banks, and municipal officials in more than one thousand cities, aimed to improve or repair at least twenty million houses.[46] Recommended interventions included new wings, updated kitchens, and remodeled bathrooms, modernization efforts that were widely promoted in corporate and FHA literature of the period.

World War II had taught thousands of American men and women manual and technical skills, and the postwar skilled worker shortage and rising labor rates meant that, by the 1950s, middle-class homeowners did far more with their own hands than their nineteenth-century forebears.[47] In 1953, *This Week* magazine reported that sixty million Americans engaged in some form of do-it-yourself, making DIY the nation's number one hobby.[48] The US Department of Labor reported that, in the same year, American homeowners applied 75 percent of the nation's paint, installed 60 percent of its wallpaper, laid half of its asphalt tile, and purchased 25 million power tools and 500 million square feet of plywood.[49] The DIY movement provided millions of homeowners with opportunities for practical, economic, and aesthetic self-sufficiency.[50] Especially for owners of older or historic houses in need or want of modern updates, "do-it-yourself [made] possible luxuries that once existed only in their dreams."[51]

Mediated Modernism

The middle-class house remained essentially traditional in the decades following World War I, with many historicizing revival styles remaining popular. However, as R. W. Sexton observed in 1931, "architects are unanimous in the opinion that the period idea has been carried too far ... They still seek inspiration in the past, but instead of being slavishly imitative they are learning to be interpretive."[52] In new construction of the 1930s and beyond, traditional and modern elements were often combined to create a comfortable, mediated Modernism, what *House Beautiful* called the "American Style."[53] The simplified revival styles used to historicize newly built houses were promoted in shelter magazines; employed in well-known subdivisions of the period, such as the pared-down Cape Cods of Levittown; and included in advertising materials for home-builders and materials manufacturers that highlighted the designs' compatibility with the demands of modern family life. Ideal homes were described in terms of their modern technologies and finishes, such as oil-fired furnaces, porcelain bathroom suites, and electric kitchen appliances. Publications and promotional materials tended to emphasize "the effects of technologies"—comfort, economy, cleanliness, ease—"rather than the technologies themselves," reflecting the widespread focus on the experiential outcomes of modernization rather than a strictly modern aesthetic.[54]

Modernizing alterations brought older and historic houses in line with the hybrid modernity that characterized new residential construction. Publications and manufacturers recommended the removal of older houses' late-nineteenth-century features, such as dormers, gables, porches, and towers, to create simplified exteriors.[55] The clean lines of Modernism were often equated with the spare forms of the Colonial or Colonial Revival styles in both home and furniture design, especially in DIY literature.[56] The aesthetic preference for early American styles mirrored historic preservation activities of the period, which tended to prioritize colonial buildings; reflected the widespread disdain for Victorian architectural styles held by modernists and traditionalists alike; and marked a continuation of the Colonial style-remodeling trend first seen during the late nineteenth century.[57]

The removal of historic detail in the name of modernization was a common theme of the FHA's *Better Housing News Flashes*. *News Flashes* "No. 3" featured Cleveland architect Bloodgood Tuttle modernizing an "ugly Victorian dwelling" into a "charming Colonial-type home." Animation shows the modernization of the house as "bric-a-brac is stripped off." Before viewers' eyes, large chimneys, "overemphasized dormers," a "useless tower," overhanging eaves, iron cresting, a porch, and a porte-cochère are removed and replaced with smaller, white-painted brick chimneys; smaller dormers; a narrow Colonial-style cornice; new window sash; white-painted brick; a modern rear porch; a Colonial entry; and a white picket fence. Despite the many historicizing features that remained or were introduced, the narrator proclaimed that the "house of the gay nineties [had] gone completely 1935."[58]

News Flashes "No. 6" highlighted a display sponsored by the local Better Housing committee at the California Pacific International Exposition, in which a mechanized display of flipping models ("First it's old, then presto it's new!") showed visitors how older houses might be transformed. A bungalow whose owners were in need of more space was modernized with a spacious attic and new wing. A Victorian house was presented as "a relic of the gay nineties—until the gingerbread trimmings are ripped off. Then it becomes a modern, up to date abode."[59] Similarly, "101 Practical Suggestions for Home Improvements," published by the Johns-Manville Corporation (a manufacturer of insulation, roofing materials, and other building products) in 1934, featured a "down at the heels" Gothic Revival cottage transformed into a vaguely Colonial-style "modern home" through the removal of a cross gable and porch, altered eave and chimney details, and addition of shutters (Figure 5.4).[60] In each example, an older house's original form was exchanged for a new, historic–modern hybrid.

Opposing conceptions of the "house of tomorrow" provide insight into the divergent notions of domestic modernity that characterized the interwar period. Architect George Fred Keck's "house of tomorrow" was exhibited as part of the Homes of Tomorrow Exhibition at the Century of Progress Exposition held in Chicago from 1933 to 1934. Keck's design was a three-story, glass and aluminum dodecagon with an experimental air-conditioning system, solar heating, and airplane hanger at its base. The house's modernity was defined through technology and materials, but style and form were no less important. While obviously designed for show, the house embodies a high-style architectural vision for the modern American home.

In contrast, "101 Practical Suggestions for Home Improvements" invites readers to "Make your house the 'Home of Tomorrow.'"[61] Beneath an image of a Craftsman-style house set within a manicured lawn and garden (Figure 5.4), the ideal home is described as "attractive, reflecting good taste—comfortable and modern," with a fireproof roof, a redesigned porch, modernized kitchen, updated interior finishes, and efficient heating and cooling systems.[62] Modernity was not limited to a specific architectural style or form but was instead defined in terms of the overall experience of the domestic environment, what David Smiley calls the "Modernism of inhabitation."[63] A home's modernity was not necessarily expressed through its appearance, but rather by its ability to comfortably house the modern family.

While exteriors tended to remain fairly traditional, even when remodeled with asbestos siding, aluminum windows, asphalt shingles, Masonite, and other modern materials, interiors were more fluid, integrating modern innovations and space patterns. Owners of older and historic houses were encouraged to create simplified, open living spaces by demolishing partition walls, removing doors, and expanding openings between rooms.[64] Using an American Foursquare remodel designed by architect and preservationist L. Morgan Yost as an example (Figure 5.5), the United States Gypsum Company suggested, "Simplification is the best approach in modernization, for interior arrangements as well as exterior appearance."[65] In this clean-lined remodel, living and dining spaces were swapped, a front porch was removed and replaced with a Georgian-style double stair, and the living room was opened to a rear deck, mirroring contemporary house plans. Even with the retained or new historicizing elements, the remodeled house was nevertheless classified as "modern" due to its refreshed plan and materials. Modernization was thus distinct from Modernism. Rather than an aesthetic or ideological end in and of itself, it was an effective means to achieve a more comfortable, up-to-date home.

Figure 5.4 Opposing conceptions of the "house of tomorrow" provide insight into the divergent notions of domestic modernity that characterized the interwar period.

This hybrid, mediated domestic modernity was widely criticized by architectural elites; such houses were neither adequately historic nor acceptably modern. According to Smiley, who addressed this "modified modern" in relation to postwar new construction, "many architects and critics considered these houses degraded and hopelessly compromised as aesthetic objects. The ideas of organic unity and wholeness that undergirded the spirit of 'high' modernism were not compatible with the discontinuities, fragments, and syntheses

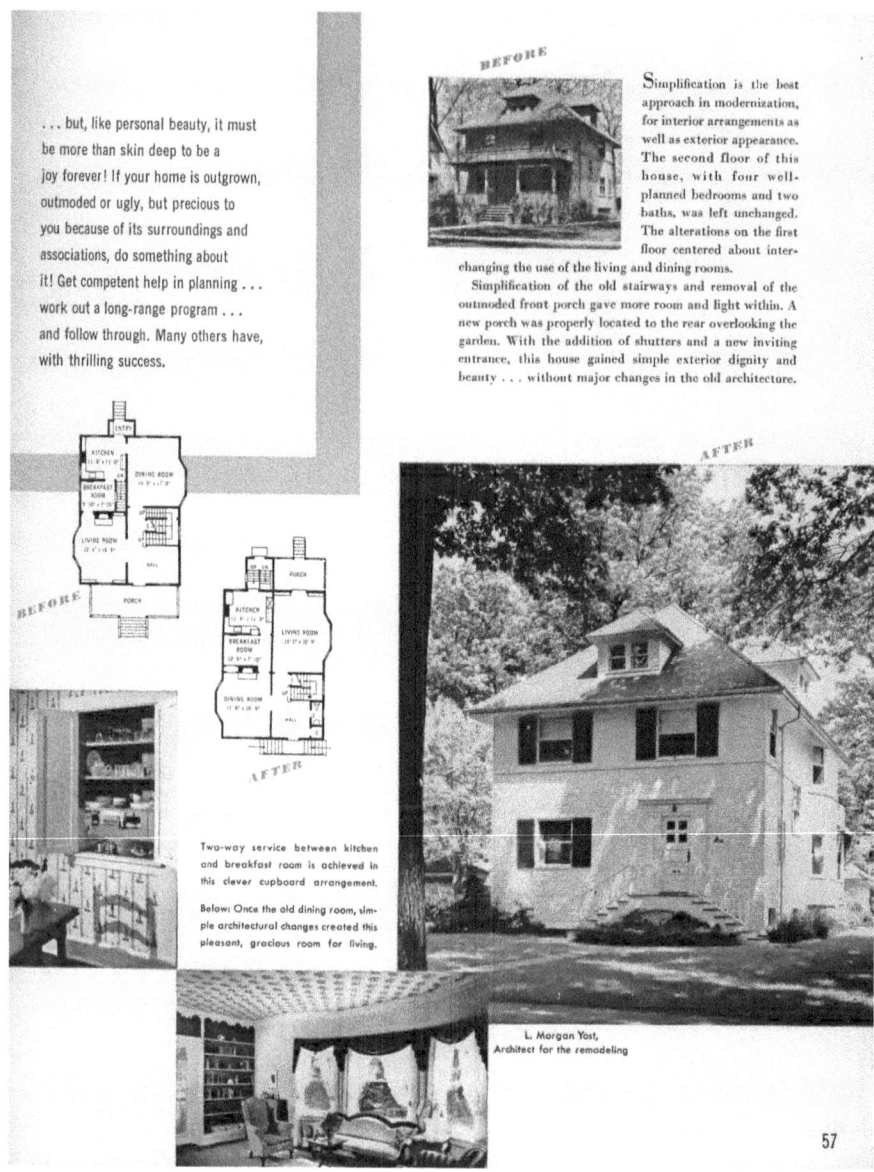

Figure 5.5 Publications and advertisements often recommended the removal of certain architectural features, such as dormers, gables, porches, and towers, to create simplified exteriors, as in this modernization scheme designed by L. Morgan Yost.

introduced by middlebrow or 'modified' domestic practices."[66] However, this mediated Modernism allowed for two of the most oppositional modernist ideologies, individualism and universal design solutions, to exist in concert, albeit within a more ambiguously modern context. Homeowners exerted agency over their design decisions, but solutions were standardized and corporatized, with products and solutions marketed as effective across a range of housing types and forms.

As Paul Atkinson observed, the modernization strategies put forth by mass-circulation publications, promotional materials, and corporate advertisers during the interwar and postwar periods "allowed people from a range of backgrounds, living in housing stock of various ages to engage with modernist design principles without employing expensive architectural advisors."[67] In creating these hybrid historic–modern domestic environments, Modernism was mediated by the publisher, advertiser, or designer of each intervention; by the subject house's existing style and form; by building materials and household technology; and, ultimately, by the homeowner's own choices.

Modernization as preservation

While some homeowners valued old houses for their "special charm" or "warm lived-in feeling," older or historic houses were more often positioned as outdated, lackluster, or unattractive, in contrast to the visual, social, and economic homogeneity of postwar suburbia.[68] The historic or architectural significance of these ordinary houses was, for the most part, overlooked. Instead, they were positioned as spaces that could be rethought and rejuvenated to suit the modern family. *Better Housing News Flashes* "No. 6," for example, urged homeowners to "consult an architect or builder to determine whether there is a more useful and valuable building under your old one."[69] Even when taking on a new identity, however, modernized houses overwhelmingly retained historicizing elements, albeit often from a different period from the one in which the house was originally built or original features re-exposed after late-nineteenth-century accretions were stripped away.

What People Want When They Buy a House, prepared by the Housing and Home Finance Agency and published by the US Department of Commerce in 1955, provides valuable insight into how homebuyers perceived older and historic houses at mid-century. The study was based primarily on two surveys conducted in 1949 and 1950 in which 1,000 buyers of both old and new houses were interviewed in regard to their housing preferences: 40 percent of buyers preferred a new house, while 20 percent preferred an old one (the study defined "old" houses as any house that had been previously occupied).[70] Of those who favored old houses, 61 percent cited quality of construction as old houses' leading attribute, with 18 percent citing price as their most attractive feature.[71] Size was also a draw: older houses tended to have more stories, more rooms, and were more likely to have a dining room.[72] Interestingly, the appearance of a house was of little importance to either group; only 3 percent of all buyers preferred a certain architectural style.[73] This suggests that the experiential aspects of domestic modernity, such as comfort and ease, were more important to homebuyers than a modern aesthetic.

The modernized houses presented in publications and advertisements of the late postwar period were more ambiguous than earlier examples and yet more honest, with historic and modern elements existing side by side. Some of the recommended interventions are problematic from a contemporary preservation perspective, such as the alterations presented in "The Home Improvement Pictorial," published by the Celotex Corporation (a manufacturer of roofing and insulation materials) in 1961 (Figure 5.6). Many original elements of the featured house, built in 1903, were obscured

Prescription for 11 million homes . . .

COMPLETE HOUSE REMODELING

ACROSS the country there are some 11,000,000 basically sound homes now being slowly attacked by blight and neglect. Not yet lost, they can still be brought to proper living standards by professional skill and a reasonable investment of money.

Here we show what can be done by private enterprise—in this case, the Amber Lumber and Supply Co., Pittsburgh, Pa., and ACTION, a national organization concerned with homes in so-called "gray areas" where homes can still be saved. The old home was purchased for $5,000, and just under $11,000 was spent for every conceivable improvement. A more typical renovation would be much less.

AFTER: (photo below) Paneling for the walls and fiberboard acoustical ceiling tile resulted in this modern interior.

BEFORE: (photo above) The living room area dated this home built in 1903 with its dark wood work, cracked walls and ceilings.

Figure 5.6 The modernized houses presented in publications and advertisements of the late postwar period were often more ambiguous than earlier examples, with historic and modern elements existing side by side.

or removed: "dated" dark wood trim and cracked plaster walls were covered with wood paneling and acoustical ceiling tiles, a front porch was eliminated, and the house's entrance was moved to what had originally been a side elevation.[74] While some of these alterations negatively affected the house's architectural integrity, the remodel nevertheless resulted in its preservation, maintaining its essential historic form and use.

The unabashed complexity of such modernized houses was in direct opposition to the "galloping restorationitis" that plagued many idealized reconstructions, in which historic buildings were perfected and sanitized.[75] Large-scale restorations and reconstructions, such as Colonial Williamsburg and Greenfield Village, while certainly attractive, were not reflective of the layers that accrue as architecture necessarily changes over time; Ada Louise Huxtable called Williamsburg an "extraordinary, conscientious and expensive exercise in historical play-acting in which real and imitation ... are carelessly confused."[76] These reconceived historic environments were similar to the modernized older house of the interwar period, stripped down or built up to reflect past styles and forms within the context of the present.

While it was much more frequently promoted in mass-circulation publications and promotional materials, modernization was not the only option available to owners of older houses during the interwar and postwar periods. Reproduction building materials were first introduced in the 1930s, when professionals working on the restoration of Colonial Williamsburg partnered with manufactures to create a range of Williamsburg-branded "approved reproduction" materials that included historic paint colors, wallpaper, moldings, interior tile, and fences. These were marketed both to homeowners interested in remodeling or restoring their houses with greater attention to historic accuracy and to those who wished to imbue newly constructed homes with "correct" historicizing details.[77] Other homeowners engaged in more traditional preservation activities, completing historically accurate restorations based on careful research and attention to existing building fabric.

These homeowners tended to be in the minority, however, reflecting the "activity of a few upper-class antiquarians" as opposed to the actions of ordinary homeowners.[78] The consumer-driven modernization under discussion here in many ways mirrors the findings and recommendations of *With Heritage So Rich*, the seminal report on the state of American preservation published in 1966, which concluded, "If the preservation movement is to be successful, it must go beyond saving bricks and mortar. It must go beyond saving occasional historic houses and opening museums. It must be more than a cult of antiquarians. It must do more than revere a few precious national shrines."[79] The report recommended increased government support (both financial and programmatic) and expanded public–private efforts in order to maintain historic buildings as living parts of communities, something already achieved by homeowners' individual modernization efforts.[80]

The passage of the National Historic Preservation Act in 1966 codified American historic preservation activities, establishing federal and state oversight and standardized guidelines for the treatment of historic buildings. By the late 1970s, preservation was an accepted part of the DIY movement, with some homeowners increasingly interested in the careful restoration of historic houses and manufacturers producing a broader range of historically appropriate building materials.[81] Iconic television program *This*

Old House premiered in 1979, paying closer attention to the accuracy of materials and details but continuing to emphasize the adaptation of historic houses to accommodate modern needs and technologies.

Examining interwar and postwar modernization efforts within the context of design history challenges essential conceptions about the nature of design and preservation and forces historians to reconsider whether such actions must be consciously undertaken in order to be considered valid. While it is unlikely that the homeowners at whom these advertisements, publications, and other materials were directed were primarily motivated by a desire to preserve, the user-driven remodeling of older and historic houses encouraged by this body of literature was ultimately an act of both preservation and of modernization, completing a cycle of design and creating a hybrid domestic identity that allowed homeowners to embrace modern living within the safe confines of a mediated American past. As Fitch shrewdly observed, "In architecture there are no spectators: there are only participants."[82] While modernization didn't often result in aesthetically or ideologically pure iterations of Modernism, it did create numerous domestic environments—and homeowners—that engaged with modern ideas, technologies, and finishes in all their complexity.

Notes

1. James Marston Fitch, "How to Merge What You've Got (the Past) with What You Want (the Future)," *House Beautiful* (February 1952): 60–1.
2. Ibid., 61.
3. Many of the documents referenced in this chapter are part of the Building Technology Heritage Library (BTHL), a collection of American and Canadian, pre-1964 architectural trade catalogs, house plan books, and technical building guides maintained by the Internet Archive in conjunction with the Association for Preservation Technology International.
4. Steven M. Gelber, "Do-It-Yourself: Constructing, Repairing, and Maintaining Domestic Masculinity," *American Quarterly*, 49 (March 1997): 79.
5. Armstrong Cork Co., "Ideas for Rooms Old and New from the Scrapbook of Hazel Dell Brown," 1944, 1, https://archive.org/details/IdeasForOldRoomsAndNew.
6. Richard S. Tedlow, *New and Improved: The Story of Mass Marketing in America* (New York: Basic Books, 1990), p. 375.
7. Architect Julius Gregory touched on this theme in *House and Garden* in "Keep Your Home from Slipping Back" (October 1933) and the "Remodeling Number" (November 1934), in which he observed, "Contrary to popular belief, houses don't stand still. They either march forward, or they slip back."
8. Elizabeth Gordon, "The Threat to the Next America," *House Beautiful* (April 1953): 126–31, 250–1.
9. Armstrong Cork Co., "A Houseful of Decorating Ideas," 1953, 1, https://archive.org/details/AHousefulOfDecoratingIdeas.
   Benjamin Moore Co., "How to Protect and Preserve America's Homes," 1940, 1, https://archive.org/details/HowToProtectAndPreserveAmericaHomes.
10. Notable recent studies of postwar housing include Barbara Miller Lane's *Houses for a New World: Builders and Buyers in American Suburbs, 1945–1965* (Princeton:

Princeton University Press, 2015) and James A. Jacob's *Detached America: Building Houses in Postwar Suburbia* (Charlottesville: University of Virginia Press, 2015). Histories of the American historic preservation movement include *Giving Preservation a History: Histories of Historic Preservation in the United States*, edited by Max Page and Randall Mason (New York: Routledge, 2003) and *Keeping Time: The History and Theory of Preservation in America* by William J. Murtagh (Hoboken: Wiley, third edition, 2005). These tend not to address the smaller-scale actions of individual homeowners in preserving older and historic houses, especially the manner in which houses have changed over time as a result of user-driven interventions. Barbara M. Kelly's *Expanding the American Dream: Building and Rebuilding Levittown* (Albany: State University of New York Press, 1993) does address ways in which homeowners have altered their homes, but her analysis is limited to a specific postwar housing development. Important studies of DIY include *Building a Market: The Rise of the Home Improvement Industry, 1914–1960* by Richard Harris (Chicago: University of Chicago Press, 2012) and Carolyn M. Goldstein's *Do It Yourself: Home Improvement in 20th-Century America* (New York: Princeton Architectural Press, 1998), which accompanied an exhibition at the National Building Museum. The *Journal of Design History* addressed DIY in a special issue in 2006.
11 "Historical Census of Housing Tables: Homeownership," US Census Bureau, last modified October 31, 2011, https://www.census.gov/hhes/www/housing/census/historic/owner.html.
12 Richard Harris, *Building a Market: The Rise of the Home Improvement Industry, 1914–1960* (Chicago: University of Chicago Press, 2012), p. 9.
13 Carolyn M. Goldstein, *Do It Yourself: Home Improvement in 20th-Century America* (New York: Princeton Architectural Press, 1998), p. 17. Richard Harris, "The Birth of the North American Home Improvement Store, 1905–1929," *Enterprise & Society*, 10 (December 2009): 698.
14 Goldstein, *Do It Yourself*, p. 25.
15 Gelber, "Do-It-Yourself," p. 79.
16 Karen E. Altman, "Consuming Ideology: The Better Homes in America Campaign," *Critical Studies in Mass Communication*, 7 (1990): 286.
17 Harris, *Building a Market*, p. 162.
18 Goldstein, *Do It Yourself*, p. 25.
19 National Steel Fabric, "New Homes from Old Houses," c. 1920, https://archive.org/details/NewHomesFromOldHouses_901.
Weatherbest Stained Shingle Company, "Making Old Houses into Charming Homes," c. 1925, https://archive.org/details/MakingOldHousesIntoCharmingHomesWithWeatherbestStainedShingles.
Barrett Company, "Better Homes from Old Houses: How to Make Your Old House More Comfortable, More Attractive and Worth More Money," 1924, https://archive.org/details/BetterHomesFromOldHousesHowToMakeYourOldHouseMoreComfortable.
20 Weatherbest Stained Shingle Company, "Making Old Houses into Charming Homes," 12. Barrett Company, "Better Homes from Old Houses," 1.
21 Weatherbest Stained Shingle Company, "Making Old Houses into Charming Homes," 5.
22 US Census Bureau, "Historical Census of Housing Tables: Homeownership." Kenneth T. Jackson, *Crabgrass Frontier: The Suburbanization of the United States* (New York: Oxford University Press, 1987), p. 193.
23 Harris, *Building a Market*, p. 15.

24 John Normile, "Better Homes & Gardens Awards $1,000 Sweepstakes Prize," *Better Homes & Gardens* (April 1934): 13.
25 Federal Housing Administration, *Bulletin for Manufacturers, Advertising Agencies & Publishers* (Washington, DC: US Government, 1934), p. 13.
26 Goldstein, *Do It Yourself*, p. 19.
27 Ibid., pp. 19–20.
28 Record Group 31, National Archives and Records Administration, Washington, DC, sound recording 3, part 2, quoted in Goldstein, *Do It Yourself*, p. 26.
29 Goldstein, *Do It Yourself*, p. 26.
30 Theodore E. Damm, "How the Paint Manufacturer Can Profit from the National Housing Act," *Oil, Paint, and Drug Reporter*, October 21, 1935, p. 27. Gabrielle Esperdy, *Modernizing Main Street: Architecture and Consumer Culture in the New Deal* (Chicago: University of Chicago Press, 2008), p. 64.
31 Goldstein, *Do It Yourself*, p. 26. Harris argues in *Building a Market* that this is a generous figure, as it includes landlords and property owners who may have held multiple modernization loans.
32 *Sixth Annual Report of the Federal Housing Administration* (Washington, DC: Government Printing Office, 1940), pp. 87, 93.
33 Ibid., p. 94.
34 Ibid., p. 92.
35 Bird & Sons, Inc., "Are You Going to Build or Repair," 1935, https://archive.org/details/AreYouGoingToBuildOrRepair.
Eljer Company, "Modern as Tomorrow," 1939, https://archive.org/details/ModernAsTomorrow.
Weyerhaeuser Sales Co., "Good Homes Never Grow Old," 1935, https://archive.org/details/GoodHomesNeverGrowOldAManualForHomeOwnersOnTheEconomical.
Montgomery Ward, "Complete Catalog of Plumbing, Heating, Building Materials," 1935, https://archive.org/details/WardsCompleteCatalogOfPlumbingHeatingBuildingMaterials.
36 Sears, Roebuck and Company catalog, spring/summer 1940, pp. 636–7. Montgomery Ward, "Complete Catalog of Plumbing, Heating, Building Materials."
37 Goldstein, *Do It Yourself*, pp. 23–4.
38 Sears, Roebuck and Company catalog, spring/summer 1940, pp. 566–7.
39 US Census Bureau, "Historical Census of Housing Tables: Homeownership."
40 Jackson, *Crabgrass Frontier*, p. 232.
41 Ibid., p. 233.
42 US Census Bureau, "Historical Census of Housing Tables: Homeownership." "Historical Census of Housing Tables: Homeownership by Selected Demographic and Housing Characteristics," US Census Bureau, last modified October 31, 2011, https://www.census.gov/hhes/www/housing/census/historic/ownerchar.html.
43 "1956 as National Home Improvement Year," *Marriage and Family Living*, 18(2) (1956): 150.
44 Edward Thurber Paxton, *What People Want When They Buy a House: A Guide for Architects and Builders* (Washington, DC: Government Printing Office, 1955), p. 80.
45 See William Crouse's *Home Guide to Repair, Upkeep, and Remodeling* (New York: McGraw Hill, 1947), Reginald Hawkins and C. H. Abbe's *New Houses from Old: A Guide to the Planning and Practice of House Remodeling* (New York: McGraw Hill, 1948), and Henry Lionel Williams and Ottalie K. Williams, *Modernizing Old Houses* (Garden City, NY: Doubleday, 1948).

46 "1956 as National Home Improvement Year," p. 150. Harris, *Building a Market*, p. 312.
47 Steven Gelber, *Hobbies: Leisure and the Culture of Work in America* (New York: Columbia University Press, 1999), p. 268.
48 *This Week*, June 3, 1956, p. 12, cited in Albert Roland, "Do-it-Yourself: A Walden for the Millions?," *American Quarterly*, 10(2) (Summer 1958): 155.
49 "The Shoulder Trade," *Time*, August 2, 1954, p. 62.
50 Paul Atkinson, "Do It Yourself: Democracy and Design," *Journal of Design History*, 19(1) (March 2006): 7.
51 "The Shoulder Trade," quoted in Atkinson, "Do It Yourself," p. 7.
52 R. W. Sexton, "The Use of Style in Architecture Today," in *The Better Homes Manual*, ed. Blanche Halbert (Chicago: University of Chicago Press, 1931), pp. 149–50.
53 James Marston Fitch, "The New American Architecture Started 70 Years Ago," *House Beautiful*, May 1950, pp. 134–7.
54 Sandy Isenstadt, "Modern in the Middle," *Perspecta*, 36 (2005): 67.
55 Goldstein, *Do It Yourself*, p. 20.
56 Gelber, *Hobbies*, p. 272.
57 Betsy Hunter Bradley, "Reviving Colonials and Colonial as Revival," in *Re-Creating the American Past: Essays on the Colonial Revival*, ed. Richard Guy Wilson, Shaun Eyring, and Kenny Marotta (Charlottesville: University of Virginia Press, 2006).
58 Federal Housing Administration, *Better Housing News Flashes* "No. 3," National Archives Record Group 31: Records of the Federal Housing Administration, 1930–1974.
59 Federal Housing Administration, *Better Housing News Flashes* "No. 6," National Archives Record Group 31: Records of the Federal Housing Administration, 1930–1974.
60 "101 Practical Suggestions for Home Improvements," Johns-Manville Corporation, 1934, 1, https://archive.org/details/101PracticalSuggestionsForHomeImprovements-1934.
61 Ibid.
62 Ibid.
63 David Smiley, "Making the Modified Modern," *Perspecta*, 32 (2001): 51.
64 Goldstein, *Do It Yourself*, p. 20.
65 United States Gypsum Co., "Popular Home's Ideas Galore: How to Build, Buy, Modernize and Decorate," 1946, 57, https://archive.org/details/UnitedStatesGypsumCo.0001.
66 Smiley, "Making the Modified Modern," p. 51.
67 Atkinson, "Do It Yourself," p. 7.
68 United States Gypsum Co., "Popular Home's Ideas Galore," pp. 53, 59.
69 Federal Housing Administration, *Better Housing News Flashes* "No. 6."
70 Paxton, *What People Want*, p. 12.
71 Ibid., p. 83.
72 Ibid., pp. 81, 36.
73 Ibid., pp. 83, 16.
74 Celotex Corporation, "Home Improvement Pictorial," 1961, https://archive.org/details/HomeImprovementPictorial.
75 Ada Louise Huxtable, "Lively Original U.S. Dead Copy," *New York Times*, May 9, 1965, https://timesmachine.nytimes.com/timesmachine/1965/05/09/97198780.html?pageNumber=482.
76 Ibid.
77 Goldstein, *Do It Yourself*, pp. 90, 91.

78 "Focus on Preservation," *Architectural Record* (March 1991), p. 152.
79 United States Conference of Mayors Special Committee on Historic Preservation, *With Heritage So Rich* (Washington, DC: Preservation Books, 1999), p. 193.
80 Ibid., p. 194.
81 Goldstein, *Do It Yourself*, p. 94.
82 James Marston Fitch, "The Future of Architecture," in *James Marston Fitch: Selected Writings on Architecture, Preservation, and the Built Environment*, ed. Martica Sawin (New York: W. W. Norton, 2007), p. 280.

Section 2

Intermediaries

Representing modern architecture in *The Rockford Files*, 1974–1980

Christopher S. Wilson

Rockford

The Rockford Files was a 1970s weekly American television series that narrated the exploits of Los Angeles private investigator Jim Rockford, played by Hollywood veteran James Garner (1928–2014). Rockford, a pardoned convict, was not like other "private eyes" who had been previously depicted on either stage or screen. Paul Green, biographer of *Rockford Files* co-creator Roy Huggins, has described Jim Rockford as "an everyman and not impossible tough guy figure removed from the experience of the viewer. He loses his teeth in fights, can't afford fancy restaurants, asks his father for aspirin and often doesn't get paid for his efforts. He struggles to get along."[1] In the words of James Garner:

> [Rockford is] a quirky character who turns all the private eye clichés inside out: he works out of a broken-down trailer at the beach instead of a seedy downtown office; he's got a telephone answering machine rather than a leggy secretary; and while most private eyes are loners without families, Rockford has his dad, Rocky.[2]

Jim Rockford was cautious; he was not a tough guy who thrived on danger. He would rather run away than fight, believing that "bravery gets you nothing but hurt."[3] In fact, Rockford does not like to hit people because it hurts his hand. He owns a gun, but keeps it in a cookie jar on his kitchen counter. He rarely carried it because, as he said, "If I carry a gun, I may have to shoot somebody."[4] Jim Rockford was an ordinary guy, with a slight paunch because of his weakness for tacos and Oreos. Rockford has little ambition beyond being able to pay his bills, go fishing with his dad, and drink beer while watching TV.

The main character of *The Rockford Files* was not the only aspect of the show that made it different from other TV shows of the time; it was also how the weekly stories were filmed and how they were portrayed on the television screen. Speaking to this aspect of *The Rockford Files*, James Garner has said:

> In the 1970s, Universal was a factory for prime-time television series: *Columbo, Quincy, The Six Million Dollar Man, The Bionic Woman*—all the shows had a similar style, or lack of it. Bland. Cookie-cutter. The studio cared more about

getting them out than getting them good. I didn't want Rockford to be tainted by that attitude, so I hired my own production crew and bought my own location equipment. I wanted to get off Universal's back lot, and I wanted the camera to follow Rockford wherever he went, so we shot more than half the scenes on location.[5]

A total of 122 episodes of *The Rockford Files* were created over six seasons between 1974 and 1980, with more than half of each show taking place outside and/or in the actual streets of Los Angeles. Besides Jim Rockford's trailer, the show's set was basically the city of Los Angeles itself. Rockford frequently impersonated different characters to get the information required for his investigations, which resulted in seeing him at various Los Angeles locales as he talked his way into and out of many different situations. A look at the shooting call sheets published in a *Rockford Files* anthology reveals locations such as: Exterior, Airport; Exterior, Industrial Area; Exterior, Museum; Exterior, Embassy; Exterior, Hot Dog Stand; Exterior Payphone; Interior, Bank; and Interior, Bar. Advanced locations on these same sheets are listed as: Exterior, Donut Shop; Exterior, Mexican Restaurant; Exterior, Raceway; Exterior, Shopping Mall; Interior, Beauty Parlor; and of course, Exterior, Rockford Trailer.[6] This predominance of outside filming was in stark contrast to other television shows at the same time—some listed above—that were mostly shot inside sterile studio conditions or outside on the fake streets of a studio's back lot. Watching *The Rockford Files* each week meant personally following Jim Rockford around the streets of Los Angeles as he pursued various clues, hunches, and leads, until he finally solved the mystery of that episode. That is, watching *The Rockford Files* was like traveling around Los Angeles itself. Because of this, the image of 1970s Los Angeles owes a lot to *The Rockford Files*—and vice-versa: the two seem to be inextricably intertwined.

Modern architecture

A major component of Los Angeles' image as depicted in *The Rockford Files* is the occurrence of modern architecture in the background or as a backdrop to the action. To understand the significance of modern architecture in the 1970s, one must first understand its origins and development. Modern architecture first appeared around the turn of the twentieth century in Europe, particularly in Germany, the Netherlands, and France. Following the industrialization of the nineteenth century, architects and designers began to feel that new buildings and objects should take on new forms to match the new age. This resulted in undecorated, geometrical forms with flat roofs and large expanses of floor-to-ceiling glass that utilized the new materials of iron, steel, and reinforced concrete. Experimentation in the 1920s and 1930s led to a general acceptance of this new style in Europe. However, it took until the 1950s for modern architecture to become commonplace in North America. This acceptance came about partly because of economics—modern architecture was less expensive to construct than traditional architecture—but also partly because of the forward-looking attitude that characterized the style and matched the optimistic post-World War II spirit of the time period. As summarized by architectural historian William J. R. Curtis, "The 1950s in the United States was a period of unparalleled prosperity and relative optimism, in which scientific and technological ingenuity allowed an increasing sophistication in the construction, servicing and detailing of buildings."[7]

By the 1970s, however, modern architecture and its stark minimalism began to be questioned, by architects, designers, and the public at large. Specifically, architects started to challenge the notion that buildings should be, in the words of famous Swiss modern architect Le Corbusier, "machines for living."[8] They started to look back at the merits of historical precedents and merged them with the modern architecture experiments of the twentieth century, resulting in a sort of mash-up style that has been labeled "Post-Modern Architecture." Architectural historian Charles Jencks has tongue-in-cheekly proclaimed that "Modern Architecture died in St. Louis, Missouri on July 15, 1972 at 3:32 pm (or thereabouts) when the infamous Pruitt Igoe scheme, or rather several of its slab blocks, were given the final *coup de grâce* by dynamite."[9]

The result of this questioning of modern architecture was a change in the general meaning and/or understanding of it. As argued by architect Robert Venturi in *Complexity and Contradiction in Architecture*, characteristics such as pure, simple, clean, and straightforward can also be interpreted as impersonal, boring, conventional, and redundant.[10] And so, whereas modern before the 1970s meant new, futuristic, progressive, and avant-garde, after the 1970s modern came to mean inhuman, cold, brutal, and outdated. This is where Los Angeles and *The Rockford Files* comes in: despite the gangsters, pimps, schemes, scams, dirty deals, and double-crossing that takes place in the stories of *The Rockford Files*, the image of Los Angeles that is projected is generally a positive one. It is a place where mysteries are solved, a place where the bad guys get punished, a place where the underdog is supported, and, being southern California, a place where the sun is always shining. A major component of this positive image is the modern architecture in the background of most scenes, both inside and outside. That is, in *The Rockford Files*, the modern built environment is depicted as an optimistic place in which everyday life occurs. The modern architecture of *The Rockford Files* is far from inhuman or outdated; if anything, it is the backdrop for the drama lived out every day of one's life.

This positive image is in contrast to the negative image of 1970s New York portrayed in television and cinema of the time—crumbling, seedy, crime-ridden—that also contains modern architecture in the background. Television shows contemporaneous to *The Rockford Files* depict the streets of New York as a dirty place to retreat from into the safety of one's personal apartment (*The Odd Couple*, 1970–1975), or where controversial (and therefore unsafe) social issues of the time period played out (*All in the Family*, 1971–1979), or where bad things could happen to good people (*Kojak*, 1973–1978). Similarly, contemporaneous films depict the streets of New York as full of gun-toting, bank-robbing, hi-jacking thugs. *The Taking of Pelham One Two Three* (1974) follows four criminals with machine guns as they attempt to hi-jack a New York City subway car with seventeen passengers as hostages in exchange for one million dollars. *A Dog Day Afternoon* (1975) narrates a botched bank robbery on a hot summer's day that also involves hostages. *Taxi Driver* (1976) follows the eponymous character around New York as a vigilante fighting against the city's sleaze, corruption, and prostitution. In these depictions, the modern, urban, and advanced New York is a place where just walking down the street, using the subway, or even going to the bank is a dangerous proposition.

Conversely, in *The Rockford Files*, modern-styled office buildings, schools, hospitals, courthouses, universities, museums, apartment buildings, hotels, and even parking garages serve as a backdrop representing Los Angeles as a modern, forward-looking, and progressive city. As opposed to modern and dirty New York, Los Angeles is modern and clean. While the storylines of *The Rockford Files* reveal just as much sleaze, crime, and corruption as the New York TV shows and films described above, this is mitigated by the pleasant modern built environment that serves as a backdrop to the action. That is, in the Los Angeles of *The Rockford Files*, there still may be gun-toting, bank-robbing, hi-jacking thugs, but the pleasant and modern built environment makes them less noticeable. And, being southern California, the thugs also wear sunglasses and frequent the beach.

For example, in Season 2, Episode 14, Rockford's former cellmate Gandolph Finch is released from prison after twenty years and seeks Rockford's help in proving his innocence. One of their first stops is Finch's former employer, loan shark and pimp Charles R. Runkin, who, in the years that Finch was in prison, had transitioned to the respectable world of suits and lawyers. Proof of this respectability is the modern office building where Rockford and Finch find Mr. Runkin (Figure 6.1). In fact, the building

Figure 6.1 Respectability made three-dimensional through modern architecture: The "Charles R. Runkin Building," Season 2, Episode 14.

Figure 6.2 Jim Rockford [right] and former cellmate Gandolph Finch [left] at the entrance to the "Charles R. Runkin Building," Season 2, Episode 14.

is even named after him; "The Runkin Building" (Figure 6.2) is a tall, gleaming, modern concrete structure that seems to confirm Mr. Runkin's decency. Finch even comments: "Well, after all these years . . . it looks like he done pretty good for himself." The modern structure, however, is just an appearance of respectability, because when Finch asks Runkin for his pre-prison "muscle" job back, Runkin admits that the few times a year when he does need muscle, he brings it in from out of town.

Another example, from Season 5, Episode 3, is when Rockford is framed for murder. The initial hearing for the case takes place at the Santa Monica County Courthouse. Following this hearing, wherein enough doubt was cast to drop the charges, Rockford and his lawyer "Coop" Cooper discuss the possibilities about who may have actually committed the murder as they make their way back to their respective cars (Figure 6.3). All throughout this back-and-forth discussion, which lasts a good three minutes, the modern courthouse looms in the background, ubiquitous and ever-present (Figure 6.4). The courthouse in this scene is literally the backdrop for the intense discussion, serving exactly like a backdrop in a theater: to provide the context in which to place the dialog. It is as if the modern courthouse building—with its flat roof, undecorated geometric surfaces, and plain coloring—represents, in the background, the dispenser of modern justice.

The Rockford Files contains many scenes similar to this in which Rockford and another person, usually his lawyer, discuss a subject and walk at the same time, resulting in a series of buildings or interiors moving in the background (Figures 6.5 and 6.6).

Figure 6.3 Jim Rockford [right] and lawyer "Coop" Cooper [left] exit the modern "Santa Monica County Building," Season 5, Episode 3.

Figure 6.4 Jim Rockford [right] and lawyer "Coop" Cooper [left] debate in the parking lot of the modern "Santa Monica County Building," Season 5, Episode 3.

Figure 6.5 Jim Rockford [right] and stewardess friend Lori Jenivan [left] walking through LAX airport, Season 3, Episode 1.

Figure 6.6 Jim Rockford [right] discussing a contract with lawyer Beth Davenport [middle] and friend Aaron Ironwood [left], Season 2, Episode 1.

These buildings and interiors are always modern, and they always present a positive image of Los Angeles. When looking at the entire six years (and eight TV movies) of *The Rockford Files*, what emerges is a picture of Los Angeles as a modern, forward-looking, and progressive city. This image, however, is conveyed without the use of any of the canonical modern architectural gems of Los Angeles such as Frank Lloyd Wright's textile-block houses, the white boxes of Richard Neutra and Rudolph Schindler, the Case Study Houses sponsored by the magazine *Arts + Architecture*, John Lautner's Chemosphere House, or Pereira and Luckman's Union Oil Center, just to name a few. That is, the architectural aesthetics of *The Rockford Files* were more oriented towards "the everyday" than they were towards "the canon." A sort-of "vernacular modernism" is portrayed—modern architecture as background architecture, rather than standing out from the rest.

Vernacular modernism

The idea of "vernacular" is not unique to architecture. The term is derived from the Latin *vernaculus*, meaning "native." It is most commonly used in the field of linguistics, to describe a common or shared language amongst a group of people. Other uses of the word include vernacular art (those objects made by ordinary people, not designers), vernacular culture (those practices, mostly ritualistic, performed by ordinary people), and vernacular geography (the sense of place revealed by a society's local surroundings). Anthropologist Margaret Lantis has defined the components of the vernacular as: values and goals, time and place, common knowledge, attitude systems, relationship systems, sanctions, and communication, underlining the fact that "the vernacular" is just as much a viable concept to study as "the canonical."[11]

Vernacular architecture is defined as those buildings constructed that are based on local needs, utilizing local construction materials, and usually reflecting local traditions. Its forms vary in shape, style, and material—from the Bali rice barn to the British thatched cottage to the American "shotgun shack." Typically, design professionals are rarely—if ever—involved in the production of vernacular architecture, as revealed in the title of Bernard Rudofsky's 1964 landmark book, *Architecture without Architects: A Short Introduction to Non-Pedigreed Architecture*.[12] University of California Berkeley Professor Nezar AlSayyad has defined vernacular architecture as "native or unique to a specific place, produced without the need for imported components and processes, and possibly built by the individuals who occupy it," but continues this sentence by acknowledging that such a definition is changing in the twenty-first century: "as culture and tradition are becoming less place-rooted and more information-based, these particular attributes of the vernacular have to be recalibrated to reflect these changes."[13]

I use the term "vernacular modernism" to describe the architectural aesthetics of *The Rockford Files* not because those buildings were produced by the local population with local materials, but because they are buildings that were produced without a heroic designer. Identified by architect and graphic designer Martin Treu as a form of "commercial architecture,"[14] it is the strip malls, banks, drugstores, gas stations, furniture stores, food stands, beauty parlors, and supermarkets that proliferated the built environment, especially in North America, after the acceptance of high modernism following World War II (Figures 6.7 to 6.10). Such buildings have all the characteristics of modern architecture—flat roofs, large plate-glass windows, and no traditional decoration—but are not necessarily icons worthy of being included in the architectural history textbooks because they were not designed by some great master like Frank Lloyd Wright. Such buildings are indeed designed and constructed by professionals—architects, planners, interiors designers, etc.—they just do not have the same pedigree as other, more heroic buildings. In addition to these commercial buildings, the other component to vernacular modernism is the "stuff in-between" them—the parking lots, highways, billboards, and signage that come with such an automobile-oriented environment—brilliantly analyzed by architects Robert Venturi, Denise Scott Brown, and Steven Izenour in their landmark 1972 book, *Learning from Las Vegas*.[15]

Returning to Los Angeles and *The Rockford Files*, the modern architecture that serves as a background in most scenes is composed of this vernacular modernism of strip malls, gas stations, parking garages, and supermarkets. Matching the character of Jim Rockford, who is not a glamorous personality but a sort of "everyman," the background architecture of *The Rockford Files* consists of the "everyday" environment of Los Angeles, not of dazzling locations with breathtaking views. That is, Rockford the

Figure 6.7 "Vernacular modernism": Jim Rockford's car driving on a Los Angeles freeway in the opening credits to *The Rockford Files*.

Figure 6.8 "Vernacular modernism": A motel as seen in Season 1, Episode 10.

Figure 6.9 "Vernacular modernism": Jim Rockford [left] at a fast-food stand with friend and client Rita Capkovic [right], Season 4, Episode 16.

Figure 6.10 "Vernacular modernism": Two thugs search for Jim Rockford in a concrete parking garage, Season 5, Episode 14.

"everyman" experiences his life—each weekly episode—in the streets of vernacular Los Angeles. Let's not forget that, after all, Rockford lives in a trailer.

Some may say that the background architecture of *The Rockford Files* is nothing special. After all, the series was filmed on the streets of a city that had major post-World War II development, coinciding—as explained above—with the rise of modern architecture in the USA. This might explain the strip malls, gas stations, and hot dog stands, but does not explain the set-up shots that are constantly used throughout the episodes to inform the viewer where the action is about to take place. These are three- to four-second shots, almost stills, that focus on a building—always modern—resulting in stereotypical building images: hotel, university, federal building, museum, etc. (Figures 6.11 to 6.14). In addition to these specific set-up shots of modern architecture, there are often other, more general, shots of modern Los Angeles (office buildings, skylines, bridges, etc.) that also "set the scene." Such set-up shots primarily reinforce Los Angeles as a modern city, but they also work to validate these stereotypical building images in their modern form. That is, in the nineteenth century—during the period of "the styles"—certain building types became associated with certain styles (banks and government buildings = Classical temples; educational buildings = Gothic; libraries = Romanesque, etc.). With the advent of modern architecture, this all changed stylistically but not ideologically: various building types—particularly institutional buildings—have a stereotypical modern version, which is being reinforced by these *Rockford Files* set-up scenes.

Figure 6.11 The image of "hotel," as seen in Season 5, Episode 8.

Figure 6.12 The image of "university," as seen in Season 4, Episode 13.

Figure 6.13 The image of "federal building," as seen in Season 2, Episode 15.

Figure 6.14 The image of "museum," as seen in Season 5, Episode 20.

Multiple modernisms

The relevance of this discussion of the architecture depicted in *The Rockford Files* to this book's topic of looking "beyond the canon" is two-fold. Firstly, examining such popular culture staples as television shows is worth the time of the design historian because such shows cannot take place within a vacuum or against a blank screen. During each show, the characters will be dressed in a certain way, they will be surrounded with and use designed objects, and the action will take place inside specific interiors and around specific exteriors—all of which can be identified and analyzed for historical purposes.

More specifically, however, this analysis of the architecture depicted in *The Rockford Files* has revealed that modern architecture is not just simply what can be found in the textbooks. That side of modern architecture is a grand (hi)story composed of iconic structures that were designed by iconic architects. Such buildings are photographed in majestic sweeping views—often without people—and distributed via architectural magazines, journals, textbooks, and, most recently, the internet. An entire culture (or cult) of architectural tourism has evolved in recent years in which people travel from place to place just to see these icons, often to take the exact same photograph as they have seen in the magazine or textbook. But what has been revealed in this chapter is that there is another side to modern architecture—a vernacular modernism—which is just as relevant and deserves the attention of the design historian. Such an analysis opens up the possibility, not only in architecture but in all areas of design history, of "multiple modernisms." Not just one, single modernism, but a multiplicity of modernisms that co-exist parallel to each other, sometimes informing each other and at other times not. It is the recognition that not all buildings are destined to become design icons—even the reassurance that this should not be the case (imagine a world where every single building screams out "I am an icon!"). It is the recognition that "the everyday" is just as important—if not more so—as "the extraordinary," a point that can easily be made both inside and outside the classroom. And, in the end, the recognition and acceptance of such multiplicities is the very definition of looking "beyond the canon."

Notes

1 Paul Green, *Roy Huggins: Creator of "Maverick," "77 Sunset Strip," "The Fugitive" and "The Rockford Files"* (Jefferson, NC: McFarland & Co., 2014), p. 126.
2 James Garner and Jon Winokur, *The Garner Files: A Memoir* (New York: Simon & Schuster, 2011), p. 128.
3 Ibid.
4 Ibid.
5 Ibid., p. 126.
6 Ed Robertson, *Thirty Years of THE ROCKFORD FILES: An Inside Look at America's Greatest Detective Series* (New York: ASJA Press, 2005), pp. 322, 330, 362, and 365.
7 William J. R. Curtis, *Modern Architecture since 1900* (Upper Saddle River, NJ: Prentice Hall, 1996), p. 400.
8 Le Corbusier, *Towards a New Architecture* (1923), trans. Frederick Etchells (New York: Dover Publications, 1986), p. 4.

9 Charles Jencks, *The New Paradigm in Architecture: The Language of Post-Modernism* (New Haven: Yale University Press, 2001), p. 10.
10 Robert Venturi, *Complexity and Contradiction in Architecture* (New York: The Museum of Modern Art, 1966), p. 16.
11 Margaret Lantis, "Vernacular Culture," *American Anthropologist*, 2 (1960): 206.
12 Bernard Rudofsky, *Architecture without Architects: A Short Introduction to Non-Pedigreed Architecture* (Garden City, NY: Doubleday, 1964).
13 Nezar Al Sayyad, "Foreword," *Vernacular Architecture in the 21st Century: Theory, Education and Practice* (London: Taylor & Francis, 2006), p. xvii.
14 Martin Treu, *Signs, Streets, and Storefronts: A History of Architecture and Graphics along America's Commercial Corridors* (Baltimore: The Johns Hopkins University Press, 2012).
15 Robert Venturi, Denise Scott Bown, and Steven Izenour, *Learning from Las Vegas: The Forgotten Symbolism of Architectural Form* (Cambridge, MA: MIT Press, 1972).

CLOTHES CLOTHES CLOTHES PUNK PUNK PUNK WOMEN WOMEN WOMEN

Maria Elena Buszek

On July 14, 2016, Viv Albertine—of the legendary, all-woman band The Slits—arrived at the British Library to speak as part of its *Punk 1976–78* exhibition. The library had been collecting material from the British punk movement since the 1970s, and the exhibition was organized as part of the year-long, city-wide *Punk.London* celebrations commemorating the "40th anniversary" of the movement in the UK, which most participants and scholars agree coalesced around the first performances of the Sex Pistols in 1976.[1] Albertine's talk was organized—like other events that included The Raincoats' Gina Birch, punk-musician-turned-scholar Helen "McCookerybook" Reddington of The Chefs, and Albertine's fellow Slits member Tessa Pollitt—as part of the library's efforts to encourage discussion regarding the significant contributions of women to punk's foundations during these formative years. And, yet, in ways reflective of the very clichés these speakers were coordinated to contradict, the exhibition's checklist and labels perpetuated the perspective that UK punk was a near-entirely male phenomenon.

Albertine strode onto the British Library's stage, clearly a bit hot under the collar, and opened her talk by asking the audience whether they had seen the exhibition's introductory "yellow panel," name-checking a series of bands listed there as pioneers of the movement: "The Sex Pistols, The Buzzcocks, la-la-la ... they didn't mention the female bands!" She then added, mischievously, "There is now, if you want to go around and have a look"[2] (Figure 7.1). As was reported by the music press in the ensuing days, Albertine had vandalized the exhibition's introductory label and "corrected" it to include some of the listed bands' women contemporaries and collaborators—not a stretch, considering, as the punk-era music journalist Caroline Coon has confidently asserted: "It would be possible to write the whole history of punk music without mentioning any male bands at all."[3] And yet, Albertine lamented, the battle for women's visibility in punk history continues: "It's a fight that, honestly, never, ever ends."[4]

Albertine's critically acclaimed 2014 autobiography CLOTHES CLOTHES CLOTHES MUSIC MUSIC MUSIC BOYS BOYS BOYS—titled after her mother's exasperated mantra during Albertine's adolescence, filled as it was with these very obsessions—goes a long way in correcting the historical record. (So, too, have more recent autobiographies by contemporaries such as Chrissie Hynde, Grace Jones, and

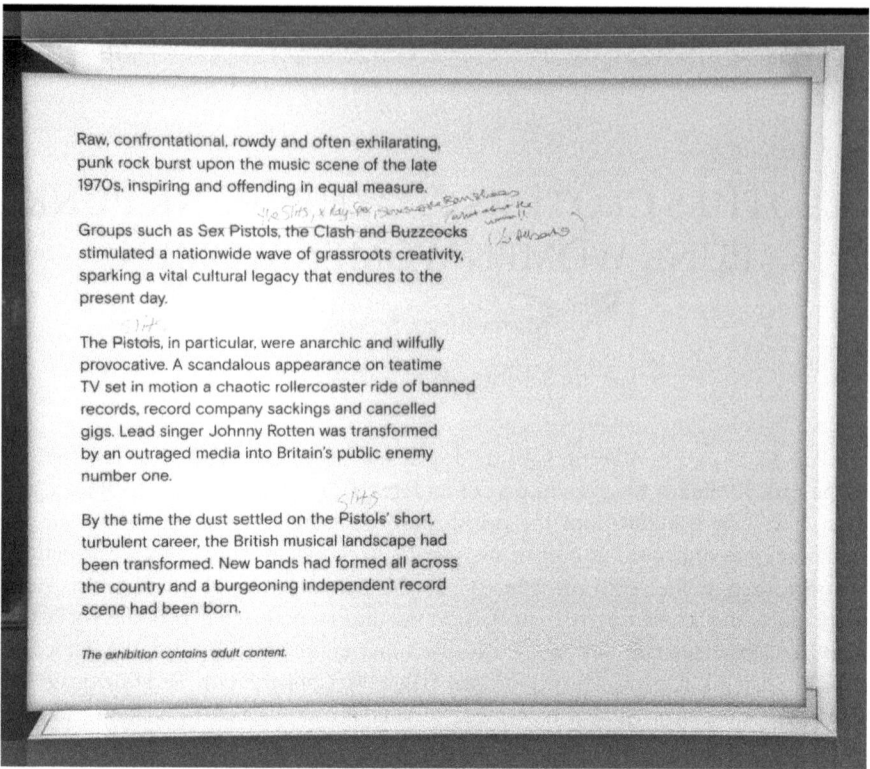

Figure 7.1 Detail of Viv Albertine's "corrected" introductory label to the *Punk 1976–78* exhibition, 2016.

Cosey Fanny Tutti.) The book was a bestseller among music fans, but scholars of art and design history would do well to read this art-school dropout's insights into the interconnectedness of the visual, musical, and performance cultures of punk, as well as punk's role as a feminist incubator for many in her generation. In particular, and as evidenced by the primacy of "CLOTHES" in the book's title, Albertine champions the fact that fashion was the first way in which punk culture expressed itself, its participants found one another, and perhaps the one subject on which women were looked to as authorities at punk's start. This authority was reflected in the significance of women as professional designers and do-it-yourself pioneers in punk fashion, and also instilled in many an agency that extended to other parts of their lives. Because recent anniversaries around punk's fourth decade have seen a burst of interest in establishing a canon of its foundational figures that too often marginalize, or outright ignore, the contributions of women, I would like to address the pivotal roles of both fashion and women as "intermediaries" in the gestation of UK punk, with a focus on influential figures for whom clothing served as an empowering extension of their creative practice and, for several, a realization of their feminist politics.

"I thought the fashion was much more important than the music. Punk was the sound of that fashion."[5]

Malcolm McLaren

While the precise origins and birthplace of punk are too nebulous and contested to be fleshed out in any detail here, there is general agreement that between the mutation of an aggressive American garage-rock sound represented by Detroit's Iggy and the Stooges in the late 1960s and the first public performances of London's Sex Pistols in 1976, a youth subculture recognized as "punk" emerged. The movement's labeling is often credited to the New York City fanzine *Punk*, founded in 1975 by John Holstrom and Legs McNeil to document the stripped-down, grungy rock scene that began to revolve around writer-musician Patti Smith and the club CBGB's in the mid-1970s. However, the term first entered popular culture decades earlier, arguably through the writings of William S. Burroughs, whose chronicles of queer life often referenced this underground term for young, gay hoodlums. "Punk" was first appropriated by popular music in 1971, when *Creem* magazine's Dave Marsh used the term "punk rock" in a piece about the flamboyant, working-class style and exuberantly messy sound of Chicano one-hit wonders ? and the Mysterians, and again in 1973 by his *Rolling Stone* colleague Greg Shaw (and publisher of the music 'zine *Who Put the Bomp?*) in his review of the garage-rock compilation *Nuggets: Original Artyfacts from the First Psychedelic Era*. Here, Shaw defines punk as "the arrogant underbelly of Sixties pop:" proudly unschooled, unhinged, and primitive.[6] The fact that this style caught on in the midst of a ballooning economic crisis in the West during the 1970s is no coincidence. Scholars Dick Hebdige and Simon Frith influentially added to the earliest definitions of punk the notion that the decade's recession, poverty, and political turmoil led this subculture toward a rejection of hippie optimism and "glam-rock" decadence in favor of a gritty, angry expression of what Frith, by way of Hebdige, called "an oblique challenge to hegemony."[7]

But before it coalesced into a full-blown musical genre, as McLaren's quote above asserts, punk was recognized as a "look" rather than a "sound"—and both evolved from the increasingly visible queer culture that its roots in Burroughs' writing acknowledges. As one of the first journalists for London's music weeklies to write about the then-emergent punks, Coon noted in the summer of 1976 that all its strands seemed to lead to David Bowie, who had at that point abandoned his flashy, glam-rock "Ziggy Stardust"-era personae, adopted a sleek, minimalist look and sound, and moved to Berlin with Iggy Pop in an effort to immerse himself in the city's lingering, Dada-era vibes.[8] Important, too, was Bowie collaborator Lou Reed's recent incarnation as a *Rock'n'Roll Animal*, through which Reed adopted a similarly theatrical, if less fey, persona: studded-leather-clad, head shaved, eyes ringed in thick black eyeliner.[9] These stark, Weimar Republic inspirations would have been instantly recognized by the art-school students who dominated the early UK punk scene, bringing with them a knowledge of the Dada and Surrealist art crucially rediscovered and taught by their professors who came of age in the Pop Art era.[10] So, too, was this era a rediscovered touchstone for the city's queer clubs of the mid-1970s, where interwar-inspired get-ups proliferated following the 1972 hit film *Cabaret*'s popularization of Weimar *kabarett* glamour, and dovetailed neatly with glam-rock androgyny.[11] These scenes merged as the future founders of the Sex Pistols, Siouxsie and the Banshees, The Clash, and The Slits gravitated toward London clubs associated with the city's gay and lesbian scenes, such as Chaugerama's (eventually, and famously, rechristened The Roxy), the Masquerade Club, and Louise's, as would the Manchester punks who eventually formed The Buzzcocks and Ludus frequent that city's drag bar, Dickens. All these clubs were known for playing the dance-oriented glam-rock of Bowie and Roxy Music, as well as the sensuous soul of Barry White and Isaac Hayes—music miles away from the chart-making, squeaky-clean sounds of The Bay City Rollers and Brotherhood of Man that dominated the British airwaves in 1976. As Siouxsie Sioux would reminisce about punk before "punk:" "Before it got a label it was a club for misfits. Waifs, male gays, female gays, bisexuals, non-sexuals, everything. No one was criticized for their sexual preferences [...] we attracted that ambiguous sexuality."[12] And cultivating this "ambiguously"-gendered, Weimar-inspired look meant that soon enough the few shops that specialized in the unusual, provocative clothing that went over in these scenes themselves became clubhouses—none more influential than the boutique at 430 King's Road run by Vivienne Westwood and Malcolm McLaren, the latter determined to put a "sound" to the look.

In 1971, Westwood and McLaren had taken over the storefront of the former Paradise Garage on the King's Road fashion strip in London, peddling the vintage dead-stock that appealed to London's "Teddy Boys," and clothing of their own design inspired by the Teds' Edwardian-England-meets-50s-rockabilly look. They rechristened the shop first as Let It Rock, then in 1973 changed it to Too Fast To Live Too Young To Die, whereupon it became a constantly evolving storefront in the mold of Granny Takes a Trip, established a few doors down in 1963. Granny Takes a Trip was founded at the then-unfashionable side of the King's Road known as "World's End," but would eventually bookend the strip that was arguably first established when Mod maven Mary Quant's boutique opened at the opposite end in 1955. Granny Takes a Trip was curated with a Pop Art sensibility, organized events, printed poster art, and even produced an album.[13] As English designer and curator Jane Withers would later write, this model of "the pop boutique" "offered the possibility of an environment that was both an artistic and a commercial outlet—a fusion of studio and gallery, court and stage."[14] To peripatetic art student McLaren, 430 Kings Road offered him an opportunity to put his interests in conceptual art—which he studied at Central St Martin's, Chiswick Polytechnic, Croydon College of Art, Harrow Art College, and Goldsmiths (without ever graduating from any of them)—into real-life practice, in the manner of neighboring Granny's.

McLaren had also been associated with the King Mob group, formed by a group of Brits inspired by the Situationist International (SI) movement, which had emerged in continental Europe after World War II. Claiming themselves heirs to the interwar Dada movement, the Paris-based SI espoused the idea of *detournement*, or the strategy of appropriating and then manipulating pre-existing imagery, texts, narratives, and technology from the so-called "spectacle" of popular culture in order to undermine the status quo it propped up. According to Situationist theory, these "*detourned*" projects would stealthily re-enter pop culture, whereupon their seeming familiarity would lend them an audience, but their contradictory, anti-consumption, anti-capitalist messages would instigate a wave of critical thinking, protest, and even revolution to overthrow what they saw as a complacent, bourgeois postwar order.[15] In its publications and interventions, the British King Mob group held up American lesbian feminist Valerie Solanas as an exemplar for the putting radical theory of her *S.C.U.M Manifesto* into practice in her (unsuccessful) plot to assassinate Andy Warhol in 1968—the same year that SI-affiliated youth helped successfully shut down the city and suburbs of Paris in the May '68 uprising. McLaren was convinced that the working-class, often violent subcultures of the Teds and, later, *The Wild Ones*-emulating "Rockers" to whom his boutique catered might be ideal collaborators (or, at the very least, minions) for the SI-inspired projects that he had in mind.[16]

Westwood was, if anything, more fueled by and dedicated to the activist underpinnings of the Situationists, though she lacked the formal education in their principles that McLaren enjoyed. Born into a working-class family in the northern county of Derbyshire, Westwood went to Harrow Art School for just one year, studying silversmithing and painting, but quit and put herself through secretarial school and teacher's college. Supporting her family—son Ben from her first marriage, Joe from her relationship with McLaren, and McLaren himself—with a meager teacher's salary, McLaren pulled her into the shop at 430 King's Road after he took it over, in hopes that her modern copies of 1950s fashions might supplement his unsuccessful scheme of selling at a mark-up the vintage records he had spent his art-school grants buying. Westwood had grown up in relative poverty (in the era of post-World War II rationing, no less), and was a self-taught seamstress, making her own clothing since adolescence.[17] What began as an exercise in pattern-making—as she literally took apart vintage clothing to learn how to recreate desirable "drape" jackets and zoot suits for the Teds— quickly took over the store, as the couple's increasingly modern and, eventually, wildly original twists on and repurposing of vintage fashions took over the shop's aesthetic.

Westwood and McLaren began experimenting with more and more aggressive and confrontational "rocker" styles—leather, metal studs, zips, and even bicycle-tire and chicken-bone embellishments—in unisex styles and sizes. Following their SI influences, they also began hand-printing texts, slogans, and lists onto their clothes using a toy printing set and stencils, marker pens, and fabric dye: "The Barrier Between Friend and Foe is Thin," "At Certain Times of the Day There Are Only Us," "Create Hell and Get Away With It," "Be Reasonable Demand The Impossible."[18] By 1974, these experiments had led them toward increasingly pornographic designs and materials, studying BDSM fetish gear long custom-tailored and sold by mail-order and at underground establishments like London Leatherman, and yet another change of name for 430 King's Road, now provocatively dubbed SEX. The shop was a magnet for the mostly teenaged "misfits" who had been congregating at clubs like Louise's, and vice-versa.[19]

The store's growing popularity with this new youth subculture inspired McLaren— no doubt remembering the fictional pop group whose name King Mob had invented and sprayed around Victoria Station as one of their many efforts to create hype around their politics[20]—to piece together a phony band of, essentially, mannequins to shill the store's wares. Their name first appeared well before the group existed, on a screen-printed SEX T-shirt of 1974, cooked up by the shop's sometime manager and fellow SI enthusiast Bernard Rhodes, with contributions from McLaren, and which served as something of a manifesto for the shop's aims. Often called the "Loves/Hates T-shirt,"

(Figure 7.2) it began with the ominous statement: "you're gonna wake up one morning and <u>know</u> what side of the bed you've been lying on!" followed by a list of hated, establishment cultural phenomena ("the ICA and its symposiums" "THE ARTS COUNCIL" "David Hockney & Victorianism" "POP STARS who are thick and useless"), separated by a diagonal line of white space dividing it from a list of, presumably, approved ideas and individuals. Significantly, the "loves" list not only includes obvious SI and King Mob heroes (Valerie Solanas and her "Society for Cutting Up Men," Alex Trocchi, Buenaventura Durutti), but the fake band "Kutie Jones and his SEX PISTOLS." Within a year, McLaren had cobbled together a group of young men who hung out and

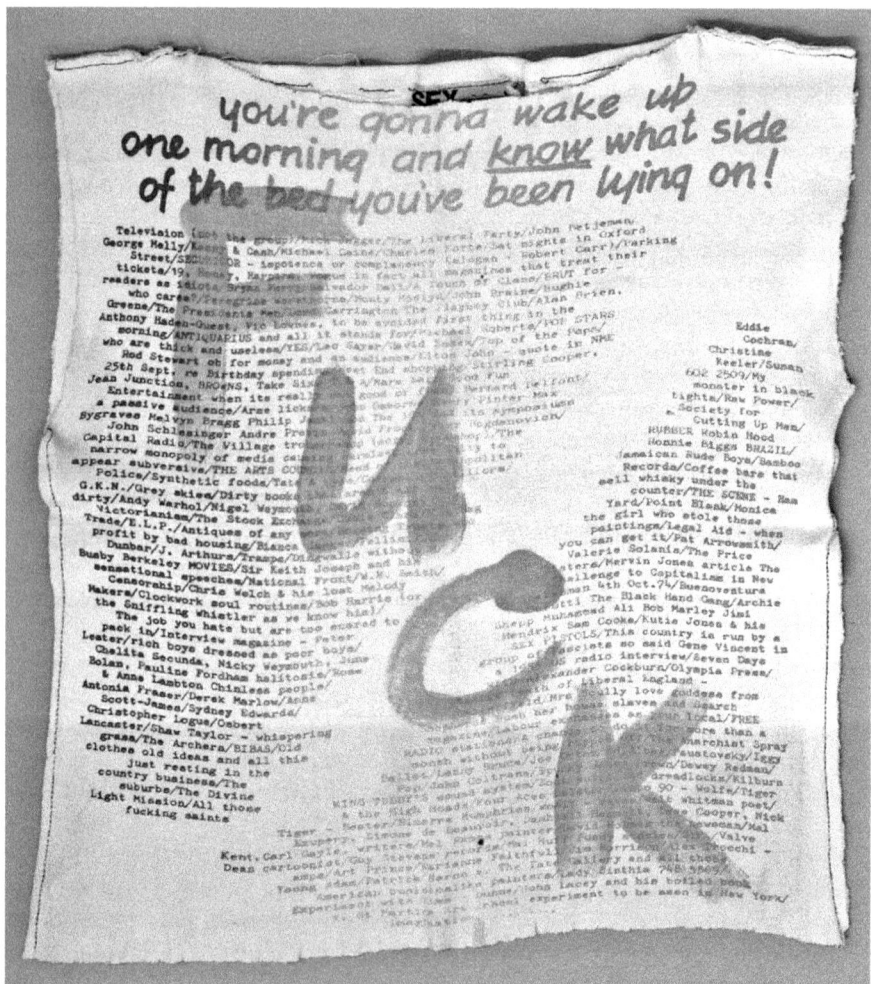

Figure 7.2 Malcolm McLaren, Vivienne Westwood, and Bernie Rhodes: "You're gonna wake up one morning and know what side of the bed you've been lying on" T-shirt, SEX *c.* 1976.

worked at SEX to essentially *become* its "Pistols," who would wear the store's gear and act out McLaren and Westwood's Situationist-inspired fantasies in the shambolic gigs that followed—and ultimately, ironically, eclipse both the store's and the designers' influence in pop-cultural history.[21]

Returning to the "Loves/Hates" T-shirt, it is interesting that, while the garment has gained fame for its prefiguring the pioneering punk band, rarely discussed is the fact that so, too, does the shirt reference many women, and specifically feminist women, as heroes on the "loves" half: from pop-cultural underminers of the British status quo like Christine Keeler and Marianne Faithfull, to convicted IRA terrorists The Price Sisters and Rose Dugdale. More surprising is the presence of feminist philosopher Simone de Beauvoir and, along with the infamous Solanas, fellow lesbian activist Pat Arrowsmith. While both Westwood and McLaren consistently shunned the label "feminist" throughout their lives, Rhodes' dedication to radical causes and more organized politics—which eventually led to his breaking from both SEX and the Pistols and organizing his own band to manage, The Clash—suggests his influence in these figures' inclusion. (Indeed, Rhodes wearing this very T-shirt at the same 1975 gig that future Clash guitarist Mick Jones wore his own led to their fateful introduction.)[22] That said, the fact that the "graffiti" that adorned the walls of SEX was derived from Solanas' *S.C.U.M. Manifesto*[23] is further evidence that, at the very least, British punk's original headquarters admired and sought to emulate the radical ideologies of the feminist figures name-checked in SEX's shop and garments.

There is no question, however, that SEX attracted many women to its staff and clientele, for whom the shop's clothing and community nurtured a transgressive sensibility—indeed, it is often remarked upon that the shop's now-legendary saleswoman Jordan (neé Pamela Rooke) was, as music critic and punk historian Jon Savage put it, "the first Sex Pistol."[24] The late film director and gay activist Derek Jarman, who would cast her as the heroine Amyl Nitrate in his 1977 punk epic *Jubilee*, concurred: "As far as I was concerned, Jordan was the original. Without Jordan, the shop wouldn't have worked. She was the original Sex Pistol. Everyone else came in and saw Jordan dressed up, and the attitude, and it took off from there. She was the Godfather, the Godmother if you like."[25] Short and zaftig, with variously colored hair teased and swept into spikes or an asymmetrical bouffant, and makeup that often separated her plain features into Mondrian-like planes, Jordan was an unlikely high-fashion muse. But her insouciant confidence, and dedication to extreme sartorial self-expression, influenced not only Westwood toward increasingly button-pushing ensembles, but the growing community of misfit club kids who discovered the store and emulated her look. And the influence was reciprocated, as Westwood—a generation older than most of her staff and patrons—became a mentor to many of them from her perch at SEX. In 1976, the shop was renamed Seditionaries, befitting Westwood and McLaren's increasingly assertive use of the shop's clothing as a Situationist intervention, as it found its way into the world on the backs of a rapidly multiplying set of kids calling themselves punk rockers. Jordan herself remembered Westwood's view of her fashion as kind of consciousness-raising: "You could never just buy something in the shop. It was always *why* are you buying it? [...] She could always make it into some political statement about the world today. [She...] worked as a teacher, and has never lost that attitude, of teaching and wanting to teach."²⁶ The result was a new community centered around the shop, which resembled Andy Warhol's studio "the Factory" a decade earlier, but revolving around McLaren and Westwood. And, as Savage has written, while McLaren was cultivating the Pistols "during the latter part of 1975 and the first half of 1976, Vivienne cultivated her own inner circle of performers, mainly women, who would act out the implications of the Sex Pistols [...and] their wildest fantasies. By doing so, they became part of the Sex Pistols and gave punk its Warholian edge."²⁷

And, of course, these women gave punk its sartorial "edge," focusing as Westwood did on the costuming of this burgeoning scene, with Jordan as its first, and singular, intermediary across borders of genre and gender. Today, the most visible images of Jordan in pop culture—like those of the era's punk women in general—tend to represent her in the most outrageously hyper-sexual ensembles sold at the store. To many of the women who frequented SEX and Seditionaries, this overtly sexual costuming felt liberating; journalist and music scholar Lucy O'Brien (formerly of The Catholic Girls) reminds us that the hard-edged, fetish-style gear many punk women chose was not only pointedly confrontational in public vs. private, but appeared against "the [mid-1970s] backdrop of tiered flowery skirts, flicks and flares, and the crushing conformity of what it meant to be a female in a Britain still tinged by post-war austerity."²⁸ (Although, interestingly enough, while Jordan's outrageous outfits often so piqued fellow public-transport passengers on her commute into London from her suburban council flat that she would be physically attacked, it was her co-worker Alan Jones who was arrested for "exposing to public view an indecent exhibition" while wearing McLaren and Westwood's "Naked Cowboy" shirt, featuring a *detourned* 1969 Jim French illustration of two pantsless cowboys in the style of Tom of Finland.)²⁹ However, a closer look at the historical record suggests that Jordan's style, overwhelmingly reflected in the garments sold at SEX and Seditionaries, was—like that of the era's punk women in general—often rather androgynous. To Caroline Coon, the real story of punk fashion was the way it "demonstrated a progressive political story of how patriarchal, orthodox, binary sex and gender stereotyping was being blurred if not collapsing."³⁰

Then, as now, Westwood's bestsellers weren't the rubber and mesh, lingerie-inspired outfits Jordan wears in today's most-reproduced imagery of London punk's heyday, but the stores' unisex, silkscreened T-shirts. Her perhaps most infamous model, the "Tits T-shirt," (Figure 7.3) is a hilariously simple example of the kind of gender play at work in the store's early punk fashions. As infamous for allegations that Westwood and McLaren had "*detourned*" the idea (and possibly the image itself) directly from a T-shirt produced since the late 1960s by the San Francisco-based Jizz, Inc. label as the concept itself,³¹ the shirt featured a chest-height "window" onto a silkscreened, *trompe-l'oeil* pair of women's breasts. Needless to say, the effect was different, but equally baffling no matter the gender of the shirt's wearer. The Sex Pistols' guitarist Steve Jones wore a version on the band's legendary appearance on Bill Grundy's *Today* show, when Jones called Grundy a "fucking rotter" on live TV in December 1976 (and effectively put the band on the mass-culture radar as a result of the scandal); with Jones' burly frame and working-class, macho demeanor, its juxtaposition came across as an obscene joke. On willowy, blonde Viv Albertine, however, the T-shirt's image invited, then mocked, the illusion of bare women's breasts that it suggests. In such cases, the double-

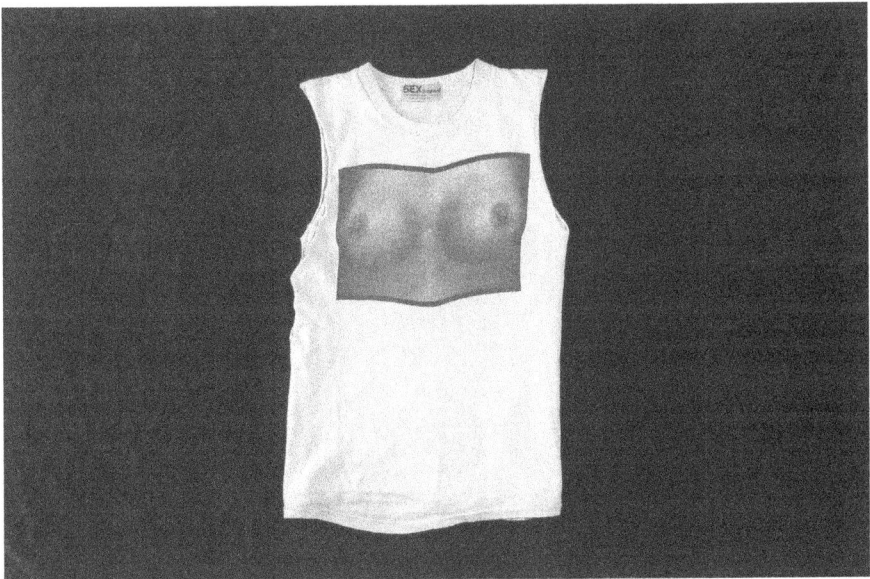

Figure 7.3 Malcolm McLaren and Vivienne Westwood, "Tits" T-shirt, SEX, previously owned by Helen Wellington-Lloyd, c. 1976.

takes that the shirt encouraged were of a different, if no less provocative, sort; musing over the effect of such garments worn by femmes such as herself, Albertine would later write, "men look at me and they are confused, they don't know whether they want to fuck me or kill me. This sartorial ensemble really messes with their heads. Good."[32]

Subtler in its unisex appeal, and perhaps the first Westwood ensemble to clearly cross into haute-couture, was the iconic 1977 "bondage suit" (Figure 7.4). The original suit was inspired by Westwood's studied mash-up of US Army trousers she'd found during a trunk-show trip to New York City, the zip-and-strap-laden fetishwear for which SEX had gained notoriety, and a straightjacket; first made of the polished, black satin cotton that British Rail used for its uniforms, followed by a range of wool tartans. The suit came in two variations: one with a jacket in a boxy "military style," the other a more form-fitted "civilian style."[33] Its trousers—legs connected (and long strides hobbled) by a strap at the knees—had attachments for an optional kilt "flap" to add to the ensemble, and the pant-zip went from front-to-back along the crotch seam, making closing them up a tricky endeavor, especially where men's more dangly bits were concerned. While the suit today tends to be identified as menswear, both archival photographs and films, and accounts of participants from the original London punk scene, confirm that the Seditionaries bondage suit was made for, sought after, and worn by punks of all genders.[34] Indeed, as seen in Jane England's photograph of Westwood and Jordan in the shop (Figure 7.4), throughout 1977 Jordan was summoned by Westwood to model the unisex suit for photographers and the press—notably, in the first documentary on punk to be aired on British television, Janet Street-Porter's *The*

Figure 7.4 Jane England, *Vivienne Westwood and Jordan, Seditionaries, London,* 1977.

Year of Punk. Here, Jordan languidly poses while Westwood's voice-over reels off the garment's historical influences, asserting deadpan that the suit is "something that you might have seen at the Battle of Culloden," and holding forth on the political significance of British craft, haughtily informing Street-Porter: "I don't go to Hong Kong and get something made up cheaply. I rely on English craftsmen," adding "If I were the Prime Minister, one of the things I would do to help the economy of this country is to take more care of English craftsmen."[35]

For all these reasons, women were drawn to punk fashion, and Westwood and Jordan as its earliest female icons, which would eventually nurture the consciousness of overtly feminist punks who would emerge from the scene. Coon—who came of age during the hippie years, and was recognized as a prominent British activist while barely out of her teens[36]—was one of the most public, vocal feminists of early punk. She not only went out of her way to speak to gender issues in her very earliest articles on the movement for *Melody Maker*, but often made a point of asking the women she interviewed their perspectives on women's liberation.[37] Coon, however, was among the notable exceptions; to most punks, the feminist movement was negatively lumped in with hippie culture. The label was rejected, if only—like punks' appropriation of the swastika in the years before skinhead punk took Nazi ideology to heart—as another strategy to shock or claim independence from liberals of the previous generation. Artist and fashion designer Alex Michon reflected on her own, class-based take on the term at the time: "feminism seemed to belong to another era. I saw it as a mostly middle-class thing, something that posh mothers did."[38] When pressed by Coon in a 1977 interview with The Slits to speak to what the journalist felt was the band's feminism, Albertine disdainfully responded, "we're just not interested in questions about Women's Liberation. [...] All that chauvinism stuff doesn't matter a fuck to us. [...] You either think chauvinism is shit or you don't. We think it's shit."[39] In her autobiography, Albertine summarized the contradictory feeling of young women like herself at that moment, who identified with feminism's aims, but not its "isms": "I read a lot about feminism, and I'm a feminist, apply it to everything I think and do, but I don't want to be labeled in any way."[40] But, from Coon's perspective today, reflecting back on the type of evolving political consciousness very much in evidence in biographies like Albertine's, "as they matured and understood the world, in various ways, all these women realized that they did need feminism—indeed, they embraced the term."[41] Of Westwood herself, and the deeply feminist lessons Albertine feels she learned by way of fashion at 430 King's Road (regardless of the designer's rejection of the term), she wrote admirably: "[Westwood is] uncompromising in every way: what she says, what she stands for, what she expects from you, and how she dresses. She's [...] made me conscious of the signs and signals I'm giving off with my clothes. I've become much more visually aware from going to the shop, more than from any art-school teaching."[42] In such ways, through her politically motivated design and consciousness-raising, Westwood became an intermediary between not just fashion and music, but punk and feminism.

Linder Sterling, artist and founder of the Manchester band Ludus, was (like many figures from that city's scene) less worried about how her political affiliations might be "labeled" by the London crowd. Then, as now, Manchester proudly identified as the radical, working-class home of England's suffrage movement, and pioneering punks from the area often actively embraced its activist history.[43] With her friend Savage, a queer punk himself allied with the aims of both the women's and gay liberation movements, she co-authored the 'zine *The Secret Public*, which featured Linder's collages inspired by her studies of art and literature in the feminist magazine *Spare Rib*. Linder cautions we should "never underestimate the power of the first pair of bondage trousers that Vivienne Westwood made—it was beautifully crafted and subtly subversive," and notes that like many punk women she wore hers as a badge of honor, even though she was threatened and even beaten by strangers for wearing them in public.[44] Linder additionally credits the ways in which Westwood's shop encouraged "women like Jordan, over size 12, daring to wear fantastic clothes. Up North, too, there were big lumpy punks around. A lot of the punk women weren't 'ideal' prizes, but they had small skirts on if they wanted [...] There was something glorious about all those shapes and sizes of bodies on show."[45] As is evident in this photograph of women congregating at The Roxy during London punk's crescendo in 1977 (Figure 7.5), the looks ran the gamut from obviously homemade, slashed-and-chained approximations

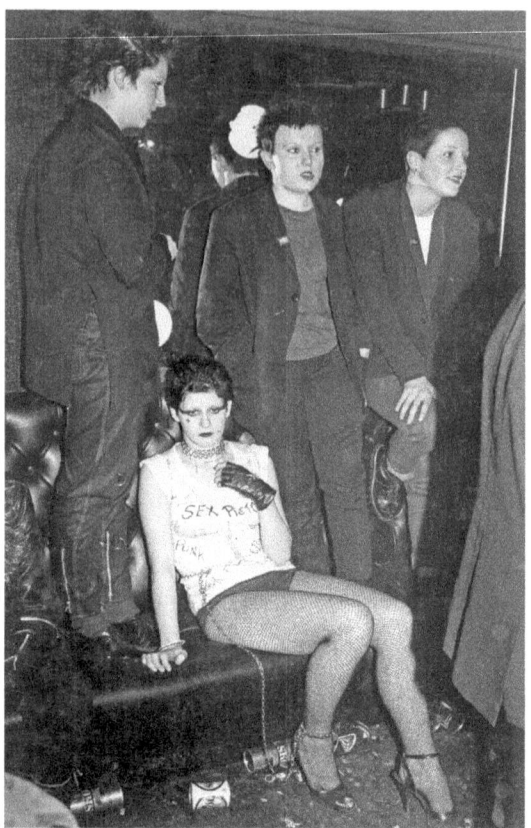

Figure 7.5 Punks at The Roxy, London, April 1977.

of fetish styles to "lumpy," butch blazer-and-dungaree ensembles; stilettos and Doc Martens.

This anything-goes approach was furthered by the do-it-yourself ethos of punk, including punk fashion; seeing as McLaren and Westwood started their own careers as designers by copying historical fashions, evolving out of the cut-and-paste, "jumble-sale" aesthetic of the early 1970s, this should be unsurprising. And while the pair were quick to develop an elitist, hierarchical attitude toward London's punk fashion scene—especially after competitors such as Acme Attractions sprung up elsewhere on King's Road, and dozens of Pistols-inspired bands cropped up in their wake—the scene they helped foster was not bound to McLaren's and Westwood's shop for its uniform. This was significant in no small part because their work was so expensive because it was largely hand-made locally—and, in the case of the bondage suits, of heritage fabric—often by Westwood herself in her family's tiny council flat in Clapham. (In 1976, for example, a Seditionaries button-up "anarchy shirt" ran upwards of £25, or approximately £170 at the time of this book's printing.)[46] But, the fact of the couple's own DIY ethos was also inspiration to many punks to create their own clothing rather than buy the pricey gear at 430 King's Road—especially women, used to being taught or expected to make clothes for themselves and their families, and long encouraged to pay careful attention to their sense of style.

"Oh Bondage! Up Yours!"[47]

Poly Styrene

Indeed, the late musician Poly Styrene suggested her pioneering punk band X-Ray Spex's first single, 1977's "Oh Bondage! Up Yours!" was something of an anti-Seditionaries rejoinder. Styrene herself (born Marianne Joan Elliott-Said of Scottish-Irish and Somali descent) was, like Jordan, among the earliest models of punk femininity in London, but without the name-brand stylist. After running away from home at the age of fifteen, she supported herself out of a tiny vintage-clothing stall at the same rabbit-warren of boutiques at the Beaufort Market on King's Road from which Acme Attractions first emerged. As Acme's head clerk, DJ, musician, and filmmaker Don Letts has said of Beaufort Market's shops, they were not just friendlier and less elitist, but also struck the British-born Jamaican Letts as less racist than the scene at 430 King's Road: "It was about multi-culturalism, whereas Vivienne and Malcolm were always more Eurocentric. [...] The kids who came to [Beaufort Market] were intelligent enough to know that there is something aesthetically wrong with a punk thing being ready-made and sold for £60."[48] Bi-racial and pixyish, with a mouth full of braces and a head topped by wild, natural curls, Styrene was one of these "kids."

Always dressed eclectically in the same rag-picked, second-hand clothing she sold inexpensively at her stall (Figure 7.6), Styrene embodied both the DIY and anti-consumerist spirit that was fomented by punk women beyond the clique at Westwood's and McLaren's shop, as well as the significant contributions of Britons of color to UK punk's origins—like women, too often forgotten in histories of the scene. Many of her thrifted ensembles (as seen in Figure 7.6) riffed on the perma-prest looks of 1960s Mods and the natty "rude-boy" styles of Afro-Caribbean British immigrants. But Styrene would often undermine these "cool" sources with comical, kitschy additions such as pom-poms, feathers, and even fake-fruit arrangements that read as more grandmotherly than vanguard, but no less feminist in its sartorial potential. Styrene's style is reflected in the comfortable, make-and-mend aesthetic captured in a photograph of music journalist and musician Vivien Goldman and musician Neneh Cherry by Coon (Figure 7.7). First-generation punk fans, both these women would go on to pioneer reggae-inspired dub and hip-hop sounds in their musical projects of the 1980s; genres to which Goldman additionally gave some of their first attention in her writing, as well as her work as Bob Marley's first UK publicist.[49] This frumpy, DIY look featured layers of cheaply won, second-hand separates, purposely pairing contradictory combinations like socks and sandals, sheaths and baggy cardigans. The effect was summarized by Simon Frith and Howard Horne in their book *Art into Pop* as a look in which iconography "consistent in patriarchal ideology—woman as innocent/slut/mother/fool—was rendered ludicrous by *all being worn at once*."[50]

Figure 7.6 Marianne Joan Elliott-Said, more commonly known as Poly Styrene, lead singer with the pioneering punk group X-Ray Spex, December 18, 1977.

The style thumbed its nose at the self-serious elitism of the crew at 430 Kings Road. In "Oh Bondage! Up Yours!" Styrene's lyrics mock not just the literal "bondage gear" sold there, but McLaren and Westwood's contradictory political/business model: "It was about being in bondage to material life. In other words, it was a call for liberation. It was saying 'Bondage? Forget it! I am not going to be bound by the laws of consumerism.'"[51] But, the song also became a (much-covered) feminist anthem, opening as it does with the now-legendary introduction that sets up Styrene's anti-consumerist manifesto, which adds a gendered critique to the concept of "bondage" when she speaks/screams: "Some people think little girls should be seen and not heard / But I think '*OH BONDAGE! UP YOURS!*'"

Fellow DIY enthusiast Alex Michon took the philosophy in a different direction, after she met Bernard Rhodes following her foundation year of art school, and was hoping to put together a portfolio with the goal of transferring to prestigious Goldsmiths College. Supporting herself in the meantime doing work for a small bathing-suit manufacturer in London's West End, she used this experience to essentially

Figure 7.7 Journalist and musician Vivien Goldman [left] and musician Neneh Cherry [right], dressed in jumble-shop style, late 1970s.

bluff her way into a position as The Clash's "in-house" designer. As addressed above, Rhodes viewed himself as the most rigorously political of the SEX associates, and felt that the women's and gay liberation movements offered models and allies for punk progressivism—indeed, he sent musicians he managed into bookstores to buy *Gay News* and *Spare Rib* not just for the journals' content, but to experience what it meant to publicly associate with these marginalized movements in the transaction.[52] Rhodes' mother was also a Russian-Jewish evacuee during World War II, and he was among the few original UK punks to consistently and vocally take issue with the scene's flippant uses of the swastika—vetoing The Clash's early name of "London S.S." by confronting them with ugly Nazi paraphernalia, and refusing to let Siouxsie and The Banshees borrow The Clash's gear for their first performance due to the former's swastika-laden costumes.[53]

After Rhodes acrimoniously parted ways with SEX, he grew determined to outdo McLaren's band with his own, more overtly political group, and The Clash's early mantra "we're anti-fascist, we're anti-violence, we're anti-racist, and we're pro-creative"[54] was meant to be the positive-image response to the Pistols' negative-image nihilism. Like Michon, the three founding members of the band were all former art students, and had responded to the Pistols' flashy Westwood costuming with dingy jumble-sale suits and coveralls, spattered with paint in a style meant to reference both the uniforms of working men and the "creative work" of art-world heroes like Jackson Pollock. However, in the words of the band's late singer and guitarist Joe Strummer, they realized "painting dead men's clothes had gone as far as it would go;"[55] Michon was brought on as a collaborator to create clothing that matched the band's political as well as creative ambitions. But, Rhodes also instilled in her the confidence that her move into fashion might be an extension of her art practice, fueled by the Dada and Situationist ideas that were by 1977 very much a part of the punk *Zeitgeist*, as well as conceptual art influences to which she'd been introduced by her foundation-year faculty associated with the UK Art & Language group. As Michon wrote in her diary that year, Rhodes reminded her: "You have to remember Alex that everything in art that is important, initially started as a revolutionary movement."[56]

Michon's earliest costumes for the band riffed on their earlier, Abstract Expressionist-inspired look, using zippers to emulate the hard bars of paint underpinning Pollock's drip paintings, or the famous "zips" of Barnett Newman's canvases. In retrospect, Michon muses, she was working with many of the same ideas about functional and hard-wearing street-protest clothes that American artist Jae Jarrell was making in the 1960s as part of the AfriCOBRA (African Commune of Bad Relevant Artists) collective,[57] which, like The Clash and its collaborators in the band's earliest years, not only saw all their creative and political work as intertwined, but worked and even lived communally.[58] She designed and constructed her clothing for the band knowing it would be hard-worn, because the band wore them both on stage and off.[59] Clash bassist Paul Simonon contrasted Michon's designs with Westwood's: "If you got chased down the road with bondage trousers on you'd never get away. With Clash trousers [...] you were ready for anything. Ready to leap over a wall or escape."[60] At this point, the possibility was not simply a romantic notion: besides the oft-noted reality of punks being met with violence on the streets due solely to their willfully unique and provocative style, Simonon, Strummer, and Rhodes had been caught up battling London police alongside friend Don Letts in the race riots that flared up during the annual West Indian Notting Hill Carnival in 1976—photos from which (by another Clash associate, Rocco Redondo) materialized on two different Clash albums, and were silk-screened on several Michon designs (Figure 7.5). The experience inspired Rhodes to demand of Michon, "The clothes have to be hard wearing as there is going to be fighting on the streets!"[61]

While this would ultimately prove a bit of Rhodes' typically Situationist hyperbole, the battle-themed and social-justice underpinnings of the band nonetheless became an important part of their image. And, like many young women of her generation, Michon's activist sensibilities gradually turned to gender injustice when Rhodes pressured her to create a womenswear line. Michon pushed back, arguing that her designs, while ostensibly made for an all-male band were, like the band's politics and community-building, for all genders, writing in her diary "Can't think separately for girls!"[62] In fact, her archives are filled with the designer herself modeling samples or wearing variations of the same clothing she created for The Clash: zip-ornamented trousers, tailored shirts inspired by the same rude-boy style that impressed Poly Styrene (as in Figure 7.8), and what she dubbed a "boxer shirt" with a cowl neck inspired by the look of fighters toweling off in the ring, many in collaboration with her friend and Central St. Martin's fashion student (today, Nottingham fashion professor) Krystyna Kolowska (Figure 7.9). Indeed, as Coon recounts, when Michon and Kolowska would arrive at The Clash's rehearsal spaces and squats with "armfuls [of] their wonderful clothes—the result of their style collaboration with the band—and the band would try on items and decide who should wear what," the rest were often divided up and worn by women in the band's circle. This included Coon, who briefly managed the band, and was photographed in 1978 wearing a pair of "Clash trousers" deemed too small for Simonon (Figure 7.10), topped with a studded, black-leather motorcycle jacket, looking glamorous and dangerous. Reflecting back upon how Michon and Kolowska's unisex styles felt from a feminist perspective, Coon said they were "representative of the hard-style clothing that I/we found so necessary, protective and liberating as the often violent, misogynist backlash against women in the workplace ramped up in the 1970s."[63]

Michon's and Kolowska's clothing for The Clash was noted negatively by Savage at the time, writing in his diaries shortly after the band had signed to CBS: "All I can think of, when The Clash come on, is that they jettisoned their great Pollock look for a more

Figure 7.8 Alex Michon wears Michon and Kolowska "running policeman" pocket shirt and "zip trousers." The policeman photograph was taken by Rocco Redondo during the riot that broke out at the 1976 Notting Hill Carnival, and also reproduced on two different Clash album covers.

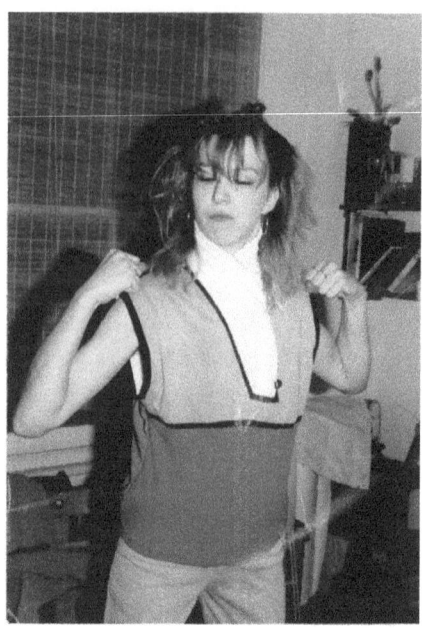

Figure 7.9 Macho posturing: Alex Michon trying on masculinity for size, wearing the Michon and Kolowska, Genet-inspired "Boxer" top, 1980–1981.

Figure 7.10 Caroline Coon, a regular on the punk scene, pictured March 1978, photographed in a pair of Michon and Kolowska "Clash trousers."

militaristic uniform of zippers and epaulettes. It makes them look like rock stars."[64] But, Michon's inspiration came from a surprisingly queer source: "I was totally obsessed with the writings of Jean Genet at the time, [and] the male-only machismo of gay desire, toughs and crime, bruised masculinity."[65] In another surprising bit of gender-bending for the otherwise famously butch Clash aesthetic, Michon created for Strummer what the two of them dubbed his "silk-stocking sleeve" shirt, in which the see-through, black fabric sleeves of a cotton button-up of her design were double-hemmed in such a way that they looked like the tops of ladies' silk stockings, draped like lingerie over his biceps (Figure 7.11). The name, she says now, "was just a piss take, really. But, yes [...] conceptually it was a big deal!"[66] This explicitly feminine bit of detailing in fact reflects the forgotten first impressions of even this most macho of punk bands, whose members Savage remembers hitting the scene seeming "quite vulnerable [...] like hurt, scared boys,"[67] and whose complex masculinity Michon recognized and wanted to express through such design subtleties.

Alas, by the time Alex Michon accompanied the band to the United States in 1981 for their now-legendary, seventeen-day residency at New York City's Bond's Casino—where The Clash's ongoing dedication to supporting women musicians and musicians of color saw them include opening acts like The Slits, Grandmaster Flash and The Furious Five, ESG, Lee "Scratch" Perry, and Pearl Harbor—punk culture was jettisoning its eclectic origins, and already canonizing originators as straight, white, and male. For those, like Savage, who witnessed punk's origins in the UK, punk had been "made for and by outsiders. And that meant outsiders of every hue, and that meant weird boys, hopeless boys, strong women, and gay men and women."[68] Yet in no time at all "that whole explosive moment," Savage lamented, was "tidied up within current laddish rock modes."[69]

This is as true of our understanding of punk fashion as punk music, evidenced by recent bids to similarly declare a canon of punk design (in which Westwood is the token woman), contradictorily established along a strict, binary gender norm, and with men as its style leaders. This sensibility was evident in the two recent "blockbuster" shows featuring UK punk fashions at the Metropolitan Museum of Art's Costume Institute, *Anglomania* and *Punk: Chaos to Couture*. In the former, all the unisex punk fashions were exhibited on male mannequins in the gallery entitled "The Gentlemen's Club." In the latter, curators unimaginatively dressed its mannequins in a predominantly binary fashion, with close-fitting, corseted, and skirted ensembles on hyper-slender, female-bodied mannequins; rough-and-ready, less-formal trouser ensembles on taller, muscular, male-bodied mannequins. Neither exhibition catalog included a single woman contributor. In the exhibition and catalog for *Chaos to Couture*, over and over men designers and punk figures are held up as representatives of the original movement, whereas women's "contributions" were predominantly represented by professional models wearing couture clothing (near-exclusively by men designers) in the decades since, rather than the pioneering women who were the acknowledged style-makers at its start.

Now that these institutional shots have been parted, the time seems right to challenge this emergent design canon to recognize the presence and the style of the punk women who served as crucial intermediaries—between music and fashion, haute-couture and DIY, punk and feminism—at the origins of this explosive moment in popular culture.

106 Design History Beyond the Canon

Figure 7.11 Cover of 1981 *Best* magazine on which Joe Strummer wears Alex Michon's "silk-stocking sleeve shirt."

Notes

1 See *Punk.London: 40 Years of Subversive Culture*: http://punk.london/
2 Kate Mossman interview with Viv Albertine at the British Library (July 14, 2016): https://www.youtube.com/watch?v=MpzuxyakTb0
3 Quoted in Helen Reddington, *The Lost Women of Rock Music: Female Musicians of the Punk Era* (Bristol, CT: Equinox, 2012), p. 2.
4 Kate Mossman interview with Viv Albertine at the British Library (July 14, 2016): https://www.youtube.com/watch?v=MpzuxyakTb0
5 Nigel Farndale, "Malcolm McLaren: Punk? It Made My Day," *The Telegraph*, September 30, 2007: http://www.telegraph.co.uk/culture/3668263/Malcolm-McLaren-Punk-it-made-my-day.html
6 Needless to say—like any exercise in genre—the roots and definition of punk are much disputed and continue to be debated. This chapter included. In any case, a recent, handy round-up of the many positions and debates on the matter can be found in Nicholas Rombes, *A Cultural Dictionary of Punk: 1974–1982* (New York and London: Continuum, 2009).
7 See Dick Hebdige, *Subculture: The Meaning of Style*, 10th edn (London: Routledge, 1991); and Simon Frith, *Sound Effects: Youth, Leisure, and the Politics of Rock'n'Roll* (New York: Pantheon, 1981).
8 See Caroline Coon, "Rock Revolution," *Melody Maker*, July 28, 1976, in *1988: Punk Rock New Wave Explosion* (New York: Hawthorn Books, 1977), p. 13.
9 See Mary Harron's recollections of Reed's influential look, in Jon Savage, *The England's Dreaming Tapes* (Minneapolis: University of Minnesota Press, 2010), p. 136.
10 For an excellent summary of the "art-school" trajectory for many British musicians after World War II, see Simon Frith and Howard Horne, *Art into Pop* (London: Methuen, 1987).
11 The film *Cabaret* had legitimate, Weimar-era origins, based as it was on Christopher Isherwood's 1939 novel inspired by his participation in the gay culture of this era, *Goodbye to Berlin*. The material from this book was first turned into the 1951 play *I am a Camera*, and later the Broadway musical version of *Cabaret*, which debuted in 1966.
12 "Siouxsie Sioux," in Savage, *The England's Dreaming Tapes*, pp. 341, 345.
13 See Paul Gorman, *The Look: Adventures in Rock and Pop Fashion* (London: Adelita, 2006), pp. 64–8.
14 Jane Withers, "From *Let It Rock* to *World's End*: 430 Kings Road," in *Impresario: Malcolm McLaren and the British New Wave* (New York: New Museum of Contemporary Art, 1988), p. 55.
15 See Guy Debord, *Society of the Spectacle*, 1st English edn (Kalamazoo, MI: Black and Red, 1970).
16 For arguably the most thorough history of punk rock's relationship to the Situationists, see Greil Marcus, *Lipstick Traces: A Secret History of the 20th Century* (Cambridge, MA: Harvard University Press, 1989).
17 See Vivienne Westwood and Ian Kelly, *Vivienne Westwood* (London: Picador, 2014), pp. 41–161.
18 See Stephanie Talbot, *Slogan T-Shirts: Cult and Culture* (London: Bloomsbury, 2013), pp. 24–30.
19 Savage addresses the relevance of gay clubs in general, and Louise's in particular, in bringing together what would become London's punk community in *England's Dreaming*, pp. 183–8. So, too, do Savage's interviews with Berlin, Siouxsie Sioux, Viv

Albertine, John Ingham, Johnny Rotten, Barbara Harwood, Steve Walsh, and Nils Stevenson all make note of Louise's "clubhouse" atmosphere in Savage's *England's Dreaming Tapes*. Many thanks to Andrew Wilson for his suggestion regarding the fuzzy timeline between Louise's pre- and post-punk history (in email correspondence with the author, January 13, 2018).

20 This history of the (non-existent) Chris Gray Band is briefly addressed in David Wise et al., *King Mob: A Critical Hidden History* (London: Bread and Circuses, 2014). With thanks to Paul Stolper and Andrew Wilson for their thoughts on the relevance of Gray's work—especially his SI anthology *Leaving the 20th Century*—to both King Mob and McLaren's foundations.

21 Needless to say: this is not the story of The Sex Pistols. But a blow-by-blow—literally, month-by-month—history of the band is lovingly documented in Jon Savage's *England's Dreaming: Anarchy Sex Pistols, Punk Rock, and Beyond*, 2nd edn (New York: St. Martin's Griffin, 2001).

22 See Mick Jones' and Tony James' recollections of Rhodes' first meeting with Jones in Pat Gilbert, *Passion Is Fashion: The Real Story of The Clash* (Cambridge, MA: DaCapo Books, 2005), p. 60; and Chris Salewicz, *Redemption Song: The Ballad of Joe Strummer* (New York: Faber and Faber, 2006), pp. 134–5.

23 See recollections of Chrissie Hynde, Jordan, and Adam Ant, in Savage, *The England's Dreaming Tapes*.

24 Savage, *England's Dreaming*, p. 55.

25 "Derek Jarman," in Savage, *England's Dreaming*, pp. 662–3.

26 Savage, *England's Dreaming*, p. 183.

27 Ibid., p. 183.

28 Lucy O'Brien, "The Woman Punk Made Me," in *Punk Rock: So What? The Cultural Legacy of Punk*, edited by Roger Sabin (London and New York: Routledge, 1999), p. 186.

29 Savage, *England's Dreaming*, p. 103.

30 Caroline Coon, email correspondence with the author (July 9, 2017).

31 Pop-culture historian Paul Gorman published his fascinating study on the "tits T-shirt's" history on his blog: http://rockpopfashion.com/blog/?p=178

32 Viv Albertine, *Clothes, Clothes, Clothes, Music, Music, Music, Boys, Boys, Boys* (New York: St. Martin's Press, 2014), p. 112.

33 See Matteo Guarnaccia, *Vivienne Westwood: Fashion Unfolds* (Milan: Moleskin, 2015), p. 32.

34 It's telling that, forty years after Jordan, Westwood, and Seditionaries salesgirl Debbi Juvenile were photographed together wearing bondage suits next to the shop, Westwood's "World's End" website continues to photograph women in the suit, still in production, as its ideal wearer: http://worldsendshop.co.uk/bondage-suit/ (Accessed August 6, 2017). And yet, the Victoria and Albert's file on the suit in their collection contradictorily identifies it as both "a genderless matching two-piece jacket and trousers" and a "suit consisting of a man's jacket and trousers." See "Bondage suit, Vivienne Westwood," in the V&A digital collections, https://collections.vam.ac.uk/item/O72586/bondage-suit-vivienne-westwood/

35 Janet Street-Porter, *The Year of Punk* (London: LWT Broadcast, 1977): https://www.youtube.com/watch?v=4jal1D_7NaQ

36 See Coon's appearance (as the only woman) in "Who's Who in the Underground," *The Observer* color supplement (December 3, 1967): 8–9.

37 Her persistent feminist probing of her subjects and the scene is very much on display in one of the first books to be published on the subject of punk, the anthology of

Coon's reportage entitled *1988: Punk Rock New Wave Explosion* (New York: Hawthorn Books, 1977), p. 108.
38 Alex Michon, email correspondence with the author (July 25, 2017).
39 Quoted in Caroline Coon, "The Slits," *Melody Maker*, June 16, 1977, in *1988: Punk Rock New Wave Explosion*, p. 106.
40 Viv Albertine, *Clothes, Clothes, Clothes, Music, Music, Music, Boys, Boys, Boys* (New York: St. Martin's Press, 2014), p. 153.
41 Caroline Coon, email correspondence with the author (July 9, 2017).
42 Albertine, *Clothes, Clothes, Clothes, Music, Music, Music, Boys, Boys, Boys*, pp. 126, 129.
43 See *Suffragette Legacy: How Does the History of Feminism Inspire Current Thinking in Manchester?*, edited by Camilla Mork Rostvik and Ella Louise Sutherland (Cambridge: Cambridge Scholars Publishing, 2015).
44 "Linder Sterling," in *Totally Wired: Postpunk Interviews and Overviews*, edited by Simon Reynolds (New York: Soft Skull Press, 2010), p. 218.
45 Quoted in O'Brien, "The Woman Punk Made Me," p. 191.
46 Albertine's autobiography is filled with longing remembrances of items from Westwood's shop she could not, or literally starved herself to afford to, buy; Adam Ant similarly noted "I knew that the clothes in SEX at the time were expensive. They were well made, but thirty-five pounds or forty guineas for a pair of leather trousers was a lot of money. The suede boots were thirty pounds. You really had to save for that stuff, you had to want it bad. I remember it said on their handles, 'sartorial correctness'—it was expensive." Quoted in Savage, *The England's Dreaming Tapes*, p. 275. It's also worth noting that a considerable amount of the Metropolitan Museum of Art's collection of McLaren and Westwood designs was purchased from Ant in 2006.
47 Poly Styrene, lyrics from X-Ray Spex, "Oh Bondage! Up Yours!" 7″ single (b/w "I am a Cliché"), Virgin Records (VS 189, 1977).
48 Quoted in Paul Gorman, *The Look*, p. 144.
49 See Evelyn McDonnell's "Do Everything Yourself: The Lessons of Punk Renaissance Woman Vivien Goldman," *National Public Radio: The Record*, July 21, 2016: https://www.npr.org/sections/therecord/2016/07/21/486885368/do-everything-yourself-the-lessons-of-punk-renaissance-woman-vivien-goldman
50 Frith and Horne, *Art into Pop*, p. 155.
51 Savage, *England's Dreaming*, p. 327.
52 See "Tony James" in Savage, *The England's Dreaming Tapes*, p. 281; and Gilbert, *Passion is Fashion*, p. 62.
53 See Gilbert, *Passion Is a Fashion*, pp. 63–4; Sean Egan, *The Clash: The Only Band That Mattered* (Lanham, MD: Rowman and Littlefield, 2014), p. 66; and Savage, *England's Dreaming*, pp. 172, 219.
54 See, for example, the mantra's appearance in the very early, international punk anthology, Isabelle Anscombe and Dike Blair, eds., *Punk: Rock/Style/Stance/People/Stars* (New York: Urizen Books, 1978), unpaginated.
55 Savage, *England's Dreaming*, p. 305.
56 From Alex Michon's diaries (1977), Alex Michon personal archives.
57 Alex Michon, email correspondence with the author (July 25, 2017).
58 For an excellent survey of AfriCOBRA's history and influence, see Bill Day, *AfriCOBRA: The First Twenty Years* (Atlanta, GA: Nexus Contemporary Art Center, 1990).
59 See Gilbert, *Passion Is a Fashion*, p. 170.

60 Quoted in Gilbert, *Passion Is a Fashion*, p. 169.
61 Alex Michon, email correspondence with the author (July 12, 2017).
62 From Alex Michon's diaries (1981), Alex Michon personal archives.
63 Caroline Coon, email correspondence with the author (January 4, 2018). In a testament to their hard-wearing properties, Coon still owns the trousers—which also still fit her slender frame.
64 Savage, *England's Dreaming*, p. 305.
65 Alex Michon, email correspondence with the author (July 25, 2017).
66 Alex Michon, email correspondence with the author (August 4, 2017).
67 Savage quoted in Gilbert, *Passion Is a Fashion*, p. 186.
68 Jamie Thomson, "Jon Savage On Black Hole & Why The Brits Don't Own Punk," *The Quietus*, November 9, 2010: http://thequietus.com/articles/05250-jon-savage-interview-black-hole-england-s-dreaming
69 Savage, *England's Dreaming*, p. xi.

Using digital tools to work around the canon

Matthew Bird

A tiny percentage of today's design students will create iconic, enduring objects that find their way into museum collections and textbooks. The rest will work to change the world by introducing improved medical equipment, responsibly manufactured sneakers, and better birthday presents for your dad. This work will be forgotten by tomorrow's design historians, as so many of the humble, utilitarian designs of the last hundred years have been. This is as it should be; designers for industry sign up for a life of productive anonymity. But design history, as taught today, is not as useful to young designers as it could (and should) be. Focusing disproportionally on luxury objects and the renown of a designer does not do much to explain why we need design in our world, or help students find ways to do it better. No amount of statement tea kettles, sculptural chairs, or limited-production sports cars improves our understanding of the complexities of addressing user limitations and needs.

An object's inclusion in a textbook is usually linked to its existence in high-resolution studio photographs and affordable image permission rights, often provided by museums and archives. As a result, items used to illustrate design history are limited to these sources, and this limitation is self-perpetuating. Understandably, museum collections don't tend to include everyday objects; a paying public has little interest in can-openers, prosthetics, or deodorant bottles. There are scant sources for studio photographs of vintage utilitarian objects. The existing equation helps prevent the story of design from being told by its true participants, and constrains the objects available to the small number that attain celebrity status and make it into the canon. This fixed body of objects tells a restricted version of the narrative.

Traditionally, there have not been options for learning or teaching the history of design in a way that gets past the limitations of the canon; we have been tethered to the available books and collections. With the maturing of the internet, however, we are now able to not only work past those limitations, but even accelerate the change with some intentional use of digital resources. We can harness existing tools to do better work and broaden the narrative. We can also develop new tools to help historians and teachers add more layers of information and interpretation to the existing narrative about how design happened in the past and who was involved.

The internet offers volumes of information, including primary source documents, images, advertisements, and patents, allowing us to establish new entry points into learning about objects. By harnessing non-traditional research tools, we can tailor traditional narratives to better suit an audience, however specialized its interests. Online resources are not vetted by professional editors or curators who confirm their reputations with accuracy and careful research. The challenge in successfully using the internet is finding (and teaching) ways to produce reliable, truthful, complete results. Each online resource has advantages and disadvantages, making it useful but unreliable when used in isolation as a research tool. Using web resources as a network of cross-linked tools groups their strengths to work past individual weaknesses. They are transformed from a mere curiosity to a groundbreaking resource.

Working from images

Image use is central in the investigation and discussion of design. The role of images in research has changed dramatically since the advent of the internet. Historically, an image was used as an attachment, an illustration. We worked with information, and then included the image to explain or clarify. Today, it is more common for an image to be the first contact point for an object. Any information, if it is lucky enough to stay attached, arrives later in the discovery process. Finding an image has never been easier, but finding accurate information about an image has never been more difficult. Digital images quickly become separated from the basic information we need to use the image in any meaningful way (date, maker, location, materials, ownership). Social media encourages the constant re-posting of images, making original sources difficult to locate. When Google Images was launched in 2001, it could not begin to compete with any serious library collection. Today, there are so many billions of images, it seems impossible to stay focused on a search without straying into related and enticing new territory. You may go looking for an image of the Villa Savoye and wind up lost in the world of Lego Architecture kits. Images on the internet are frequently mislabeled. Inaccurate tags and misattributions are reasons to be mistrustful of online images, but hardly reasons to discount them.

A reverse image search (which Google added to its tool box in 2011) is an effective way to find reliable information about an image, and locate its original source. This is especially useful for objects in museums. Many museum collections are viewable online, but the images do not come up in basic Google image searches. A seemingly random post on Pinterest may not lead you any farther than the first person who "pinned" it to explain their bathroom redecoration goals or the vibe of their upcoming wedding. But if you want to know about the object, a reverse image search will lead you back to that source information. Image-first browsing helps locate better-quality images of designs you already know about, discover new information sources, and also find related images. Such a search also leads to new objects and experiences that you did not already know about. Searching for "classic rotary phone" brings up the expected, canonical Henry Dreyfuss-designed 1949 Western Electric Model 500 telephone, a stellar example of good design work producing enduring solutions. It also brings up the less expected, but still canonical, Western Electric 1974 Sculptura phone (nicknamed "the doughnut"), a stellar example of design reflecting the interests of the times. But this image search succeeds where museum collections or textbooks cannot because it also brings up the 1979 Iskra phone from Yugoslavia, the 1980s Telkom phone from Poland, and any number of other examples of how designs change over time, with geography, politics, material innovation, and fashion all clearly evident.

Learning from amateurs and commerce

Internet image collections provide a quick way to harness the knowledge of both enthusiasts and commerce. Auction house websites feature search results with accurate descriptive information, reliable historical context, and provenance data that can put an object into context, connecting it with a user. The sheer volume of archived auctions offers lesser-known work by famous designers as well as familiar work by less famous designers. Most auction houses use professional photography, and they tend to be more generous with image permissions than non-commercial institutions. User-generated content sites like Flickr give the obsessive collector an audience. As a result, they also give the researcher some amazing ways to expand an investigation. Search features on image-posting platforms are clumsy, and user-generated tags often defy logic. But the breadth of images is astounding. A search for "1970s hairdryers" on Flickr turns up a remarkable variety of examples as well as vintage ads, fashion spreads, instruction manuals, salon interiors, and an immediate understanding of the variety of users, lifestyles, and hair problems we were dealing with at that time.

As with Flickr, Pinterest offers a host of frustrations that, when conquered, produce interesting and useful results. Like many online image sites, there is no authority to a Pinterest post, and the endless clicking back through previous posts of the same image will raise your blood pressure. If you want to know more about lipstick cases from the 1950s, though, there will be a collector of vintage cosmetics with images that satisfy your curiosity and lead you down new avenues of inquiry. The history of the felt-tipped pen may be best encountered through vintage office supply catalogs, and someone on Pinterest has already combed through them for you, their enthusiasm compelling them to include vintage ads and maybe even cross-linked photos of their own collection.

Academia has not traditionally valued the authority of the amateur. As the internet allows us ways to explore our peculiar interests and share them with others, the hyper-focused, specific authority of many amateurs should not be overlooked. If you want to see the history of the high-end plastic designer chair, MOMA can help you. But if you want to know the history of the tragically ubiquitous four-dollar mono-bloc chair owned globally by nearly everyone, it will not. For that, you need the help of collector Bryan Ropar, who owns one of every model Grosfillex chair ever made; his YouTube videos and Flickr photographs are more useful than anything that has been (or will ever be) published in a book or would ever be included in a museum collection.[1]

The online auction site eBay offers a global database of nearly everything ever industrially-produced. By combining the best (and sometimes worst) of user-created content, specific targeted knowledge of the amateur, and commerce, eBay can be a rewarding research tool. Because pictures are used to sell an item, they clearly show its condition, and that clarity frequently offers exciting bonuses. The original packaging for a coffee-maker might show pictures of intended users, indicate the regions of availability by offering information in multiple languages, or include an original price tag. Close-up views show construction methods and manufacturing. The MOMA's collection includes a beautiful 1956 Braun SK4 record player. It is a sleek and daringly futuristic example of German Rationalism in gleaming white metal and shiny acrylic. But if you want to see more than merely the exterior surfaces, eBay is a better resource. To sell an SK4 on eBay, a seller will remove the bottom to show that all the inside components are intact. This provides a view of the vacuum tubes and wiring, offering a contrast to the sleek exterior. We can also appreciate some smart design decisions because the main housing is made of one simple piece of bent sheet metal with convenient attachment points for all of the internal engineering cleverly stamped in.

eBay descriptions are also useful. They tell us about the use that objects have endured. We learn about a design's flaws (cracked plastic, missing knobs, even chewed doll fingers). This information tells us how design and manufacturing may have failed, and how later versions might have been altered. By only considering pristine museum-quality objects, we see only the designer's intent, not how well or poorly that intent aged with the use and abuse it was meant to survive.

Using video

YouTube was launched in 2005 to create a platform for sharing user-created videos. Kitten lovers around the world have been enjoying it ever since. YouTube now claims over a billion users, with an estimated sixty hours of content uploaded every minute.[2] For whatever incomprehensible reasons, people have included close-ups of a working escapement mechanism from a 1850s Chauncey Jerome mantle clock,[3] a 1950s ad for non-breakable Victor portable radios,[4] 1970s Woodsy the Owl public service announcements,[5] an original 1984 ad for the Apple IIc,[6] and even a "Do It Yourself in Rubber" instructional from 1959 on how to decorate your home with newly available latex sheet foam.[7] These may seem random and inconsequential, but they offer immediate insight into the world to which designers were responding to. Reliving first-hand the cringe-inducing but inextricable sexism of 1956, when Charles and Ray Eames appeared on Arlene Frances's Home show brings mid-century design right into today's ongoing conversations about gender bias, women in design, and the challenges of attribution in teamwork.[8]

Vintage film can help clarify any number of research conundrums. Many utilitarian objects were created to solve problems that, when seen in the rear-view mirror, don't make a lot of sense. Lurelle Guild designed a series of lipstick cases for Revlon in 1955 (Figure 8.1). The patent drawings (Figure 8.2) show the designs in the most brutal way, making them seem generic and mediocre. YouTube allows us to watch a vintage television ad and learn that the design separated the lipstick from the case, and saved money by offering refills.[9] The line was marketed to women, but also to husbands and children as an affordable but seemingly luxurious gift. Without this TV advertisement, the design is easy to write off as mere decoration. With this added information, the design transcends mere aesthetics to address user needs, perceived value, material use, marketing, and problem-solving. Seeing the design in action gives it a life and sophistication not evident in the brutality of an elevation-view patent drawing or two-dimensional photograph.

Figure 8.1 Futurama lipstick case, collection of the author.

Print advertisements tell stories

Vintage video is not the only easy source for bringing the user back into the equation. Old print advertisements were created to communicate innovation to consumers in targeted ways that now offer valuable insights to any design historian. Print ads are useful if even "merely" as a way to appreciate how advances in typesetting, pigment manufacturing, or color photography affected graphic design. Revlon's Futurama lipstick was well advertised in print (Figure 8.3). Through these advertisements, we can celebrate how "lustrous" and "dewy" our lips will appear while also appreciating 1950s glossy color printing. An object in a museum is a sculpture with only an implication of utility. Print ads show us what a finished design looked like, while also explaining the intended use.

A 1947 advertisement for a new metal desktop tape dispenser (Figure 8.4) lets us appreciate it aesthetically (in a fascinating image that uses a combination of photography, collage, and rendering to arrive at something printable and descriptive). We can also learn that the world did not yet fully appreciate the problems this device would solve. It is billed as a "handy new gift for Scotch tape fans" including homemakers, handymen, company presidents as well as office boys, teachers, and mothers. It can be used "*with one hand!*" (they were intentionally heavy) which makes the period between the introduction of cellulose tape in 1925 and this 1947 advertisement seem like the gift-wrapping dark ages. We can also understand the business side of design from vintage ads. The Scotch desk dispenser cost $1.89 in 1947 and came with a roll of tape, in a plaid gift box. The Futurama lipstick ads tell the researcher that they sold for as little as $1.35 and as much as $37.50, making it a curiously broad intended demographic. These details are not

United States Patent Office

Des. 178,187
Patented July 3, 1956

178,187
LIPSTICK CONTAINER

Lurelle Guild, New York, N. Y., and Raymond W. Wolff, Bridgeport, Conn., assignors to Revlon, Inc., New York, N. Y., a corporation of Delaware

Application February 28, 1956, Serial No. 40,386

Term of patent 14 years

(Cl. D86—10)

FIG. 1

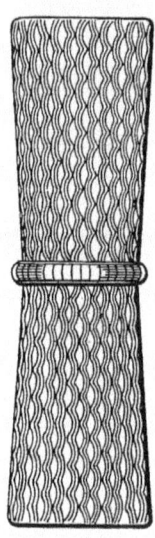

FIG. 2

FIG. 3

Fig. 1 is a view in elevation of a lipstick container showing our new design;
Fig. 2 is a top end view; and
Fig. 3 is a bottom end view.
We claim:
The ornamental design for a lipstick container, as shown.

References Cited in the file of this patent
UNITED STATES PATENTS

D. 176,326	Guild et al.	Dec. 13, 1955
D. 176,327	Guild et al.	Dec. 13, 1955

Figure 8.2 Futurama lipstick case patent, 1956, United States Patent Office.

Figure 8.3 1957 advertisement for Futurama lipstick for Revlon.

available elsewhere. They may seem small when considered independently, but they enable us to look at manufactured objects in the world they inhabited, not just in a lighted case in a museum. This is an important distinction; it allows us to learn about the people who used objects, the flaws of existing designs, material and manufacturing advances, and many more areas of inquiry that bring designs to life.

Figure 8.4 1947 advertisement for DD-1 desk dispenser for Scotch brand cellulose tape.

Was it really affordable?

Purchase price is rarely considered as part of design history. It is easy to find textbooks that tell us an 1869 Thonet #14 Consumer Chair cost less than a bottle of wine, which conveys an impression of affordability. That folklore doesn't really give us the information we need to understand who could buy the chair and where it would be used because there is a wide range of prices even with wine. This is, a rare example of cost being recorded at all. We usually assume that people could afford the objects we see in books and museums, when in fact they were largely out of reach for most consumers. Iconic designs now live completely separated from any understanding of their original price tag.

Is it useful to design historians to know that a 1963 Barbie Fashion Queen doll is worth 300 dollars today? To learn about the world this doll was designed for, we need to know what it cost new, in 1963. Vintage ads and online mail-order catalogs allow us to do so.[10] When we discover that this particular Barbie cost just 3 dollars and 69 cents, we are closer to knowing who would own it, but there is still one huge hurdle to get over: 4 dollars seems cheap for a toy because we are understanding the price using today's dollar. Online inflation calculators offer a truer perspective by telling us that today the same doll would cost around 30 dollars, making it an expensive toy.[11] Using a few internet resources quickly together connects value and cost, transforming our understanding of a product and removing many of the barriers that time and distance have erected.

Patent searches

The best digital tool for expanding the reach of design historians has to be the availability of online patent searches. Google introduced its search engine for US patents in 2006. Since then, it has expanded to include a number of other databases (Germany, Canada, China, Japan, Korea, and the European Patent Office) with more promised as other countries digitize their patent archives. Patent systems were created to protect and disseminate innovation, and their use has been an integral part of the design process since the dawn of industrialization; the two have matured together. The first US patent was granted in 1790, linking innovation to record-keeping in a way that now gives researchers access to over eight million cross-linked primary-source US patent records from any computer, at any time. The implications of this availability have changed how research can happen, and will continue to enable new kinds of research and new conversations. We can now consider in new ways which designs and innovations matter, how we assign credit for a design, and how innovations are linked, influencing later work.

One example of patents allowing (or forcing) a re-evaluation of the canon is the Waring blender. Waring Commercial Products' company history states that it began in 1937 when the popular band leader Fred Waring introduced the world to the kitchen blender.[12] Design historians add more information to that story by giving Peter Muller-Munk credit for actually designing the blender. But US design patent #104,289-S, filed in 1937, tells us that Frederick J. Osius invented and patented the device. Waring used his fame as a popular musician (and his collegiate engineering education) to perfect and market the device. Muller-Munk created the elegant "waterfall" housing that transformed the device from mere mechanism to household appliance. Part of what makes the blender work is the interior clover-leaf shape of the pitcher, which creates the vortex necessary to get all ingredients evenly chopped. Much of what we think of as Muller-Munk's design is in fact Osius's engineering. The canon of design history has had room only for Muller-Munk, but we now have the tools to reconsider the object, reposition it (and its creators), and maybe even reconsider the boundaries between design and engineering.

Patents also allow researchers to reassess designs already in the canon. They also empower us to disregard the canon altogether and use any patented object to investigate a trend, identify a pattern, or explore a technology with the accuracy of primary source documents. We can identify the anonymous work of known designers such as Dave Chapman at Montgomery Ward or Charles Harrison at Sears, who worked under a corporate umbrella that was not in the business of promoting individual designers. We can also identify unknown designers of iconic (but not "important") designs. The passage of time and new generations of researchers will discover just how far down how many different paths we can get with this powerful resource.

Combining tools

The real magic happens when all of these digital tools are combined. Using them in concert allows easy access to people, innovation, and history that was impossible to identify before the internet, and has been overlooked or forgotten in traditional information sources. That cast metal tape dispenser in the 1947 3M print ad (Figure 8.5) is ubiquitous enough to be familiar to almost everyone. It is a classic example of American streamline design of the late 1930s and early 1940s. It is not familiar from museum collections or coffee-table books, but from everyday life. It was on your grandparent's counter top, your tax assessor's desk, and in every junk shop in the country. A simple Google image search using "metal streamline tape dispenser" returns hundreds of pictures of it, and reveals that it has an amusing nickname. An eBay search for "whale tail tape dispenser" offers any number of them, in two sizes and a variety of colors. One eBay seller has posted particularly clear images, with the interior label clearly visible: Scotch Desk Dispenser, Minnesota Mining & Mfg. Co., US Patent 2,221,213 US Design Patent 127,388. A Google patent search finds both patents, and the design history of this overlooked object is clear in under five minutes.

The utility patent is from 1936 and shows a functional tape dispenser that ignored aesthetics. The design patent from 1941 shows the same basic mechanism now housed in a beautifully considered shell, with Jean Otis Reinecke listed as the designer. Because digital patent searches are cross-linked, a click on his name takes us to other patents that he was granted. It turns out that, in addition to the "whale tail," he also designed the first low-cost stamped sheet metal tape dispensers (1939 US Design Patent #116,599, 1951 US Design Patent #170,429), the iconic and omnipresent plastic tape dispenser

Figure 8.5 3M DD-1 desk dispenser, collection of the author.

(1939 US Design Patent #118,629), dispensers with levers to spit out a controlled amount of tape (1936 US Patent #2,221,213, 1941 US Design Patent #126,732), and the unavoidable 1959 plastic desk dispenser that is so ubiquitous it has become part of our collective subconscious (US Design Patent #190,781). In short, Jean Otis Reinecke, who is not included in any important design history books, can clearly be crowned the "king of tape dispenser design." He created a number of designs that are as central to the twentieth-century experience as anything iconic designers Henry Dreyfuss or Raymond Loewy ever designed. Reinecke also patented designs for toasters, juicers, radios, can-openers, lawn sprinklers, cameras, refrigerators, corncob holders, and more. Armed with his name, we can now find other shards of information about Reinecke. We may not be able to reconstruct an entire archive of information or rebuild his entire career using these quick tools, but in a short time, with little effort, we can find an astounding amount of useful and accurate information that, a mere ten years ago, would not have been available or connectable.

Reinecke is hardly an unknown designer. There is a brief biography on the Industrial Design Society of America (IDSA) website.[13] He was president of its predecessor—the Society of Industrial Designers—and inducted into the IDSA Academy of Fellows in 1952. His work is included in a glancing way in a number of overviews of design. His career illustrates the birth of the profession of industrial design, when engineering and manufacturing were combined and improved with added considerations like aesthetics, ergonomics, an improved understanding of the user, and marketing. But, he is not considered a major presence in the canon of design history. If design success is measured by the number of people whose lives are improved through a designer's work, surely Reinecke is a major success. Yet, without this way of working backwards from object to designer, we have little to consider him with.

Along this discovery route, all sorts of other avenues of inquiry open up. How and why did the Minnesota Mining & Manufacturing Co. venture from mineral production into tape manufacturing, reinventing itself as 3M? When did 3M start making tape in two sizes, requiring two versions of the tape dispenser? How do the colors offered reflect ideas about décor from that time period? Was Reinecke an employee of 3M, or did he work as a consultant designer? Did he work for a flat fee or a royalty? If the bits of convenient biographical information are true and he really did employ a staff of over 300, did he even design the tape dispensers, or did a still unnamed underling?

Patent searches are often inconclusive, and create as many new questions as they manage to answer. Patent archives are scanned using OCR (Optical Character Recognition) software that sometimes invents new ways of spelling things. Reinecke has patents as himself, but also as Reineeke and Iteinecke. As Jean O. Reinecke, J. O. Reinecke, and J.o. Reinecke. The cross-linking between patents is not completely reliable: the patent for Reinecke's 1961 redesign is a linking conundrum. It does not appear at all in the list of his patents, even though the name on the patent is correct. Clicking the link on his name in this patent does bring you to his other patents, but you can't go in the reverse direction. This one patent is floating alone in the database, unfindable through normal channels. In this case, having the patent number (thanks to another clear eBay auction photo) was the only path to that actual patent. There is a certain amount of sleuthing and tenacity required, but that is always true in research, and it seems a small price to pay for the value of such a rich resource.

Who gets to decide?

Some might argue that "lesser" designs should be forgotten, leaving the more elevated and pure examples of good design to represent our times. Would it be such a tragedy if coffee percolators, picture frames, and cafeteria dishes were not treasured a century after their creation? The danger in this reasoning is that there is no definition of "good design" that is time-resistant and universal. There are too many subjective factors in the equation to arrive at anything reliable. Purging the majority of manufactured objects to perpetuate a selected few is problematic because it leaves the history-writing and the taste-making in the same hands. It may well be that objects which were (or are) examples of what someone considers bad taste have more to teach us about their times and might deserve a better final resting place than the junk heap.

Design history is full of arguments about how good design should be defined and determined. One such argument is found in *What Is Modern Design?*, written in 1950 by Edgar Kaufmann, Jr., for the Museum of Modern Art, where he was Director of Industrial Design. An illustration from that book (Figure 8.6) contrasts a drawing of an airplane with a drawing of Jean Reinecke's 1941 tape dispenser (although no credit is given for either design). The caption states that the engineered streamlining of the airplane is "naïvely echoed on the Scotch-tape dispenser." The section attached to the illustration is titled "Streamlining is not good design." There you have it: The MOMA tells us that Jean Reinecke's work is not good design. Kaufmann goes on to delineate

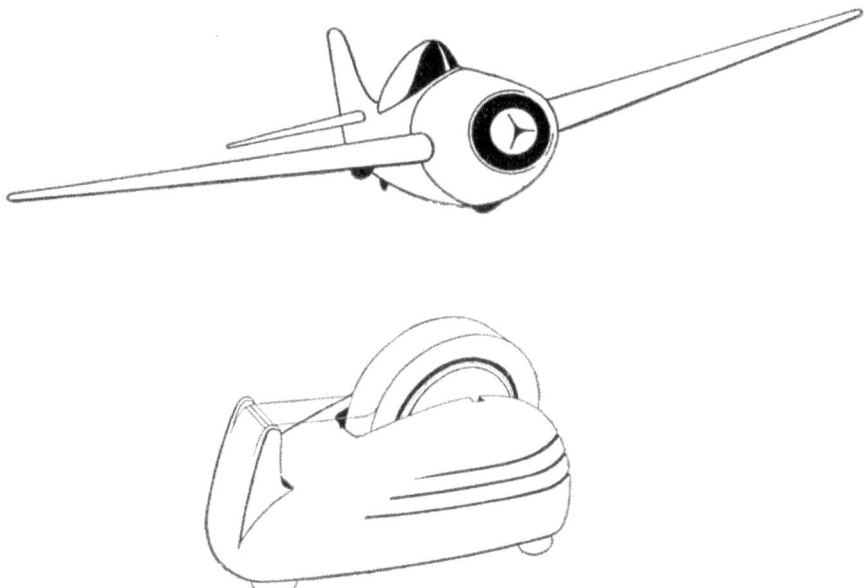

Figure 8.6 Edgar Kaufmann, *What Is Modern Design?*, 1950.

"twelve precepts of modern design" to help us avoid the pitfalls of bad taste. He proclaims that modern design should be practical, useful, express the spirit of the time, investigate new materials, improve the use of existing materials, relate form to function in ways that visually explain instead of confuse, use materials honestly (not in imitation of other materials), celebrate mass production by letting manufacturing methods determine aesthetics, be simple, and serve the widest public possible by being affordable to all.

With a little distance from 1950 and from the prejudices of the author, every one of those precepts is irrefutably true for Reinecke's tape dispenser. It was inexpensive, available to all. It used cast iron, an old material and manufacturing technique, to create forms that were contemporary instead of mimicking a previous era. It celebrated the arrival of new materials by getting cellophane adhesive tape into every home. Its form and material choice were derived from analysis of how and where it would be used. Its use is obvious without instruction, and all functioning parts are visible and expressed visually, creating the form and the aesthetic. In addition, the normal life-cycle of a designed object is short because materials, techniques, demand, and style change frequently. When Kaufmann was critiquing it, this tape dispenser was already a decade old and had earned its slightly-out-of-fashion status; expecting it to remain "modern" for that long is unfair. It continued in manufacture and in use for nearly a decade after Kaufmann condemned it, which ought to count for something when gauging success.

By selecting only the parts of our design and manufacturing efforts that reflect the image we want to see when we look at our past, we craft an intentional, artificial narrative about design progress. We may remove objects we consider ugly or cheap or in bad taste or too revealing about our real interests and our baser instincts. These removed and forgotten objects may well offer a truer portrait of who we were and who we are. If design historians want to find greater diversity of race, gender, income level, or even merely of interests, it is all available in the tape dispensers, drinking glasses, and patio furniture that live on in non-traditional sources, outside of the canonical archives. The online research tools we now have available are making it possible, even easy, to learn about less celebrated objects and incorporate them into our narratives, our publications, and our teaching.

One way to broaden the canon is to continue working on inclusion. There are so many female designers left to learn about and get woven back into the story. There are new ways to consider and discuss colonialism and find better ways to include racial diversity in the story. We need to continue these efforts and continue improving the tools we have available for communicating the story of design history. Today's students of design need—and want—to know more about the figures lurking in the shadows. We can also identify new narratives, however specific and tailored they may be, and support those narratives with a rich inter-connected group of reliable primary source documents. By focusing on an object first and what we can learn about manufacturing techniques, material advances, user demands, trade restrictions, legal constraints, and then finally, last, designers, we don't need to expand the canon. We can work around it.

Notes

1 For example: Bryan Ropar, "Comprehensive 'Definitive' Grosfillex Malaga Chair Video," YouTube video, 4:34, posted by Bryan Ropar in July 2017, https://www.youtube.com/watch?time_continue=1&v=2iwcfigzJ4Q.

2 YouTube, "For Press," https://www.youtube.com/yt/about/press/, last accessed on March 17, 2018.

3 Bill Stoddard, "Escapement of Chauncey Jerome 'Union' one-day shelf clock, 1850s," YouTube video, 00:37, posted by Bill Stoddard in May 2010, https://www.youtube.com/watch?v=iYwpjE9APHQ&list=PL0E333130D122304D.

4 RCA, "Old RCA Victor Portable Radio Commercial," YouTube video, 01:15, posted by "Thompsontech1" in November 2011, https://www.youtube.com/watch?v=dyxVVX5xMak.

5 "Woodsy Owl 1977 TV public service announcement," YouTube video 00:30, posted by "robatsea2009" in August 2009, https://www.youtube.com/watch?v=gZB7gSQRIuM.

6 Apple Computers, "Apple Inc commercial," YouTube video, 00:30, posted by "Patrick R" in February 2007, https://www.youtube.com/watch?v=ZZ6u9lvnQ-s&list=PL5ABDBBC1BB1E9181.

7 "Latex in the Home: Do-It-Yourself Rubber (1959)," YouTube video 01:55, posted by British Pathé in April 2014, https://www.youtube.com/watch?v=WVfwoduCays&list=PLEANvcdpJW0muKgJQ9aTViqOXJm1opAOU.

8 "Eames Lounge Chair debut in 1956 on NBC [1/2]," YouTube video, 4:25, posted by "omidimo" in August 2007, https://www.youtube.com/watch?v=zfzLzOl795E&list=PL678758830FA293A6

9 Revlon, "Revlon Futurama Lipstick Commercial 1956," YouTube video 01:25, posted by "Vintage Fanatic" in May 2013, https://www.youtube.com/watch?v=jcgZSdzS_C0.

10 Sears, "Christmas Book," 1964, p 19, scanned catalog from WishbookWeb Project: http://www.wishbookweb.com/FB/1964_Sears_Christmas_Book/#21/z, last accessed on March 17, 2018.
11 "Inflation Calculator," https://westegg.com/inflation/, last accessed on March 17, 2018.
12 Waring Commercial Products, "History," http://www.waringcommercialproducts.com/content.php?page=history last accessed on March 17, 2018.
13 IDSA, "Jean Otis Reinecke, FIDSA", http://www.idsa.org/content/jean-otis-reinecke-fidsa, last accessed on March 17, 2018.

Section 3

Designers

Confronting racial stereotypes in graphic design history

Karen L. Carter

This chapter begins with a vivid memory of encountering racist imagery almost thirty years ago in, of all places, a London supermarket.[1] I had grabbed a jar of Robertson's jam from the shelf and was shocked to see on the label a caricature of a figure with jet-black skin, wide white eyes, and spiked hair. Although I was not aware of the figure's name at the time (only later did I learn it was called a "golliwog," a character from *The Adventures of Two Dutch Dolls and a Golliwog*, the 1895 book by Florence Kate Upton), I took this racist representation to be a colonized British subject that was intended to ridicule and humiliate blacks.[2] The moment has stuck with me because I stood in the aisle for several minutes contemplating what to do next. I eventually placed the jar back on the shelf because I did not want to purchase such an item, but the confrontation of racism really rattled me. As an outsider to the United Kingdom, I remembered this encounter with a sense of disgust and bewilderment about why an internationally distributed brand would ally itself with a racist stereotype.[3] As it turns out, the "golly" had already come under public scrutiny and by 1988 was no longer used in television advertising. In 2002, "golly" was eventually dropped as the mascot of the Robertson's Jam Company, and even discussing the "golliwog" image on the Robertson's jam label is today considered racist in Great Britain.[4]

A parallel situation exists in the United States, where the racist roots of advertising images are still largely neglected by an American public that is often ignorant of the history of race and its consequences, although recent politics are forcing a national conversation about racist monuments.[5] One potent example is the iconic Aunt Jemima, a stereotyped mammy figure used to advertise Aunt Jemima Brand maple syrup and pancakes (owned by Quaker Oats Company). The "mammy" caricature is believed to be a holdover from the female house slave from the antebellum period (although there is scholarly disagreement about whether the mammy predates the Civil War), yet representations of "mammies" persist as a stereotype of African-American femininity.[6] Starting in the 1890s, the character "Aunt Jemima" was depicted on pancake mix packages as a heavy-set, African-American woman smiling widely and wearing a bandana head scarf and neckerchief. The Aunt Jemima figure is still used as the major figure of brand identity for the Aunt Jemima Company, although her image was revised in 1989 by lightening her skin, thinning her physiognomy, and dressing her in more contemporary clothing that included pearl earrings and a lace collar; these changes effaced references to the figure's antebellum roots and made her image appear more in line with black and white women who would potentially purchase these products.[7] Other racial stereotypes used in American commercial advertising include caricatures of "Uncle Tom": for example, the image of Uncle Ben on packaging for rice products (in use since the 1940s).[8] As American consumers have become acculturated to seeing racial stereotypes circulated throughout society, we often ignore these examples of graphic design. However, recent examples of racist images in contemporary advertising have received public scrutiny, as will be discussed below.

Meaningful analyses of historical representations of race in design artifacts are largely absent in textbooks used to teach graphic design history and, consequently, the topic is often difficult to broach in the college classroom. In 2009, Sarah Lichtman, a professor at Parsons, the New School of Design, challenged design historians to integrate issues of gender, race, colonialism, sexual orientation, and ethnicity into the survey of design history.[9] According to Lichtman, "not engaging with historical or academic frameworks will mean that students will be unable to fully engage with issues critical to the contemporary practice of design."[10] Despite this challenge to problematize the issues in design history, most graphic design history textbooks do not broach the topics of race, colonialism, or primitivism (the cultural appropriation of African motifs in early twentieth-century art and design) in relation to American and European graphic design.[11] For example, *Meggs' History of Graphic Design*, often referred to as the "Bible" of graphic design history, includes a lengthy discussion of the impact of modern art movements on early twentieth-century design, but the book does not mention primitivism or representations of race within those chapters.[12] Stephen Eskilson's *Graphic Design: A New History* acknowledges colonialism as a social factor in poster design, and his book features two posters (Adrian Allinson's *East African Transport—Old Style* and *East African Transport—New Style*), in which we see a contrast of a European colonist and indigenous Africans, with the white European male depicted as a superior overlord.[13] Eskilson includes two other posters designed for the 1931 Colonial Exposition held in France.[14] Despite the importance of these examples, there is not a substantial analysis of race in advertising throughout his history. Large, encyclopedic histories of design, such as Pat Kirkham's *History of Design: Decorative Arts and Material Culture, 1400–2000* and Victor Margolin's *World History of Design*, employ a more global view of design, and thereby acknowledge the contributions of non-Western designers to design history, but with their universal focus and high price tags, these studies make poor choices for a graphic design survey textbook despite their utility as a resource for the instructor.

Part of the problem, then, is this gap between the desire of design historians to teach difficult topics such as the impact of race on the history of graphic design and the lack of material in textbooks that could aid such discussions. This chapter, therefore, presents some case studies for classroom activities to help graphic design students learn to critique the use of racial stereotypes in publicity of the past and more recently. The case studies presented here—Paul Colin's La Revue nègre poster (1925) for a performance of Josephine Baker, artifacts from the Jim Crow Museum of Racist Memorabilia, and examples of contemporary advertising accused of perpetuating racist stereotypes—were integrated into a junior-level history of graphic design course (taught in 2016 and 2017) that is required for all graphic design majors at Kendall

College of Art and Design, Ferris State University. My college (KCAD for short) is located in Grand Rapids, Michigan, about an hour south of our partner institution, Ferris State University, which is located in Big Rapids, Michigan, and which also houses the Jim Crow Museum. The objectives of the learning module were: to engage students in critical thinking about racial stereotypes using artifacts from 1920s and 1930s graphic design; to have students apply those historical lessons about racial stereotypes to contemporary graphic design and advertising that had been implicated in charges of racism; and finally, to enable graphic design students to generate a set of standards for their own design practice that is sensitive to the history of racial stereotypes. The first two cases studies were historically located for the most part in the 1920s and 1930s, an era when Jim Crow Laws were still in force in the American South. At the same time, American Jazz was incredibly popular at home and abroad, and the Harlem Renaissance brought African-American culture to the forefront internationally. It is also a period when there was an active cultural appropriation of African traditional arts by American and, more particularly, European modern artists who looked to the so-called primitive arts for inspiration. Most of these European artists, however sympathetic they may have been to African and African-American culture, were nevertheless perpetuating a colonialist mindset by appropriating these cultural forms.[15]

The topic of race may be one that professors hesitate to confront in an art history or design history course. Any topic that lies outside the canon can cause discomfort because it challenges expectations and assumptions. Most of my students are Millennials (born roughly from 1980 to 2000), are Caucasian of Dutch or Polish backgrounds, come from western Michigan, and are not well acquainted with the history of racism and segregation in the United States. KCAD prioritizes new diversity and equity guidelines for teaching, staff and faculty hiring, and student recruitment, but despite these institutional initiatives, students of color are still in the minority; there are also international students who come to Michigan, mostly from China, Korea, and Japan. The students in my graphic design history courses were at first reluctant to discuss race, but eventually showed a tremendous curiosity about racial issues and the history of the United States. This reluctance may have stemmed from the perception that "race" is an issue that affects other people, rather than recognize that white is indeed a race that carries with it social, legal, and economic privileges in the United States. This inability to "see" race or to understand the complex historical and social issues makes discussing race in the classroom often difficult, because it necessarily requires the students and instructor to openly acknowledge their own identities, assumptions, and lived experiences. In any case, the make-up of the students in a class and the background of the instructor (I am a white female) will shape the direction of how the discussion unfolds and will inevitably be part of the exploration of the topic. The benefits that students gain in understanding the racial underpinnings of visual culture far outweigh the temporary discomfort that students may initially feel. It should go without saying that all classroom discussions need to be conducted in a civil manner so that all participants are treated with dignity and their opinions are respected. Even with those ground rules established, instructors who open up their classes to discussions of race should be willing to tolerate and guide the discussion in relation to remarks that can range from the bizarre to the downright ignorant.

The first case study introduced was Paul Colin's La Revue nègre poster that advertised the African-American performer, Josephine Baker. The case study can be integrated into a history of graphic design as part of the material in the category of Art Deco graphics. To begin, I provided an overview of Baker's life, from her childhood in the US through her rise to fame as a dancer in Paris and situated her biography within the context of American and European racism in the early twentieth century. Josephine Baker (born Freda Josephine MacDonald, 1906–1975) was an African American born in St. Louis, Missouri, to a poor family with few prospects given her race and social-economic background; her mother was a washerwoman and, as a young teenager, Baker also worked as a maid. At a young age, she learned to dance, and by the age of thirteen she married for the first time and later left home to become a performer, eventually traveling with a troupe from New Orleans to Philadelphia. In 1921, she joined the Dixie Steppers in Philadelphia. The same year, she married Willie Baker (her second marriage) and, although the relationship was short-lived, she kept his name for the remainder of her life.

According to her biographies, Baker was often asked to participate in performances that capitalized on African-American stereotypes, including playing a clown in blackface.[16] While traveling around the United States, Baker would have undoubtedly encountered the struggles that faced African-American performers of the time: segregationist Jim Crow Laws in the South (in effect from 1877 to the 1960s) restricted blacks' access to restaurants, lodging, transportation, bathroom facilities, and public drinking fountains. These laws effectively forced American blacks into a second-class status that not only separated whites and blacks but also sought to institutionalize a social system based on an ideology of white racial superiority. The situation of African-American performers would not have been remarkably better in other areas of the country, especially in the Midwest, where "sundown" laws made it illegal for blacks to spend the night in cities and towns. Violators were harshly penalized, and the draconian laws permitted blacks to work within these whites-only communities as long as they did not try to take up residence there. These legal restrictions were accompanied by the presence of white supremacist groups, such as the Ku Klux Klan, that reinforced a social system of white racial superiority through threats, violence, and murder, often in the form of public lynchings. Rather than operating outside the social and legal structures of American society, the Klan often had close connections with local law-enforcement and government.[17] As a black woman in the 1920s and 1930s (the height of the Great Migration), Baker would have faced tremendous prejudice, even in major urban centers in the northeastern and midwestern United States. Hazel Carby argues that the experiences of African Americans migrating from South to North varied greatly depending on gender and class, and that black women were considered at the time to be "sexually degenerate and, therefore, socially dangerous."[18]

Given these conditions of oppression, it is no surprise that in 1924, Baker took the chance to travel to Paris in order to dance and sing in La Revue nègre (The Black—or Negro—Review), and she fled the US at a time when lynchings in the South were at an all-time high. Baker had been selected by Caroline Dudley Reagan, an American socialite producer, who wanted to bring a real "negro" music and dance review to Paris. Baker joined the troupe as the lead dancer, singer, and comic, and the job marked a major turning point in her life and career. Performers who accompanied Baker included Dennis Day on trombone, Bass Hill on tuba, Percy Johnson on drums, Sidney Bechet on clarinet, composer Spencer William, and Claude Hopkins, band leader and pianist. The Mexican-born artist Miguel Covarrubias was hired to design the sets for the show.[19]

By the time the troupe arrived in Paris in October 1925, the revue was adapted to better conform to a Parisian music-hall performance, with opening night only ten days away. La Revue nègre's performance at the small Music-Hall des Champs-Elysées was therefore "tailored" for the French audience with more sexual and voyeuristic fare, and this change was reflected in the publicity for the performance. Upon the troupe's arrival, Baker's place in the company changed slightly, and she was foregrounded as a dancer rather than a comic; her costumes were replaced, and she performed a particularly provocative dance with a partner, Joe Alex, who was hired in France.[20] Both Baker and Alex performed almost nude and were outfitted in "primitive" costumes. In the publicity photographs for the show, Baker is shown topless, wearing ankle adornments made of straw and a beaded necklace. In her performance at the Music-Hall des Champs-Elysées, Baker wore almost nothing, except for a pink flamingo feather covering her groin area. As part of the *danse sauvage* (savage dance) that Baker performed, she cartwheeled on the back of Alex; the dance was described in the Parisian press as possessing the "animality" of the savage: exotic, bestial, and degenerate.[21] The performance catapulted Baker to fame.

Despite the racism of French colonialism, a cultural system in which Baker was forced to operate as a performer, France offered her the freedom that she did not have in her native United States. She was well paid and became a star virtually overnight. French women imitated her hairstyle (she endorsed the hair product "Bakerfix" that thousands of women used to mimic her slicked-down hairstyle), but she nevertheless had to conform to pre-existing notions of the African "primitive" and, at least for the early years of her career, she relied on her erotic dancing and sexuality to distinguish herself. In her early film career, she was cast in roles in which her ethnic and racial background were highlighted and in which she was presented as a colonial subject.[22] Even though for most of her life she was a singer and later became a political activist and war hero, this pivotal stage of her career as an erotic dancer assimilating the colonial racism of primitivism has been what essentially defined her for the rest of her life.

One question raised by this meteoric rise to fame in Parisian culture is what precisely was Baker's contribution to the *danse sauvage*? In other words, was she wholly responsible for the dramatic transformation of her career once she arrived in Paris? Some scholars who have written about Baker's claim that she was fully aware of the cultural impact of her *danse sauvage* and entirely responsible for its creation. Sieglinde Lemke writes about Baker's early performances as part of La Revue nègre:

> Baker herself seemed to have been aware that her stardom was predicated on her embodiment of the *primitive de luxe*, and she consciously decided to give the French what they so desperately wanted. Playing off the imagery of the jungle, she adapted the racist stereotypes by which black people had been oppressed and exploited them for her own commercial success.[23]

Lemke bases her assessment on comments that were attributed to Baker in her 1927 biography that was penned by Marcel Sauvage.[24] She also contends that Baker understood that her performances fit into a construction of the black body within the ideology of colonialism in Europe, and that she "played the role of the savage as long as she was adequately compensated."[25] As Bennetta Jules-Rosette contests, later in life Baker became a master of constructing her professional identity and embodied many performative types that were enshrined in the dioramas (with wax figures) at her residence at Château des Milandes, including the Cinderella myth, the Black Venus, and the Marian (or Mary) figure as the mother of the "rainbow tribe" of adopted children.[26] While these touristic displays at her château were no doubt the result of careful constructions of Baker's various celebrity personas by a seasoned performer, one has to at least question the ability of a nineteen-year-old American with little exposure to European audiences in 1925 to foretell the tastes and preferences (according to Lemke, the "exotic yearnings") of Parisians after having landed in France only a few days before the first performance of La Revue nègre.

Rather than attribute the transformation of La Revue nègre performance and subsequent publicity to Baker alone, there were probably others responsible for the transformation, and the creation of the *danse sauvage* should best be considered a collaboration between Baker and three men: director Rolf de Maré, André Daven (artistic director), and Jacques Charles, director of the Casino de Paris, who was asked to make the show more "African." The illustrator Paul Colin was commissioned by Maré and Daven to create the poster for the troupe. These taste intermediaries made possible the construction of Josephine Baker as a sexualized, exotic performer and subject of graphic design and publicity. Jules-Rosette also credits Baker's manager and companion, Guiseppe (Pepito) Abatino, with helping Baker construct her early persona from 1925 to 1935, the height of her career.

Paul Colin's poster (Figure 9.1), advertising La Revue nègre, then, assimilates some of these influences as it features two African-American men and a young woman dancing in the background. Colin's design incorporated an image by Miguel Covarubbias (1904–1957) that had been published in *Vanity Fair* only a few months earlier.[27] Although the style of the poster can be categorized as Art Deco because of its streamlining and use of geometrical forms, the figures nonetheless still contain gross racist stereotypes represented with large grins, wide eyes and thick lips. The female dancer also adds a clear element of sexuality as she appears to tug her short skirt up to the top of her thighs. The Art Deco style makes these stereotypes slightly more palatable and less grotesque yet still depends on a tradition of stereotyping black performers using exaggerated facial features and enhancing the sexuality of black females. In the class we compared Colin's depiction of the performers in La Revue nègre (Figure 9.1) to images of African Americans in the 1920s and 1930s, including Colin's images of Baker in *Le Tumulte noir* (Figure 9.2), a fine art series of lithographs printed in 1927 that further served to transform Baker from black urban flapper to African primitive, and to disseminate her image to the French public as a sexualized African body.[28]

Part of the class lecture on Baker included information about European colonialism and the cultural appropriation of African motifs in sexualized imagery that was used to advertise Baker's performances in Paris. We watched short clips from historical films

Confronting racial stereotypes in graphic design history 135

Figure 9.1 Paul Colin, poster for La Revue négre performance at the Music-Hall des Champs-Elysées, 1925. Posters Please, Inc., New York.

of her "banana dance" that made her famous and viewed other photographs and prints that represented Baker as a plantation slave and savage. These images and films were discussed as dependent on European colonialism, a system that was based on theories of racial inferiority and that France wholeheartedly adopted. For example, throughout the early twentieth century, the country held exhibitions of Africans and Asians in

Figure 9.2 Paul Colin, "Josephine Baker, Banana Skirt," from *Le Tumulte noir*, 1927, lithograph with *pochoir* coloring on paper. Posters Please, Inc. Artists Rights Society (ARS), New York.

human zoos and colonial villages as part of state-sponsored and organized festivals celebrating French colonialism.[29] As Jennifer Boittin maintains in *Colonial Metropolis*, "interwar Paris was a colonial space, meaning a space in which the spectre of 'empire' guided the self-identification of its residents as well as their social and political interactions."[30] Clearly, Baker was operating within this colonial space.

We discussed as a class the stereotype of the African physiognomy (the exaggerated facial features) that were circulating in Paris at the time, and compared the Colin poster (Figure 9.1) to American images and objects from the early twentieth century that are shown on the Jim Crow Museum website. While this comparison may seem a bit like comparing apples and oranges (or drawing parallels between racist American artifacts and European graphic design), the grotesque racist stereotypes seen in posters advertising American minstrel shows, for example, were widely disseminated in France in the late nineteenth and early twentieth centuries, well before Baker ever came to France.[31] One such example is the poster for the minstrel troupe, *Les Jolly Koon'ess*, for a performance at the Ambassadeurs, Champs-Elysées (Figure 9.3). While many American performers (both white and black) who came to Paris to perform minstrel acts brought their own posters with them, this one was printed by Emile Lévy, a Parisian printer and publisher, who employed his own designers.[32] The Josephine Baker case study allowed the students to link American social stereotypes to moments in graphic design history and also provided a transition to the next case study about racial stereotypes and caricatures that were displayed in the Jim Crow Museum.[33]

A second activity of the learning module was a field trip to the Jim Crow Museum of Racist Memorabilia, which is located in Big Rapids, Michigan. This field trip was planned because I wanted to capitalize on a collection of objects that was connected to my college. Dr. David Pilgrim, the founder and primary collector of material in the Jim Crow Museum, and several volunteers took the students on a guided tour of the collection and displays.[34]

Many of the students were initially hesitant to discuss racial stereotypes and seemed to be uncertain about the trip to the Jim Crow Museum. Part of the problem may have been that they thought the visit would be a kind of litmus test about race and that they would be judged in some way about their responses to racial imagery. The exhibits included information about American slavery and Jim Crow Laws and included visual documentation of segregated practices (water fountains, bathrooms). Photographs of lynchings, a replica tree with noose, and a small display about the Klan filled a central gallery. The next few galleries contained exhibits of mass-produced and distributed graphic design that caricatured and de-humanized blacks: toys, games, illustrated books, magazines, food packaging, signs, music sheets, and posters—all the categories of graphic design had been utilized in the American system of racism between the Civil War and the Civil Rights Movement. This section was overwhelming in the sheer number of artifacts that had been collected by Pilgrim or donated to the museum.[35] The students made connections between familiar products, such as Aunt Jemina Pancakes and Syrup, and the stereotype of the mammy, who has since receded from public memory, but still lurks behind the image of Aunt Jemima. The next exhibits followed the rise of the Civil Rights Movement that eventually ended Jim Crow, but as Pilgrim and his docents emphasized, the 1960s did not witness the end of racist

Figure 9.3 Emile Lévy (printer), "Ambassadeurs," Champs-Elysées, 1885

imagery. Other displays contained post-1970s artifacts including racist propaganda against President Barack Obama, most of which pledged violence and death to the former president. Some objects still capitalized on the image of blacks as sub-human— such as the game Ghettopology (designed by David Chang in 2002 and sold briefly in Urban Outfitters) complete with "pimps," "hoes," and "drug dealers,"[36] while others— such as the Oreo Barbie doll (by Mattel and Nabisco) of 1997—revealed a callous insensitivity to racial stereotypes by using the derogatory term, "oreo," which can indicate an African American "who behaves more white than black."[37]

For the most part, however, the students were remarkably quiet during the field trip, perhaps because they, like me, felt overwhelmed by what they had seen. There were two objects that were the most memorable for the students: one, a small photograph depicting black children with the legend below reading "gator bait." The actual practice of using children as "gator bait" has not been authenticated; however, the representation of black babies as gator bait was rampant and indicates the level of hatred towards blacks during the Jim Crow era. The image was striking for the students because it showed the blind contempt for black lives, even for innocent children. The Aunt Jemima ad campaign and its stereotype of the mammy was unknown to them, and they were shocked that the product was still sold by a caricatured logo until 1989, when it was revised.

The field trip had an impact, as was seen in the next classroom activity, which linked racial stereotypes seen at the Jim Crow Museum to contemporary advertising. We saw that when discussing contemporary advertising, racial stereotypes still re-emerge in contemporary media. Once the class returned to campus, the students discussed specific examples of contemporary graphic design in small groups. The examples included recent advertising that had been accused of racism on the internet and social media, including: a Burger King television commercial featuring Mary J. Blige singing about fried chicken;[38] an ad for Pizza Planet: California Meat print ad (Nexus BBDO, Bolivia, 2011), one in a series of ads with "divided" personalities to represent divided pizzas (this ad showed the California Meat pizza as a "divided" black man half dressed in a Laker's jersey and sideways ball cap and the other half shirtless and adorned in body paint feather and beads); an Intel brochure advertising its Core2 Duo processor that depicted black sprinters kneeling in front of a white man; a Sony PlayStation Portable billboard (the Netherlands) featuring a white woman (representing the "white" PlayStation) aggressively dominating a more diminutive black woman (indicating the "black" PlayStation);[39] Nivea's "White is Purity" ad campaign released on Twitter;[40] and Kendall Kardashian's infamous Pepsi television commercial set in a generic protest. Some of the ads were distributed in other countries, while others were designed and distributed in the United States. With the internet and the globalization of many design firms, racial stereotypes in graphic design have become an international problem. As we saw above, globalization of racist stereotypes existed more than a hundred years ago when American minstrel posters (Figure 9.3) were exported from America to Europe, but they are the focus of greater scrutiny and debate today. Some of the examples were not immediately recognizable to my students as potentially containing racial stereotypes (the Intel Core Duo2 processor ad in particular), but others were more evident, partly because they had been discussed in greater depth in the media, such as Kendall Kardashian's Pepsi commercial, which the students immediately recognized as appropriating a widely publicized image of a participant in a "Black Lives Matter" protest.[41] The students mostly discussed how the advertisements were examples of poor design principles. As one student remarked about the Sony PlayStation billboard, "Using skin color to market a product is never a good idea."

After we discussed these case studies together—Josephine Baker, the Jim Crow Museum, and contemporary advertising—the students were asked to write individual papers. They were given three possible assignments for their papers: they could write about contemporary examples they found that contain racial stereotypes; they could write about an artifact in the Jim Crow Museum; or they could research a female, African-American and/or a Latino designer whose work can be interpreted as attempting to challenge racial stereotypes.[42] The papers were assessed according to how well the students analyzed the ad they selected and made connections with the issues we had discussed for the past few classes. Most students chose the first two options, either writing about the Aunt Jemima ads (and conducting research on their own to trace the development of the character) or contemporary advertising. In this last category, students found and researched additional examples of racial stereotypes in advertisements (such as a Chinese television commercial for laundry detergent in which a black man is put into a washing machine and emerges several shades lighter, and a Nivea print ad for men's products [the "Re-Civilize Yourself" campaign] in which a clean-shaven black man prepares to throw a head with a long afro and full beard). One student attempted to redesign the Aunt Jemima ad from the 1930s and wrote about her choices in the design process; she first featured an updated female African-American chef, then completely omitted a person altogether and depicted instead a stack of pancakes. Another student, who talked about her Native American origins in class, wrote about cultural appropriation seen in the cover of an issue of British *Elle Magazine* (November 2014), which depicted pop star Pharrell wearing a Native American headdress.

The main objectives of these case studies were to engage students in critical thinking about cultural insensitivity and racial stereotypes using examples from graphic design history. The basic learning module can, however, be extended to include artifacts that relate to industrial design and fashion, depending on the interest of the instructor. Graphic design examples from the past and the present abound on the internet and can be used to instigate discussion with students, and ads that perpetuate racial stereotypes still circulate in our society and deserve more scrutiny in academia as the subject of research and teaching. This chapter has proposed several case studies that can be used by teaching design history "beyond the canon" as one way to confront these racist stereotypes. We owe it to our students, and to the design professions in which they will eventually practice, to help them learn to recognize, analyze, and challenge racial stereotypes while in college, so they may more productively contribute to the design professions after graduation.

Notes

1. I am indebted to Victoria Rose Pass, Assistant Professor, Maryland Institute College of Art, and Mark Fetkewicz, Professor, University of Northern Colorado, for their collaboration in the initial exploration of this pedagogical project in 2015 as part of the NEH Summer Institute: Teaching the History of Modern Design. Part of this chapter was presented at SECAC 2016 held in Roanoke, Virginia, in the panel, "The Canon and Beyond: Theory into Practice," that was chaired by Russell Flinchum.
2. For an analysis of the character of the golliwog, see David Pilgrim, "The Golliwog Caricature," The Jim Crow Museum of Racist Memorabilia, https://ferris.edu/HTMLS/news/jimcrow/golliwog/homepage.htm, accessed March 5, 2018.
3. To my knowledge, the "golly" figure was not reproduced on package labels for items exported to the US.
4. Marcus Dunk, "How the Golliwog Went from Innocent Child's Hero to Symbol of Bitter Controversy," *Daily Mail* (February 4, 2009), http://www.dailymail.co.uk/news/article-1136016/How-golliwog-went-innocent-childrens-hero-symbol-bitter-

controversy.html, accessed March 3, 2018. Claire Carter, "Discussing Robertson's Jam 'Golliwog' Label Is Racist, Judge Rules," *The Telegraph* (December 18, 2013), https://www.telegraph.co.uk/news/uknews/law-and-order/10525121/Discussing-Robertsons-jam-golliwog-label-is-racist-judge-rules.html, accessed March 3, 2018.

5   See, for example, Maggie Astor, "Protesters in Durham Topple a Confederate Monument," *New York Times* (August 14, 2017) https://www.nytimes.com/2017/08/14/us/protesters-in-durham-topple-a-confederate-monument.html (accessed March 5, 2018) and Yoni Appelbaum, "Take the Statues Down," *The Atlantic* (August 13, 2017), https://www.theatlantic.com/politics/archive/2017/08/take-the-statues-down/536727/ (accessed March 7, 2018).

6   See David Pilgrim, "The Mammy Caricature," the Jim Crow Museum of Racist Memorabilia, https://ferris.edu/HTMLS/news/jimcrow/mammies/homepage.htm, accessed March 5, 2018. Probably the best-known example of a mammy is the Mammy character in *Gone with the Wind* (1939) performed by Hattie McDaniel (1895–1952). McDaniel was the first African American to be awarded the Academy Award for Best Supporting Actress. For a short film about the Aunt Jemima character, see "I'se in Town, Honey" with excerpts from the Aunt Jemima Variety Show, posted by the Jim Crow Museum on YouTube: https://www.youtube.com/watch?v=3ipamH6EEwI, accessed March 3, 2018.

7   Many African-American artists have appropriated the image of Aunt Jemima and transformed her into a militant icon. See, for example (in chronological order): Jon Onye Lockhart, *No More* (1967), Betye Saars, *The Liberation of Aunt Jemima* (1972), and Faith Ringgold, *Who's Afraid of Aunt Jemima?* (1983). The first example is displayed at the Jim Crow Museum in Big Rapids, Michigan.

8   David Pilgrim, "The Tom Caricature," Jim Crow Museum website, https://ferris.edu/HTMLS/news/jimcrow/tom/homepage.htm, accessed March 5, 2018.

9   Sarah Lichtman, "Reconsidering the History of Design Survey," *Journal of Design History*, 22, 4 (2009): 343. Lichtman's case study is "History of Design, 1850–2000," the design history survey course taught at Parsons.

10 Ibid., p. 343.

11 Primitivism and the "primitive" are two deeply problematic terms that can refer to the impact of non-Western art in European countries, but they depend on a binary opposition of the "civilized" West to the "primitivized" Other. In the nineteenth century, the primitive could have been defined as pre-modern art ("pre-Raphael" as in the Pre-Raphaelite Brotherhood) or the rejection of industrialization in favor of rustic handicraft, as in the presumed spiritual simplicity of Breton culture or Tahitian art (in the paintings, prints, and ceramics of Paul Gauguin). Despite its elegance and sophistication, Japanese art was interpreted by artists such as Vincent van Gogh as "rustic" and could therefore be categorized as "primitive." By the early twentieth century, the primitive was overwhelmingly associated in European art with the influence of African culture that was appropriated as a direct consequence of colonialism. For an in-depth analysis of the term, see Mark Antliff and Patricia Leighten, "Primitivism" in *Critical Terms for Art History*, edited by Robert Nelson and Richard Shiff (Chicago: University of Chicago Press, 2003).

12 Philip Meggs and Alston W. Purvis, *Meggs' History of Graphic Design* (Hoboken, NJ: John Wiley and Sons, 2016). See Part IV, The Modernist Era; Chapter 13, The Influence of Modern Art; and Chapter 14, Pictorial Modernism.

13 Stephen J. Eskilson, *Graphic Design: A New History*, 2nd edn (New Haven: Yale University Press, 2012), "Art Deco and Colonialism," pp. 172–5.

14 Ibid., p. 174–5.
15 See Jody Blake, "Taking the Cake: The First Steps of Primitivism in Modernist Art," *Le Tumulte noir: Modernist Art and Popular Entertainment in Jazz-Age Paris, 1900–1930* (University Park, PA: The Pennsylvania State University Press, 1999), pp. 11–36.
16 See, for example, Jean-Claude and Chris Chase, *Josephine: The Hungry Heart* (New York: Random House, 1993) and Bennetta Jules-Rosette, *Josephine Baker in Art and Life: The Icon and the Image* (Urbana: University of Illinois Press, 2007).
17 This connection between government and Klan membership was brought to national attention in 1988 and 1992 when former grand wizard of the Klan, David Duke, ran as a presidential candidate. Duke served in the Louisiana House of Representatives from 1989 to 1993.
18 Hazel V. Carby, "Policing the Black Woman's Body in an Urban Context," *Critical Inquiry*, 18, 4, *Identities* (1992): 739.
19 Details about Baker's *danse sauvage* (savage dance) and La Revue nègre can be found in Karen C. C. Dalton and Henry Louis Gates, Jr., "Josephine Baker and Paul Colin: African American Dance Seen through Parisian Eyes," *Critical Inquiry*, 24, 4 (Summer 1998): 903–34.
20 According to Dalton and Gates, Joe Alex, possibly born in Martinique, frequented Le Grand duc, a black club in Montmartre. Dalton and Gates, "Josephine Baker and Paul Colin," p. 913.
21 For a description of the performance, see Wendy Buonaventura, *Something in the Way She Moves: Dancing Women from Salome to Madonna* (Da Capo Press, 2004), pp. 194–6. For an incisive look at the reception of Josephine Baker in Paris and beyond, see Mae G. Henderson and Charlene B. Regester, eds., *The Josephine Baker Critical Reader* (Jefferson, NC: McFarland and Company, 2017), pp. 30–125.
22 For a summary of her early films, see Jules-Rosette, pp. 72–123.
23 Sieglinde Lemke, *Primitivist Modernism: Black Culture and the Origins of Transatlantic Modernism* (Oxford: Oxford University Press, 1998), p. 103.
24 Marcel Sauvage, *Les Mémoires de Joséphine Baker* (Paris: Editions Kra, 1927), pp. 99–100, as cited in Lemke, p. 103, footnote 160.
25 "Baker knew that she was being categorized as a figure of primitivism and that she was fulfilling the exotic yearnings of Europeans. She knew that she owed her success to this dubious 'primitivismus.' Although Baker had heard about primitivism in the arts—e.g., in expressionism—she did not seem to have a thorough understanding of what *primitivismus* meant and why and how she had become a part of it. Apparently, she willingly played the role of the savage as long as she was adequately compensated." Lemke, p. 103.
26 Jules-Rosette, pp. 13–29.
27 Covarubbias's illustration is reproduced in *Josephine Baker and La Revue nègre: Paul Colin's Lithographs of Le Tumulte noir in Paris, 1927* with an introduction by Henry Louis Gates, Jr., and Karen C. C. Dalton (New York: Harry Abrams, 1998), p. 6; and Dalton and Gates, "Josephine Baker and Paul Colin," p. 913. The image, sometimes titled "Jazz Baby," was published in *Vanity Fair* (December 1924) under the title "2 A.M. at 'The Cat and the Saxophone'" as part of a two-page spread, "Enter, The New Negro, A Distinctive Type Recently Created by the Cabaret Belt in New York," pp. 60–1.
28 The title, *Le Tumulte noir* (*The Black Furor*), suggests the craze in Paris for American-African music and popular culture. Colin's series included 45 lithographs with *pochoir* printed in an edition of 500. Baker used Colin's imagery in these lithographs and his

illustrations in her 1927 biography by Marcel Sauvage to bolster her celebrity and used variations of the images in subsequent publicity posters. See Marcel Sauvage, *Les Mémoires de Joséphine Baker* (Paris: Editions Kra, 1927) with illustrations by Colin. For reproductions of *Le Tumulte noir* portfolio, see *Josephine Baker and La Revue nègre*.

29 The connection between the depictions of Josephine Baker and displays of African bodies are examined in Mae G. Henderson, "Josephine Baker and *La Revue nègre*: From Ethnography to Performance," *Text and Performance Quarterly*, 23, 2 (August 2003): 107–33, reprinted in *The Josephine Baker Critical Reader*, ed. Mae G. Henderson and Charlene B. Regester (Jefferson, NC: McFarland Publishers, 2017), pp. 67–87. For an analysis of the 1931 Colonial Exposition, see Patricia Morton, *Hybrid Modernities: Architecture and Representation at the 1931 Colonial Exposition, Paris* (Cambridge, MA: The MIT Press, 2000).

30 Jennifer Anne Boittin, *Colonial Metropolis: The Urban Grounds of Anti-Imperialism and Feminism in Interwar Paris* (Lincoln: University of Nebraska Press, 2010), p. xiv.

31 For information about the popularity of late-nineteenth-century minstrel shows and performances of the cake walk in Paris, see Blake, *Le Tumulte noir*, pp. 11–36.

32 There are many examples of posters for American minstrel shows that were exported to Paris and deposited in the collection of the National Library of France (Bibliothèque nationale de France); see the digitized collection of advertising posters in gallica.bnf.fr.

33 There is a distinction between a stereotype and a caricature. Stereotypes are usually negative characteristics foisted on a group of people, and caricatures are depictions that exaggerate physical attributes or facial features.

34 The museum and David Pilgrim were featured in *The New York Times* in a series about collecting racist objects. Logan Jaffee, "Confronting Racist Objects," *New York Times* (December 9, 2016), https://www.nytimes.com/interactive/2016/12/09/us/confronting-racist-objects.html, accessed February 26, 2018.

35 Most instructors will not have access to a collection like the Jim Crow Museum, but the museum has an excellent website with an introductory video and categories of racist stereotypes. The Jim Crow Museum of Racist Memorabilia: Using objects of intolerance to teach tolerance and promote social justice, https://ferris.edu/jimcrow/. A virtual tour of the museum has recently been added to the website, https://my.matterport.com/show/?m=8miUGt2wCtB, accessed March 15, 2018.

36 These modern figures continue the stereotypes of the "brute" and the "jezebel." Ibid.

37 *The Free Dictionary* by Farlex. According to *The Free Dictionary* (idioms), the offensive slang term "oreo" derives from the cookie, which is "black on the outside, white on the inside." https://idioms.thefreedictionary.com/oreo

38 "Mary J. Blige: Burger King Chicken Ad Fallout 'Crushed' Me," *Rolling Stone Magazine* (June 28, 2012). https://www.rollingstone.com/music/news/mary-j-blige-burger-king-chicken-ad-fallout-crushed-me-20120628, accessed March 15, 2018.

39 Steve Totilo, "Sony Pulls Dutch PSP Ad Deemed Racist by American Critics," mtv.com (July 12, 2006), http://www.mtv.com/news/1536222/sony-pulls-dutch-psp-ad-deemed-racist-by-american-critics/, accessed March 13, 2018.

40 Ivana Kottasova, "Nivea Pulls 'White is Purity' Ad after Outcry," *CNN Money* (April 5, 2017), http://money.cnn.com/2017/04/05/news/companies/nivea-white-is-purity-racist-ad/index.html, accessed March 13, 2018. For a short summary of recent ads accused of racism (Dove Soap, Nivea, Seoul Secret, and Vaseline), see "Advertising: Off-Color Ads by Beauty Brands," *Time* (October 23, 2017).

41 To see Jonathan Bachman's (Reuters) photograph of Ieshia Evans, the Black Lives Matter protester, arrested by police during a protest at Baton Rouge, Louisiana (2016), see "Baton Rouge Killing: Black Lives Matter Protest Photo Hailed as 'Legendary,'" www.bbc.com (July 11, 2016), http://www.bbc.com/news/world-us-canada-36759711, accessed March 12, 2018.

42 An excellent source of information for student research is "Race and the Design of American Life: African American in Twentieth-Century Commercial Life," The University of Chicago, Regenstein Library, Special Collections Exhibition: https://www.lib.uchicago.edu/collex/exhibits/race-and-design-american-life/. A bibliography is included under "About this Exhibit." See also issues of *The Crisis* Magazine for the period examined here, which are available online: http://onlinebooks.library.upenn.edu/webbin/serial?id=crisisnaacp, accessed March 14, 2018.

The Mangbetu coiffure: A story of cars, hats, branding, and appropriation

Victoria Rose Pass

In 1924, George Specht photographed a woman named Nobosodru (Figure 10.1). She was a member of the Mangbetu—a group of people living in what was formerly called Zaire, now the Democratic Republic of the Congo—and the wife of King Touba. Specht made the photograph as a member of La Croisière Noire (The Black Crossing), an expedition across the Sahara sponsored by the Citroën car company. While over eight thousand photographs were taken by Specht as part of this expedition, led by Georges-Marie Haardt and his second in command Louis Audouin-Dubreuil, this photograph is the image that circulated most widely in popular culture, and continues to circulate even now. I argue that the particular resonance of this image through so many different iterations in European and American design is due to the ways in which it signifies the exoticism and eroticism that was attached to Africa in the popular imagination of these audiences. Europe and America have historically defined themselves in opposition to Africa, othering the entire continent as primitive and hyper-sexual.

The photograph served in certain contexts—books, posters, and exhibitions—as evidence of what many European explorers had identified as the Mangbetu people's advanced and hierarchical society.[1] Eventually though, the publicity for the expedition and the accompanying film, Nobosodru and her Mangbetu coiffeur became a brand identity for Citroën and La Croisière Noire, and later for Belgian colonialism at the 1931 Colonial Exposition in Paris. Nobosodru was chosen as an icon of Afrocentric beauty by Harlem Renaissance graphic designer Aaron Douglas, and as an icon representing the perceived exoticism of Africa by milliner Mme Agnès and a number of other fashion designers in the 1920s and 1930s. This one image is assigned multiple significations in a complex network of Art Deco aesthetics, black beauty, and fashionable modernity. Nobosodru's elegant profile was objectified by European and American audiences as an embodiment of the modernist aesthetic becoming popular in the 1920s.

While many studies have argued for the significance of the aesthetic of primitivism and the usage of non-European and American sources by designers in this period, my study uses a specific image to unpack the ways that its meaning can change from one that is specifically about colonial power in Africa to a tool for the construction of white womanhood. By attending to a specific image and its origins, we can see how

Figure 10.1 Nobosodru, a Mangbetu woman, wife of King Touba, Niangra, Belgian Congo.

signification is structured in design and better understand the use such appropriations had for designers in this period. This chapter will trace the various design applications and appropriations of this photograph in the early twentieth century, and explore the ways its meaning changes in these various contexts. Looking at the origins of the photograph of Nobosodru and its iconic status in Art Deco design is important because this image continues to be referenced in design and popular culture, most recently by Beyoncé in *Lemonade* (2016) and the film *Black Panther* (2018). I argue that the reason for this image and the hairstyle's remarkable staying power as a generic signifier for

Africa (even as it has long fallen out of vogue with actual Mangbetu women) is the way in which it combines both the sharp angles of Art Deco and modernist streamlined aesthetics with a distinct silhouette that fits in with notions of African "otherness." Thus, it is malleable to the changing tastes of both designers and users, later allowing it to be claimed by artists and designers interested in the political aesthetic of Afro-Futurism in the early twenty-first century.

An ethnographic image

Even before the Croisière Noire expedition, images of Mangbetu women were in circulation throughout Europe. Anthropologist and chief curator at the Museum of African Art in New York, Enid Schildkrout, has traced the ways in which images of Mangbetu women have been codified and circulated both outside of and within the culture. She has identified an 1871 illustration of King Munza (Mbunza) dancing for his wives as one of the first and most enduring of these images.[2] Schildkrout has shown that the Mangbetu woman, "embodies an idealized image of African beauty, yet at the same time captures the ambivalence of the colonial attitude to African women."[3] While the European public was drawn to the beauty of these women, they were also constantly othered and treated as less than human, as evidenced in the profile pose chosen by Specht in his photograph.

Specht's photograph of Nobosodru entered most powerfully into popular European visual culture in the 1920s as a result of the "multimedia extravaganza" of the Croisière Noire.[4] This expedition from Algeria to Madagascar between October 1924 and June 1925 was originally intended to demonstrate the capability of Citroën vehicles on the unpaved roads of the jungles and deserts of Africa. The eight vehicles used by the expedition were hybrids with traditional automobile fronts and tank-like rear-ends with caterpillar treads—called a half-track caterpillar system.[5] André Citroën hoped to demonstrate the flexible capabilities of the automobile to tame the various landscapes of central Africa more easily than trains.[6] He had already shown the possibilities of these hybrid vehicles on a twenty-one-day crossing of the Sahara from December 1922 to January 1923. While he was unable to garner financial support from the French, his expedition did receive an official mission from the government as well as tasks from the French Museum of Natural History and the French Geographic Society.

The expedition was a way of showing that French industry, namely Citroën, could help the state to manage and extend the commercial possibilities of their colonial possessions. In this regard, Madagascar, the most distant of France's colonial possessions, was a significant point for the expedition to terminate as a way of demonstrating the Metropole's control over even the most distant of its colonies.[7] The importance of the mission in terms of publicity for both French colonial enterprise and Citroën is underscored by the fact that two of the eight cars on the expedition were dedicated solely to the transport of photography and film equipment in order to document this historic visit.[8] Ultimately, the expedition included the photographer Specht, a film-maker, Léon Poirier, and an artist, Alexander Jacovleff, all of whom collectively created the various visual documents of the expedition which included paintings, photographs, exhibitions, books, magazine articles, and a film, *La Croisière Noire*, 1926. Images from the expedition as well as the film were seen all over Europe and in America, including a long article written by Haardt in *National Geographic* in 1926. Film historian Alison Murray Levine has argued that this focus on the visual made this expedition unique and gave it staying power in French visual culture, writing of the expedition film:

> In short the reasons for the popularity of *La Croisière Noire* today are very similar to the explanations for its popularity in the 1920s: the rich imagery that accompanied it, an energetic public relations campaign on the part of its leaders, and the chance it offered its audience to experience a moment of escapism and high adventure that associated French technology with exciting, exotic backdrops.[9]

The inclusion of technology—cars along with photography and film cameras—is an important part of this story, marking this expedition as modern. The photographs, as well as the film, highlighted the modern cars tackling the rugged terrain and often contrasted them with the "primitive" technologies of the Africans—canoes, camels, horses, and even elephants.[10] At least nineteen of the photographs published in *National Geographic* include the cars in them, making visible Citroën's message of the technological superiority that allowed the French colonizers to master the African colonies.[11]

Many of the images made by the men on the expedition were intended to document the dress and self-presentation of the people they encountered, as was the case with the image of Nobosodru. This image shows the results of the elongation of the skull practiced by Mangbetu men and women of the ruling class, which became popular among all classes of the Mangbetu, as well as surrounding peoples, at the beginning of the twentieth century. Babies would have their skulls bound with bandages starting from birth. In the second half of the nineteenth century, Mangbetu women created beehive-shaped basketry hairstyles, often supported by reed frames and including foreign hair woven in and adorned with combs and hairpins. Men would wear hats atop their elongated coiffeurs, often with flourishes of feathers and hatpins. Around the turn of the century, styles changed and women began to embrace the funnel-shaped coiffeur we see on Nobosodru. Again, a reed framework and foreign hair were used to supplement the wearer's own hair and create this elaborate look. This was a fashionable status symbol for Mangbetu women since it took so long to create, and was only worn at public functions by members of the ruling classes.[12]

By the nineteenth century, the Mangbetu had gained a reputation for being fashionable, and were referred to as "the Parisians of Africa."[13] A 1946 ethnography by M. H. Lelong described the Bangala/Lingala word *lipombo* as essentially the same as *chic*, describing anything that was fashionable and elegant in terms of bodily adornment.[14] Elaborate hairstyles continued to be an important part of Mangbetu adornment and self-expression, even as the funnel-shaped style has gone out of fashion. While the elongation of the skull from birth was outlawed by the Belgian colonial government in the middle of the twentieth century, "the Mangbetu have always considered hairstyles that show a rich imagination to be the most appealing, and that trend continues to this day."[15] The unique funnel-shaped coiffeur, however, represents a highly specific style popular in the early part of the twentieth century, rather than an unchanging traditional style, as it was often perceived by Europeans and Americans, who connected it with Ancient Egypt.

As a document of La Croisière Noire, the photograph of Nobosodru follows ethnographic conventions, presenting her with bare breasts and clearly highlighting her hairstyle through a profile view. Enid Schildkrout explains that such images of Mangbetu women were typical among European representations, "stereotypical expressions of the Western fascination with the merged categories of erotic and exotic African."[16] The practice of skull elongation was used by Westerners "as profound and physical evidence of [the] deviance and inferiority" of those who practiced it.[17] Nobosodru's bare breasts and dark skin also mark her as other in the photograph, as does the profile pose, not a portrait of an individual as much as a representation of an ethnographic type. As with most colonial representations of women, she is available for the white male viewer's sexual gaze.

Haardt makes this ethnographic gaze explicit in his text in the book he published in 1927 on the expedition, *La Croisière Noire: Expèdition Citroën Centre-Afrique*. He describes a photograph of a row of Mangbetu women with the funnel-shaped coiffeur:

Seated in a hieratic pose on small ebony stools, the women of Mangbetou [sic] are arranged in file, like figures on an Egyptian frieze. They suddenly call up in our minds a striking picture that connects the present time to the civilization of the Pharoahs. Their bronze bodies colored a copper patina, these creatures with harmonious figures remain motionless, knees locked and heads held high. A disdainful look emanates from their narrow eyelids, dominated by the strange deformation of their heads. These have an egg-like form, according to the custom of ancient Egypt, where this allusion to their esoteric beliefs about the origins of the world was a sign of the absolute power of the Pharoahs.

A hairstyle crowned with a halo, ornamented with pins from the tibia bones of monkeys, spread out behind their ovoid heads. Wearing bracelets of copper and carved ivory, a miniscule apron held on a by a discrete elephant hair passed around the back, ornamented behind by a light basketry screen (*nekbé*) with geometric designs, these are the sole ornaments to these nude figures which give them the chastity of statues with eyes of enamel.[18]

Here, we can see clearly the ways in which these women are objectified as statues with "eyes of enamel" and reliefs as opposed to living and breathing people. They are also described as creatures with strangely deformed heads who wear adornments made from exotic materials, elephant hair, monkey tibias, and ivory. We can also see the careful way in which the sexuality of these women is managed through the evocation of "the chastity of statues," allowing the white male colonizer's gaze to examine them, without the threat that they might gaze back. The eroticism of the topless photograph of Nobosodru is key to her adoption as a symbol of the expedition and of Africa itself.[19] Brett A. Berliner rightly points out that "integral to exoticism is 'ethno-eroticism,' the state of sexual arousal and desire for a specific people solely because of their racial or ethnic identity."[20]

Josephine Baker is perhaps the most well-known example of "ethno-eroticism" in European popular culture of the 1920s and 1930s. In the context of the representation of non-white women in Hollywood film, Sarah Berry argues that "primitive constructions of femininity emphasize an edenic sexuality that is libidinal but innocent, providing a mediation of Western split femininity."[21] We can see precisely this kind of rhetoric in Haardt's description of Mangbetu women quoted above and in the celebrities like Baker who provided a middle ground in the Western dichotomy of women as madonna or whore. Baker is the keenest personification of the conflation of African, African American, and the erotic in the white imagination. In her show at the Folies-Bergère in Paris, she performed in a skirt of phallic sequined bananas in a clear parody of the primitivist erotic fantasies of her white audiences. Baker deliberately cultivated an image of herself on stage as an uninhibited jungle girl. The primitive stereotypes visualized in her performances allowed her display of uninhibited sexuality to be read as primal and innocent, not threatening to her white audience.[22]

We can see the same kind of sexuality projected on to the Mangbetu women in the context of *National Geographic*. Six photographs of the ninety-eight included in the article written by Haadt for the June 1926 issue highlighted the skull elongation of the Mangbetu. The article also includes three photographs of women with lip plates. It is clear that these, and other body modifications such as scarification and elaborate hairstyles, as well as costumes and headdresses, were perceived to be of the most interest to readers. In *National Geographic*, Nobosodru is not referred to by name, but rather as the "favorite wife of Mangebetou [sic] Chief."[23] She appears on her own in the iconic profile photograph (although her bare breasts are cropped out), as well as at the front of "the 'better halves' of a Mangebetou [sic] Chief, lined up in order of preference."[24] Here again, Haardt underlines the otherness of the Mangbetu through the practice of polygamy. Another photograph is captioned, "A Mangebetou [sic] chief, surrounded by his wives, enjoys his pipe."[25] These Mangbetu women are repeatedly described as taking special care of their appearance: "women of the upper classes do little or nothing but cook and busy themselves with their toilet. This latter takes up much more time than their scanty attire would indicate." These women are portrayed as constantly sexually available to the chief, and also subservient to him, busying themselves in their efforts to make themselves visually pleasing to him. Alexander Jacovleff appears in a photograph holding a Mangbetu child whose skull has been clearly elongated by the practice of binding. Nobosodru was also noted by viewers of the film, *La Croisière Noire* (1927). French film critic Pierre MacOrlan enthused, "I know nothing more graceful than this ebony girl stylized according to Egyptian traditions."[26] The Mangbetu practice of skull elongation, as well as that of polygamy, clearly struck a chord with the French explorers and these are prominently featured in the documentation of their trip. Both practices spoke to the French explorers' expectations of the primitive nature of the Africans they encountered, marking them as uncivilized.

Nobosodru's elegant profile clearly captured the imagination of many viewers, including sculptor Malvina Hoffman. Hoffman used her image as the model for one of her sculptures in the 1933 exhibition "The Races of Man" at the Field Museum in Chicago.[27] Hoffman, a student of Rodin, was commissioned in 1929 to create sculptures to be used by the museum to exhibit racial difference. While Hoffman insisted on sculpting specific individuals from life, traveling around the world—including extensive travel to Africa—as well as relying on immigrant populations in the US and Paris, in the case of the Mangbetu she chose to use Specht's photograph. Art Historian Jeff Rosen has shown that "the 'Mangbetu Woman' was chosen [by Hoffman] not for her characteristic racial qualities, but, it seems, for the purpose of creating an exhibition that would display both a racial deformity and a sexualized primitivism."[28] He shows how Hoffman chose to highlight "deformities" that conformed to the idea that the women she represented shaped their bodies as a way of striving towards the standards of beauty that were a part of their culture. As an American woman who had to decide what girdle and brassiere to wear and whether to bob her hair or not, the idea of the female body's malleability to changing standards of beauty must have seemed familiar to Hoffman. At the same time, the perception that the Mangbetu woman's skull was deformed through permanent modification performed since birth continues to other her, and the inclusion of her bare breasts further sexualizes and others her. Rosen explains how Nobosodru, like most popular representations of colonized women, is at once treated as sexual and innocent, "in Hoffman's survey of racial types, the Mangbetu woman is also both desirable *and* unattainable; as an emblem of a chaste 'Other,' she is at once seductive in her child-like innocence and degenerate in her abject primitivism."[29] In the context of the Field Museum, we can see how Nobosodru is used to construct white femininity, her modification of her body is extreme, marking the beauty rituals of white women—such as girdles and bras—in the US as impermanent and modern by comparison. Her primitive sexuality is set in opposition to the modern sophistication coded into the construction of whiteness.

A brand identity

"Spectacles of difference," such as the visual culture surrounding the Croisière Noire and the Field Museum's "The Races of Man," were an important part of visual culture in the 1920s and 1930s in both Europe and the United States.[30] Outside of such ethnographic spectacles, primitivism in visual and commodity culture was a means of making racial "others" available to be safely consumed by white Americans and Europeans. Creating a spectacle of difference—whether through an exhibition, a documentary or Hollywood film, or fashion (as we will see)—was a way "to normalize, contain and manage non-European cultures through the very process of creating them as spectacle."[31] By commodifying, and thus fetishizing, aspects of the "other," white consumers could contain the traits which they were at once attracted to and feared in "primitive" and "oriental" cultures. White consumers' projections of unbridled sexuality, savagery, excess, and abandon onto the ethnic other were made into a commodity through spectacle; this allowed these imagined racial others to be consumed and thus assimilated into the everyday life of white Europeans and Americans.[32] This is evident in the ways in which Nobosodru's image is used as a marketing device in the 1920s and 1930s.

Even as Nobosodru's blackness and African-ness is framed as other to white femininity in the context of anthropological representation, both visual and textual, there was (and in fact still is) an aesthetic appeal to her image. Looking back at Haardt's description, Ancient Egypt is cited as the origin of the tradition of skull elongation, and while the truth of this connection is dubious, certainly there is a visual connection to be made.[33] There is a particular resonance between Nobosodru's profile and that of the iconic bust of Nefertiti. Nobosodru's funnel-shaped coiffeur seems to sprout directly from her forehead, as does Nefertiti's distinctive crown. This similarity was perhaps apparent to Specht when he photographed Nobosodru, since he chose a profile to highlight the swooping shape of the coiffeur as it grows out from Nobosodru's head. Nefertiti would have been very much in the consciousness of Europe at that moment, since her famous bust was presented to the public in 1923 at Berlin's Museum of Antiquities after being found in 1912.[34] Profile images are standard in Ancient Egyptian painting and relief work—referred to by Haardt—and the curvature of Nobosodru's headdress also resembles that of the *hedjet*, or "white crown," of Upper Egypt as well as the *khepresh*, or "blue crown," worn by pharaohs of the New Kingdom. These visual connections help to explain the status that this photograph would attain as virtually a logo for the Croisière Noire.[35] In addition to Nefertiti, the 1823 discovery of King Tut's tomb ensured that Ancient Egyptian motifs would be a vital source of inspiration for Art Deco designers.

A stylized version of her profile appears on the cover of the catalog of the 1926 exhibition on the expedition at the Louvre, on the poster for the film (Figure 10.2), and on a deluxe leather-bound version of Haardt and Audouin-Dubreuil's 1927 *La Croisière Noire: Expédition Citroën Centre-Afrique*.[36] All of these representations stylize Nobosodru's profile. On the book cover, bands around her hair colored turquoise and short curved lines give texture to her hair until the point it begins to fan out and is represented by simple radiating stripes that reach the binding of the book. On one version of the film poster, shades of black and brown are used and Nobosodru is depicted from the neck up. The texture of her hair is carefully depicted surrounded by more stylized bands of black that refers to the binding worn around the hair. The largest portion of the halo, at the end of the coiffeur, is cut off, focusing the image on an elegant line going from the tip of her noise to the end of the coiffeur. Her face is reshaped to accomplish this, and the slanted quality of her eyes, in part a result of the practice of skill elongation, is exaggerated by the illustrator. In a horizontal version of the poster, a fuller view of the hairstyle is offered and tones of red and yellow are added. Both versions have an abstract stylized pattern as a background.

All of these objects were a part of what Bret Berliner has called the "multimedia extravaganza" of the Croisière Noire.[37] The illustration from the film poster was also slightly modified and used on the cover of *Opportunity Magazine* by African-American artist Aaron Douglas. Douglas was part of the Harlem Renaissance and chose this image for the cover of an issue of the National Urban League's magazine that focused on art from Africa and the ways it inspired contemporary European artists. This issue also included an article by French journalist Pierre Mille, on the exhibition's artist Alexander Jacovleff. Mille praises Jacovleff's ability to create "documents ... of ethnographic and near-prehistoric value," once again connecting the Mangbetu coiffeur, in this case worn by a woman named Uru, illustrated by Jacovleff, to Ancient Egypt.[38]

In each of these graphic contexts, Nobosodru's profile is turned into an iconic Art Deco illustration. Art Deco, or what was known at that time as *moderne*, or modern, was

The Mangbetu coiffure: Cars, hats, branding, appropriation 153

Figure 10.2 Poster for *La Croisière Noire*, the documentary film of the Citroën Centre-Afrique expedition, c. 1926.

a style that came into prominence in the 1920s utilizing the streamlined forms of avant-garde artistic styles such as Cubism and Futurism in tandem with machine aesthetics. Specht's staging of the photograph as a profile constructs Nobosodru's body and hairstyle in the style of a streamlined Art Deco object. Her forehead curves back and up into the funnel-sharped coiffeur, while the line to her jaw and neck as well as her breasts mimic these curves. These lines echoed those that were being formed by Art Deco designers like Peter Muller-Munk. He creates a funnel form in his iconic "Normandie" pitcher between its handle and straight spout edge. The chrome-plated surface highlights the meeting of sharp angles and curvilinear forms of this streamlined object. Russel Wright's spun aluminum pitcher (1932) captured the funnel form of Nobosodru's coiffeur even more clearly, in a less expensive form.[39] We can see these same forms in Roger Broder's poster for the French Railway Company, "Marseille Porte de l'Afrique du Nord" (1920–1932). A fascination with the streamline forms of the modern cruise ships dominated the foreground with many funnel-shaped forms, and the scenic port is relegated to the background. These aesthetics are also a strong part of the modernist art of the period. For instance, sculptor Constantin Brancusi explored similar forms in his *Le Coq* (1924; MoMA). Strong diagonals are paired with curved forms and a funnel-shaped base. Looking at Munk's pitcher, Broder's poster, and Brancusi's sculpture alongside Specht's photograph of Nobosodru, we can see how he staged the photograph to appeal to viewers versed in this formal language. The translation of photograph to illustration heightens these formal similarities, exaggerating the diagonal of Nobosodru's neck and smoothing the line from her nose to forehead and the upward sweep of her coiffeur.

Streamlining, a term coined to refer to the penchant American designers had for applying aerodynamic lines to any number of products, from cars to pencil sharpeners, in the 1930s is also embodied in Nobosodru's elegant contours. The visual vocabulary of streamlining emerged from forms discovered in the aviation industry, as well as European modernist and Art Deco styles. The ways in which the photograph of Nobosodru anticipated this aesthetic are most clear in the way her image was translated into a hood ornament for Citroën; the iconic image of Nobosodru was transformed from a logo for the expedition into a brand identity for Citroën as a whole. This is perhaps the most disturbing image since, in this context, Nobosodru's head stands in for Africa as a whole, conquered by the technology of the Citroën Corporation. The black female body, as is typical in colonial imagery, stands in for the so-called "dark continent," and occupies a place on the car often occupied by animals or sexualized women.[40] As Anne P. McClintock explains, "Africa and the Americas has become what can be called a porno-tropics for the European imagination—a fantastic magic lantern of the mind onto which Europe projected its forbidden sexual desires and fears," and the land of Africa itself was figured as feminine by explorers and colonizers.[41] In this way, it is natural that a woman rather than a man would be the face of not only the Citroën expedition, but African colonial exploration more generally. In the hood ornament, sculptor François Bazin exaggerated the angle of Nobosodru's head so that her hairstyle juts back in a line that would be perpendicular to the car she was attached to. The hair that pokes out in decorative rings in between the wrapped portion of the hairstyle is abstracted into rings of small squares, and the woven quality of the funnel shape is heightened through the metallic texture of stylized concentric circles of braid. In addition to the tilt of her head, Nobosodru's mouth is also softened into a smile, making her a more palatable "mascot" for the company. She is transformed into an elegant and compliant exotic figure in this application.

Bazin's hood ornament demonstrates the ease with which the Mangbetu woman was transformed into a commercial icon, not only for Citroën but also for the Pavillon des Tabacs at the 1931 Paris Colonial Exposition, and even for Belgian Colonialism writ-large, since the Congo was one of the most significant parts of Belgium's colonial holdings.[42] Featured on the cover of the American magazine *Opportunity* in 1927, Nobosodru's profile is essentially a copy of the film poster, but in the context of a Harlem Renaissance publication she became an Afro-centric icon of black beauty. African art was a key source of inspiration for artists like Douglas, and the Mangbetu hairstyle is referenced by him later in the first panel of his 1934 mural for the Harlem Branch of the New York Public Library, now the Schomberg Center. Sculptor Nancy Elizabeth Profit, also associated with the movement, described a bas-relief she made in 1931 based on "that strangely beautiful female with the marvelous headdress in the *Croisière Noire*."[43] The relief is now lost, but according to Theresa A. Leininger-Miller, Profit sent W. E. B. DuBois the book *La Croisière Noire*.[44] Harlem Renaissance artists and thinkers used African art to illustrate the rich history of the continent and to create a pan-African aesthetic that was uniquely African American.

One of the most striking elements of the use of Nobosodru's hairstyle as a brand identity is the use of this hairstyle by Mangbetu artists. Enid Schildkrout has demonstrated that in the early twentieth century, Mangbetu artists responded to Western collectors' interest in representational sculpture that captured this iconic image of Mangbetu identity: "around 1900, then, representations of Mangbetu women began to appear on a great variety of functional objects: on the necks of ceramic jars, on the wooden covers of bark boxes, on the arms and back of wooden steamer chairs, on handles of metal knives, on the ends of many kinds of musical instruments, and on ivory hair pins."[45] She shows that production of figural objects depicting women with the funnel-shaped coiffeur marked a significant shift in the artistic production of the Mangbetu—clearly catering to this market saturated in images from the Croisière Noire—and also sidelining female makers, who were the traditional producers of pottery and baskets, in favor of the male, who capitalized on these new markets; women "became the subject of the art of pottery and lost their stake in its production."[46]

Fashion

In addition to direct representations of racial others in visual and design culture, as we've seen in the examples above, fashion was also a potent site for white consumers, particularly female consumers, to explore racial otherness. For instance, Sarah Berry argues that the mediation offered by primitivist and Orientalist ideas of ethnic sexuality allowed American cosmetic companies to market their products not as the deceptive tools of the whore, but instead as the products that allowed any woman to become beautiful: "Orientalist beauty was offered to Western women as a means of transgressing the strictures of split femininity: by temporarily adopting signs of exotic sensuality via makeup and clothing, Western women could present themselves as a combination of (white) virtue and (nonwhite) sexuality."[47] The temporary and contingent nature of fashion and cosmetics is precisely what makes these areas ripe for the expression of fantasy and experimentation with sexual expression. This helps to explain the popularity of Nobosodru's coiffure in fashion in the 1920s and 1930s, and in fact through to the present.

The French milliner Agnès probably created the first hats inspired by Mangbetu hairstyles to appear in French and American fashion magazines in 1926, tying in directly with the release of the *Croisière Noire* film. Her turban styles reflected both the older basketry hairstyles as well as the contemporary Mangbetu fashion for the funnel-shaped hairstyle. One style wrapped grosgrain or velvet ribbon into a turban that fit closely over the ears of the wearer and extended back off of the head, approximating the backwards sweep of Nobosodru's elongated forehead.[48] Another hat in jersey and black velvet ribbon attempted to replicate the funnel shape of the more recent Mangbetu coiffeur. *L'Officiel* assured readers, "don't think in reading this title that the printer made a mistake ... No! Agnès and 'The Black Cruiser [Crossing]' are closely associated this season. As we already said Mme Agnès took most of her inspirations in looking at this beautiful film and as she told us herself: 'I thought that if the nigger women [*négresses*] often sougly [*laides*—meaning ugly] were almost pretty when wearing these becoming head-dress, how our Parisian would be charming when these same headdress would be adapted to their types [sic]."[49] This description is particularly revealing, since it clearly demonstrates the racism that is at the root of "spectacles of difference." Nobosodru herself cannot possibly be seen as beautiful by Agnès, and so her aesthetic interest in the Mangbetu woman must be projected onto her hairstyle. This statement reveals the ways in which the European representations of Nobosodru and the Mangbetu women in visual culture and fashion are deeply embedded in the rhetoric of white supremacy and colonialism.

Here, we can see how the Mangbetu-style hats are a mode of mitigating the ambivalent image of Nobosodru. It is her hairstyling that makes her beautiful, not her natural form, as Schildkrout points out, "in description after description, the African woman is beautiful, yet 'deformed'; she comes from a wild place, yet she is not part of nature; she is a work of art and a product of civilization."[50] The practice of skull-binding that is used to achieve this graceful line was seen as evidence of a culture that was "other." White women could define themselves through their difference from Nobosodru, rather than binding their skulls, permanently altering them, and weaving their hair into a basket, they simply put on a hat. Scarification, lip plates, and ear plugs were all seen in the visual materials accompanying the Croisière Noire, but the elongated skull and coiffeur of the Mangbetu was the most visually alluring of these practices to Europeans and Americans, not described in grotesque terms, as was the lip plate modification of the Ubangi. In this way, the coiffeur was distinctive enough to represent a "barbaric" form of creating a particular fashionable aesthetic, but one that appealed to the modernist Art Deco sensibility of Americans and Europeans in the 1920s and 1930s.

Josephine Baker was an early model for the funnel-shaped turban just a year after she had burst onto the Paris scene (Figure 10.3). The hat was being connected through Baker to a modernist aesthetic, not only an African and ethno-erotic one. As Anne Anlin Cheng has argued, "Baker ... became an overnight sensation and an icon of European primitivism, which is also to say an icon of European modernity."[51] Baker's modernity, constructed through her off-stage persona, elegantly dressed and accessorized by French designers, helped the French readers of *L'Officiel* to view Agnès's hat as an elegant and modern accessory rather than a grotesque costume belonging to the primitive Mangbetu woman. After all, Baker had also used her own image to sell tanning oil and hair products to French consumers, so Agnès knew how powerful her star-power was.

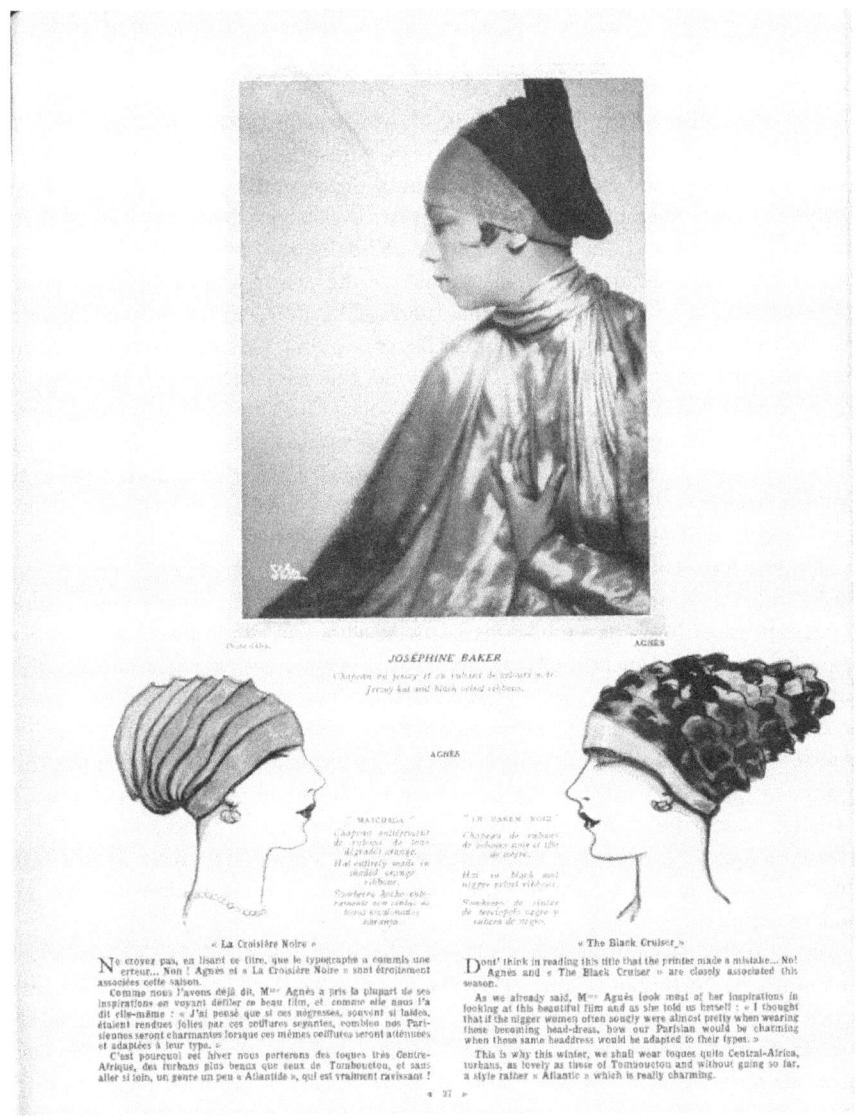

Figure 10.3 Josephine Baker modeling a hat by Agnès, photographed by d'Ora (Dora Kallmus) and two uncredited illustrations of Agnès hats, in *L'Officiel de la Couture, de la Mode de Paris*, August 1926.

The introduction of African (or Africanist) aesthetics into 1920s Art Deco stemmed particularly from the growing interest in and popularity of jazz, as well as the continued colonial presence of European powers in Africa. The continent had become a particularly fertile site for the imaginations of European and American designers and artists, inspiring popular culture of all kinds. To understand why fashionable women would have wanted to adorn themselves with African headdresses, it is crucial to understand the complex network of ideas that formed social politics of Jazz-Moderne. The Jazz-Moderne aesthetic developed from the link that European and American listeners produced between the sounds of African-American jazz music and an imagined Africa of lush jungles populated by wild dancing women and primitive men.[52] Jazz music synthesized elements of both the primitive and modern, and this combination fit in seamlessly with the rise of Art Deco style which made use of sharp staccato geometry and rhythmic patterns.[53] Visually, the Jazz-Moderne style was angular and dissonant, as was the jazz music of the period and the styles of dance associated with it. As historians have noted, during this time, Art Nouveau and Isadora Duncan were out, Art Deco and Josephine Baker were in.[54] Organic and natural forms were disposed of in favor of the angles and raucous rhythms of Jazz and its accompanying dances, such as the Charleston. Nobosodru's highly structured hairstyle fit neatly into this aesthetic. Rather than the loose waves of hair so popular on Art Nouveau posters, Nobosodru's hair was woven into a structured headdress, in the same way that Josephine Baker's bob was shellacked into a kind of shiny helmet on her head—a look emulated by many white women who bought her Bakerfix hair products.[55]

Designer Agnès frequently connected herself to this distinctive strain of modernist sensibilities, Jazz-Modern, not only in her design work but also in her self-presentation. In fact, her use of Baker as a model fits neatly into her overall marketing strategy. She frequently wore African-inspired jewelry made by Swiss designer Jean Dunand; for instance, she wore Dunand's gold giraffe necklaces on the cover of *L'Officiel* in May 1927, and in a portrait painted by Dunand that appeared in the magazine in 1926.[56] The necklace was a series of several simple bands in graduated sizes to be worn together, inspired by the jewelry worn by Massai women, and were covered with irregular motifs of triangles and stripes.[57] A similar necklace can be seen on a model wearing a different version of Agnès' Mangbetu-inspired hat in *Harper's Bazaar* (Figure 10.4). The Jazz-Moderne aesthetic was a part of Agnès' branding as a both a modern woman and modern designer.

Perhaps even more remarkable is a *Vogue* illustration in which Agnès herself models the funnel-shaped turban (Figure 10.5). She is drawn by the Russian artist Alexander Jacovleff, the very painter who participated in the Croisière Noire and documented the dress of Africans encountered on the trip. In the illustration, Agnès poses in the same three-quarter view as a Mangbetu woman named Uru who Jacovleff painted on the journey. Agnès' softly closed eyes and perfectly arched eyebrows create a crisp modernist sheen in the image. She also wears earrings that replicate the ear plugs worn by the Massai, who were also painted by Jacovleff.[58] Agnès clearly saw an opportunity to market herself and her hats as part of the Jazz-Moderne aesthetic. Josephine Baker had demonstrated the appeal of this style to French audiences, and Agnès would attempt to extend the market to the United States. The use of Baker herself as a model in the French fashion magazine cemented the connection between the hats and two of the most famous icons of black beauty at the time, Nobosodru and Baker. Baker's status as an ethno-erotic sex symbol underlines the sexuality evoked by the reference to Africa. Like Citroën, Agnès used the cultural capital of African references, and indeed the Croisière Noire itself as a way of connecting her label to modernity and French colonialism.

Figure 10.4 Baron Adolph de Meyer, a hat by Agnès, *Harper's Bazaar*, September 1926.

It is crucial to note that Baker is not used as a model in American fashion magazines in this period. Black female bodies are almost completely erased from American fashion magazines of this era, both visually and textually. In *Harper's Bazaar*, two white models pose in profile wearing Mangbetu-inspired hats, one in the funnel shape, and the other in a soft cone. Their profile poses mimic Nobosodru, but she has been entirely eliminated from the images in the magazine, only referred to indirectly as a "Congo belle."[59] Agnès' hats are described as being inspired by African headdresses, but interestingly in *Harper's Bazaar* the quote attributed to her is rather different. Marjorie Howard reports that while watching the *Croisière Noire* film, Agnès asked herself, "I who love the lines of the gown close to the body, why don't I make hats with line close to the shape of the head, outlining the skull across the front, as these beautiful black women do?"[60] A deep anxiety among whites in the US around miscegenation—and the use of Jim Crow Laws after Emancipation to prevent it—meant that the bodies of black

Figure 10.5 Alexandre Jacovleff, "Iacovleff [sic] Sketches a New Agnès Hat," *Vogue*, August 1, 1926.

women were systematically excluded from the pages of fashion magazines. Perhaps the quotation was modified with the understanding that, while black women were not present on the pages of the magazine, they might well be subscribers.[61] Even in these small bits of text, we can see the complex negotiation around race being managed by fashion intermediaries in these magazines.[62]

African-inspired Jazz-Moderne styles remained popular in Europe and the United States through the 1930s, and the Mangbetu coiffeur remained one of the most often copied styles. In 1933, *Women's Wear Daily* noted that "while not general, the Congo influence received sufficient endorsement to bear watching, and always in ultra-high effects worked out in cired [smooth or waxed] straw cloths, lacquered straw braids or matt finish silks. In the promotion of the fez, the crown treatments varied, adopting either the closed or open paper bag idea, arranged from side to side, back to front of on the diagonal."[63] The "paper bag crown," a hat in a tube shape formed close to the head and gathered at the back, allowing an extra bit of the tube to fan back out at the top, like a paper sac, is clearly a hat shape derived from the Mangbetu coiffeur.[64] The straw braid perhaps mimicked hair, as did the tubular straw used in a 1937 hat by American designer Sally Victor. She also created a funnel-shaped hat in black embellished with wooden triangles that mimics the look of the elongated skulls and upswept hairstyles of Mangbetu women.[65] These hats were likely inspired by a 1937 exhibition of hats from the Congo at Charles Ratton's gallery. The exhibition showed not only the hats, but also a series of photographs taken by the surrealist photographer Man Ray of mostly white French models wearing them. The show inspired milliners like Sally Victor and Lilly Daché who were working in the US.[66] Daché in fact bought the hat collection after the exhibition for $2,500. Like Agnès, Daché used African references as a selling point in her design work. Her branding was slightly different in that she had built a reputation as a designer who researched other cultures to create new styles. A *New Yorker* profile in 1944 lauded her process, explaining that she "studies so intently that, in her own words, 'I even know the color of the wind that blows there.'"[67] *LIFE* magazine published an article on September 13, 1937 showing how Daché used the collection of Congolese hats to inspire her own designs. This article and the designs were part of the publicity engineered for the grand opening of her new ten-story New York headquarters on East 56th Street that year. She exhibited the Congolese hats there and sent them to be shown at Marshal Fields in Chicago.[68] South of the Marshall Field's location in downtown Chicago, Malvina Hoffman's bust of Nobosodru could still be seen in the Field Museum's permanent installation "The Races of Man." Among Daché's Congolese-inspired designs for 1937 was a "lofty barbaric turban" based on the Mangbetu hairstyle.[69] This description from a Bullock's Wilshire ad highlights the way the hat was viewed as primitive, and a part of the lingering strain of Jazz-Moderne which stereotyped the Congo, and Africa more generally, in this way. Another milliner, Alix, created a hat of black lacquered straw worn at the back of the head that "suggests native Congo ways of dressing the hair."[70] The Mangbetu coiffeur was so emblematic of the Congo that even over a decade after the photograph of Nobosodru had first appeared in the US, and without a visual presence in Ratton's show, it was still referenced by these designers.

Coda: Yves Saint Laurent, Thierry Mugler, *Lemonade*, and *The Black Panther*

In the 1920s and 1930s, the image of Nobosodru and her coiffeur appealed to Art Deco and Jazz-Moderne aesthetics. Her photograph was turned into an icon for the Croisière Noire and its resulting multimedia by-products. She was used to sell magazines and cigarettes and cars. Citroën's adoption of Nobosodru as a "mascot" for the company encapsulates the way in which the company hoped to create an image which would connect them to national aspirations of colonial exploration and domination. The adoption of Nobosodru's coiffeur as an inspiration for milliners made her exotic sexuality something that could be worn by white women, but also removed. The coiffeur was used to lend designs an air of the exotic, a frisson of sexuality, or a sense of fantasy, virtually transporting the wearer to the imagined place "Africa" and allowing her to temporarily take on the ethno-erotic appeal of an imagined "African" woman. These hats allowed their white female wearers to adopt this exotic style without the permanent alteration to the body that they saw as marking the Mangbetu as radically other. This kind of fantasy space was not open to women of color, who were not, and often still are not, treated as the blank slate that white women are seen as in fashion.

What is especially striking about the image of the Mangbetu woman is the staying power of this image in European and American visual culture. Multiple fashion designers used the hairstyle on their runways, now an actual coiffeur as well as a hat. In 1967, a white model sported the hairstyle in Yves Saint Laurent's African Collection. As has often been the case throughout the twentieth century, the collection was a stylized interpretation of "African." Fashion historian Emma McClendon has explained that Saint Laurent was an "armchair explorer ... thus he developed a highly romanticized notion of the exotic as fashion fantasy based on his knowledge of French fine art, literature, and haute couture."[71] While his sculptural designs reflected the influence of African textiles, and certain forms of dress, it was mostly a bricolage of influences, filtered through "the thick lens of French culture."[72] It is especially significant, then, that among the few specific references in this collection is Nobosodru's coiffeur. This speaks to the ways in which the image is embedded in French visual representations of Africa.

The coiffeur has made appearances in other European designer collections in more recent years. If Saint Laurent's Africa is filtered through French culture, John Galliano's is filtered through Saint Laurent in his Spring 2009 ready-to-wear collection for Dior. The Mangbetu coiffeur is used by Galliano as a generic signifier, alongside raffia, beads, and reference to sculptures made by Senufo people in West Africa. It is both a shape for a hat and a hairstyle worn by white models. In 1988, Thierry Mugler used the coiffeur in a slightly different way. In his Spring–Summer collection, the coiffeur was placed alongside references to surrealist biomorphic forms, Isamu Noguchi and Alexander Calder-style accessories, and strong-shouldered silhouettes that looked back to the 1930s and 1940s. Significantly, it is worn as a hat by both black and white models and as a hairstyle by black models. Rather than use the bodies of his white models as a kind of blank canvas onto which any racial signifier can be used, Mugler's black models sport this hairstyle in ways which are more futuristic than primitive.

Mugler's show plays with his audience's perceptions of African fashions as primitive, traditional, and unchanging by showing their similarity to the space-aged biomorphism of mid-century designers. While Mugler's show is rife with stereotypical primitivist and Africanist images, he playfully and self-consciously undermines them.[73] For instance, at one moment a black model walks down a darkened runway with what seems to be an Ubangi lip plate—another key image from the Croisière Noire—but taking a bite, she holds up the remainder of a cookie.[74] Humor plays a key role in the show. Rather than a permanent body modification, the lip plate is literally a consumable object, a cookie—not to mention that the last thing we expect to see is a model eating on the runway. Mugler's collection begins to suggest a more complex appropriation of an African hairstyle on a European runway, moving beyond an evocation of primitivism and ethno-eroticism.

Contemporary African-American artists and designers have pushed this exploration even further, using references to Nobosoru as an icon of black beauty and African history. In both the films *Lemonade* (2016) and *The Black Panther* (2018), reference to Nobosodru is made as part of an Afro-futurist aesthetic which aims to critique the Euro/American view of Africa as backwards, traditional, and unchanging. The Mangbetu coiffeur appears in *Lemonade* during the song "Sorry." The costuming used in the context of this song includes a number of African references to Dutch Wax fabric, Malian mudcloth, and Massai collars. The Mangbetu coiffeur appears about half way through the song, during the bridge which marks a tonal shift both in the music and imagery. Beyoncé appears alone in an abstract space seated on the floor with legs crossed (Figure 10.6). She wears a bra by Zana Bayne that appears metallic, and the lighting also gives her skin the appearance of shining steel. The large fan-shaped earrings sparkle and shine, and reference several of the iconic publicity photographs of Josephine Baker (Figure 10.7). Her posture and movements with the coiffeur are robotic, lending the scene an air of futurism. The look plays on the sculptural quality of the hairstyle, the same streamlined form that appealed to Art Deco designers. Aaron Douglas's appropriation of the film poster image for the cover of *Opportunity* prefigures Beyoncé's use of the hairstyle as part of an aesthetic of black beauty. Both Douglas and Beyoncé deploy the hairstyle as a political tool in their Afro-centric projects. Where Douglas's image looks back in the context of a Harlem Renaissance publication, constructing a visual representation of heritage for African Americans as a part of Alain Locke's New Negro philosophy, in *Lemonade* the hairstyle becomes a part of a futuristic aesthetic, or more precisely an Afro-futurist aesthetic.

Figure 10.6 Beyoncé in *Lemonade*, directed by Kahlil Joseph, Beyoncé Knowles Carter, Melina Matsoukas, Todd Tourso, Dikayl Rimmasch, Jonas Åkerlund, and Mark Romanek, 2016.

164 *Design History Beyond the Canon*

Figure 10.7 Josephine Baker, c. 1925.

Afro-futurists such as Octavia Butler and SunRa, or more recently Janelle Monae and Wengchi Mutu, use the genres of science fiction and fantasy to place black characters at the center of their imagined futures, and to explore the politics of encounter in worlds which reflect our own, but are freed from the constraints of our own histories of race. These artists often use the freedom allowed in creating imaginative worlds to revisit historical events, or to imagine different possibilities for the future, mining images that are part of our collective consciousness. The vitality of Afro-futurism demonstrates the value of such fantasy spaces for imagining a different kind of future. While not explicitly engaged with science fiction, Beyoncé certainly imagines a different world that places black women, their stories, and their histories at the center. In the film, fashion plays a key role, along with the other visuals, in enriching the personal narrative that emerges through Beyoncé's music. It enhances and underlines the politics present sonically in the album and presents a very different way of looking at black women and their histories, which all too often are completely absent from popular culture. By mixing the Mangbetu coiffeur with contemporary fashion, Beyoncé creates an image that invokes a powerful lineage of black beauty: Nefertiti, Nobosodru, and Josephine Baker.

In the future of *Lemonade*, black women are at the center of things, they possess the power to stare, to look, to desire, to gaze uninhibited by the authority of white men or women.[75] In this context, the Mangbetu coiffeur is part of a future in which black women have agency and power within society. We see the same imaging in *The Black Panther*, in which costume designer Ruth E. Carter uses the coiffeur on Angela Basset's character Ramonda (step-mother of T'Challa, the Black Panther) as part of the construction of the fictional Wakanda, a highly advanced and intensely secretive country in Africa. While Carter has cited headdresses by married Zulu women called isicholo, the resemblance to Nobosodru's hairstyle is also unmistakable. The Zulu headdresses were, in fact, based on a hairstyle worn in the early nineteenth century which was replaced by hats made from human hair woven into basketry forms and colored with red ocher. Carter collaborated with architect and designer Julia Koerner to produce headdresses through 3D printing that mimicked the form of the Zulu isicholo, and perhaps also the Mangbetu hairstyle, but have a high-tech machine-made look.[76] Ramonda's 3D printed Zulu/Mangbetu crown appears alongside characters with scarification and lip plates, and wearing a vast array of styles related to multiple regions of Africa.

While some designers and artists have used Nobododru's image as a means of celebrating black beauty and African history, she continues to be deployed in ways that reinforce the racism of the colonialist ideology that produced the photograph of her image in the first place. The granddaughter of François Bazin, Julie Bazin, has launched a business reproducing some of Bazin's best-known hood ornaments, including the sculpture of Nobosodru. Beyond simply reproducing the sculpture of Nobosodru for her "Collection Croisière Noire," she has also created a line of jewelry based on Nobosodru's iconic profile, including abstracted disks referring to the halo ring of her coiffeur. Photographs on Bazin's Instagram—one in which she kisses the sculpture and another in which she holds a rind with the bust on it in her teeth—show the ways in which appropriations of Specht's initial photograph are still used to objectify and exploit Nobosodru.[77] Here, Nobosodru can again be worn as a colonial prize, not only on cars, but also on the bodies of white women.

Conclusion

The Mangbetu coiffeur has had a remarkable life in European and American fashion. The elegant, streamlined shape of Nobosodru's hairstyle fit seamlessly in with the aesthetic of Art Deco in the 1920s and 1930s. Evoking the elegant and otherworldly profile of the famous bust of Nefertiti, an African woman absorbed into white standards of beauty, the coiffeur also signified the otherness of the Mangbetu for Europeans and Americans, as it would only be fully realized though a careful stretching and shaping of the skull starting from birth. The style was sufficiently similar to popular aesthetics of the Art Deco style, but also carried with it enough difference to foster the excitement of exoticism. Following the image of Nobosodru through her various incarnations as a representation of the Congo, the Croisière Noire, the Citroën Car Company and their colonial exploits, Jazz-Moderne fashion, and more generic African fashion aesthetics in the second half of the twentieth and into the twenty-first century shows how design culture itself can propagate certain images and representations of entire cultures. Nobosodru's image has often been used in reductive and damaging colonialist ways, but has also been reclaimed by African-American creatives and used as an expression of African history and black beauty. By examining the life of this single image in design culture, we can understand what makes it so appealing to certain audiences, and how its meaning can change over time and in different contexts. This helps to complicate narratives of cultural appropriation, underscoring why certain appropriations of style happen in the ways that they do, and, in this case, the way that the image of this Congolese woman is used to define white femininity. It helps us to trace the events, such as the Croisière Noire, and the media through which such appropriations can happen, and how this can inflect the meaning of the resulting designed objects. The case study also reveals the importance of cross-disciplinary studies of design which include fashion. While histories of design often marginalize fashion, as Nobosodru's example shows, fashion is intertwined with other areas of design production and is often engaged with similar ideas and images. Exploring fashion alongside other forms of design not only enriches the narrative, but helps to bring identity to the fore.

Notes

1 The photograph first appeared in the book published by expedition leaders Georges-Marie Haardt and Louis Audouin-Dubreuil, *La Croisière Noire, Expedition Citroën Centre-Afrique* (Paris: Plon, 1927).
2 Enid Schildkrout, "*Les Parisiens d'Afrique*: Mangbetu Women as Works of Art," in *Black Womanhood: Images, Icons, and Ideologies of the African Body*, ed. Barbara Thompson (Hanover: Hood Museum of Art, Dartmouth College, 2008), p. 71.
3 Ibid.
4 Brett A. Berliner, *Ambivalent Desire: The Exotic Black Other in Jazz-Age France* (Amherst: University of Massachusetts Press, 2002), pp. 189–90.
5 Alison Murray Levine, "Film and Colonial Memory: *La Croisière noir* 1924–2004," in *Memory, Empire, and Postcolonialism: Legacies of French Colonialism*, ed. Alec G. Hargreaves (Lanham, MD: Lexington Books, 2005), p. 83.
6 Levine, p. 83.
7 Levine, p. 85.
8 Levine, p. 84.
9 Levine, p. 93.
10 See Georges-Marie Haardt, "Through the Deserts and Jungles of Africa by Motor," *National Geographic*, 49(6) (June 1926): 650–720. See also images in Adriane Audouin-Dubreuil, *La Croisière Noire: Sur les Traces de L'Expédition Citroën Centre-Afrique* (Grenoble: Éditions Glénat, 2014), p. 115. This celebratory volume also supports Levine's contention that the expedition remains popular as a nostalgic adventure story, the back cover notes, "Entre dans l'intimité de ces aventuriers d'un autre temps! [Enter into the private world of these adventurers of another time!] "

11 See Georges-Marie Haardt, "Through the Deserts and Jungles of Africa by Motor," pp. 650–720.
12 Els De Palmenaer, "Mangbetu Hairstyles and the Art of Seduction: Lipombo," in *Hair in African Art and Culture*, ed. Roy Sieber and Frank Herreman (New York: The Museum of African Art, 2000), pp. 117–23.
13 In the nineteenth century, "designations commonly applied to the Mangbetu were '*artistes*,' and 'the Parisians of Africa,' '*les élégants*,' and '*les jouisseurs*.'" The Mangbetu were a natural source for European milliners to draw from with their interest in adornment and stunning headwear. Enid Schildkrout and Curtis A. Keim, *African Reflections: Art from Northeastern Zaire* (Seattle: University of Washington Press, 1990), p. 30.
14 De Palmenaer, "Mangbetu Hairstyles," p. 123.
15 Ibid.
16 Enid Schildkrout, "Gender and Sexuality in Mangbetu Art," in *Unpacking Culture: Art and Commodity in Colonial and Postcolonial Worlds*, ed. Ruth Phillips and Christopher B. Steiner (Berkley: University of California Press, 1999), p. 198.
17 Jeff Rosen, "Of Monsters and Fossils: The Making of Racial Difference in Malvina Hoffman's *Hall of the Races of Mankind*," *History and Anthropology*, 12(2) (2001): 134.
18 Translation from Rosen, "Of Monsters and Fossils," p. 136. Original text: Haardt and Audouin-Dubreuil, *La Croisière Noire*, pp. 179–80, 182.
19 The fact the Aaron Douglas made Nobosodru the subject of the cover of *Opportunity*, an African-American magazine, in May 1927, reflects the image's status in both Europe and America as a representation of Africa.
20 Berliner, *Ambivalent Desire*, p. 4.
21 Sarah Berry, *Screen Style: Fashion and Femininity in 1930s Hollywood* (Minneapolis: University of Minnesota Press, 2000), p. 127.
22 Wendy Martin, "'Remembering the Jungle': Josephine Baker and Modernist Parody," in *Prehistories of the Future: The Primitivist Project and the Culture of Modernism*, ed. Elazar Barkan and Ronald Bush (Palo Alto: Stanford University Press, 1995), p. 321.
23 Haardt, "Through the Deserts and Jungles of Africa by Motor," p. 715.
24 Ibid, p. 716.
25 Ibid, p. 714.
26 Quoted in Berliner, *Ambivalent Desire*, p. 203.
27 The exhibition was seen by ten million people until it was dismantled in 1969 as these theories of racial difference were systematically disproven by scientists. The exhibition was recently remounted at the Field Museum as a way of talking about the museum's own history of constructing racial difference, as well as exploring Malvina Hoffman herself who was always uncomfortable with the scientific racism embedded in the project, writing in 1936: "I will leave the much-disputed subject of what is meant by the word 'Aryan' to be fought out between anthropologists and Mr. Hitler." Malvina Hoffman, *Heads and Tales* (New York: Charles Scribner's Sons, 1936), p. 159. Quoted in Jennifer Schuessler, "'Races of Mankind' Sculptures, Long Exiled, Return to Display at Chicago's Field Museum," *New York Times* (January 20, 2016): https://nyti.ms/2kpoFwm.
28 Rosen, "Of Monsters and Fossils," p. 135.
29 Ibid.
30 The term "spectacle of difference" comes from the work of Ella Shohat, "Gender and Culture of Empire: Toward a Feminist Ethnography of the Cinema," *Quarterly Review of Film and Video*, 13 (1991). Sarah Berry's use of the term to describe Hollywood's

commodification of ethnicity in the 1930s is particularly useful here: Berry, *Screen Style*, p. 98.
31 Caroline Evans, *Fashion at the Edge: Spectacle, Modernity, and Deathliness* (New Haven: Yale University Press, 2003), p. 31.
32 See bell hooks, "Eating the Other: Desire and Resistance," in *Black Looks: Race and Representation* (Boston: South End Press, 1992), pp. 21–40.
33 I haven't found any contemporary anthropological source that supports this theory.
34 Egypt has lobbied Germany for the sculpture's return since it was put on public display in the 1920s: "PLANNING TRIP FOR FUAD: Egyptian Foreign Minister in Berlin to Arrange for King's Visit," *New York Times*, March 23, 1929, p. 6.
35 Schildkrout, "*Les Parisiens d'Afrique*," p. 72.
36 See: *Exposition de la Croisière noire, documents rassemblés par l'expédition Citroën-Centre Afrique* (Paris: Draeger, 1926) cover, http://gallica.bnf.fr/ark:/12148/bpt6k313567x/f1.image. And: *Livres Anciens et Modernes Autographes et Manuscrits: Paris Mercredi 16 Juin 2014* (Paris: Pierre Bergé & Associés, 2014), p. 107: http://asp.zone-secure.net/v2/index.jsp?id=2637/4688/46054&lng=fr, accessed September 13, 2018.
37 Berliner, *Ambivalent Desire*, pp. 189–90.
38 Pierre Mille, "The Africa Work of Alexander Jacovleff," *Opportunity*, 5(5) (May 1927): 134.
39 See Figure 10.31 in David Raizman, *History of Modern Design*, 2nd edn. (Upper Saddle River: Pearson Prentice Hall, 2011), p. 240.
40 Africa has been figured by Europeans as feminine since at least as early as ancient Rome. See Anne P. McClintock, *Imperial Leather: Race, Gender and Sexuality in the Colonial Contest* (New York: Routledge, 1995), p. 22.
41 Ibid.
42 Enid Schildkrout explains that, "by the 1930s, the image of the 'long-headed Mangbetu woman' was virtually a logo for Belgian colonialism, featured in images at the 1931 and 1937 French expositions and on postcards, posters, guidebooks, and in art galleries. This image was simultaneously exotic, erotic, and easily aestheticized." Schildkrout, "*Les Parisiens d'Afrique*," p. 81.
43 Theresa A. Leininger-Miller, *New Negro Artists in Paris: African American Painters and Sculptors in the City of Light, 1922–1934* (New Brunswick: Rutgers University Press, 2001), p. 58.
44 Leininger-Miller, p. 58.
45 Schildkrout, "*Les Parisiens d'Afrique*," p. 86. See also pp. 85–91.
46 Ibid, p. 86.
47 Berry, *Screen Style*, p. 133.
48 One version in velvet appears in "An African Head-Dress again Inspires Agnès," *Vogue*, September 1, 1926, p. 61.
49 Articles in *L'Officiel* were printed in French, English, and Spanish. The French was the primary text and English translations do not appear to have been written by native speakers, hence the grammatical errors and awkward translations. I have tried to note words in the original French where they may affect the meaning in a significant way. *L'Officiel*, August 1926, p. 27.
50 Schildkrout, "*Les Parisiens d'Afrique*," p. 71.
51 Anne Anlin Cheng, "Skin Fashion: Josephine Baker and Dressing Race," *NKA: Journal of Contemporary African Art* (November 2015): 8.

52 Jazz clubs in Harlem were often adorned with "jungle" décor. The Cotton Club, for instance, was "decorated with palm trees, bongo drums, and African inspired geometric pattern, every element of the entertainment was geared towards white audiences' expectations of the primitive." Ghislaine Wood, "The Exotic," in *Art Deco 1910–1939*, ed. Charlotte Benton, Tim Benton, and Ghislaine Wood (London: V&A Publications, 2003), p. 137.
53 Wood, "The Exotic," p. 135.
54 Wendy Buonaventura, *Something in the Way She Moves: Dancing Women from Salome to Madonna* (Cambridge: Da Capo Press, 2004), p. 194.
55 Archer Straw, *Negrophilia*, 97. Phillis Rose, *Jazz Cleopatra: Josephine Baker in Her Time* (New York: Doubleday, 1989), pp. 100–1.
56 Working in France, he created objects of all kinds that married references to exotic Africa with a modernist streamlined aesthetic in the Jazz-Moderne style. He used a variety of metals, as well as lacquer (one of his interior design innovations) in his jewelry, introducing several African-style motifs and often working in geometric patterns featuring gold, black, and red. See, for example: Marjorie Howard, "The Latest Judgment of Paris: At a Summer Villa Near Cannes," *Harper's Bazaar*, June 1928, p. 71.
57 Laurence Mouillefarine and Evelyne Possémé, *Art Deco Jewelry: Modernist Masterworks and Their Makers* (London: Thames & Hudson, 2009), p. 235.
58 For images, see Adriane Audouin-Dubreuil, *La Croisière Noire*, p. 115.
59 Marjorie Howard, "New Feather and Fabrics," *Harper's Bazaar*, September 1926, pp. 90–1.
60 Marjorie Howard, "New Feather and Fabrics," p. 92.
61 See: "An African Head-Dress again Inspires Agnès," *Vogue*, September 1, 1926, p. 61. "Iacovleff [sic] Sketches a New Agnès Hat," *Vogue*, August 1, 1926, p. 38. And Marjorie Howard, "New Feather and Fabrics," p. 91.
62 With thanks to Regina Lee Blaszczyk for introducing this term to me during the NEH Summer Institute. See Regina Lee Blaszczyk, *Producing Fashion: Commerce, Culture, and Consumers* (Philadelphia: University of Pennsylvania Press, 2008). Regina Lee Blaszczyk, *Imagining Consumers: Design and Innovation from Wedgwood to Corning* (Baltimore: Johns Hopkins University Press, 2000).
63 "Fez Dominant Expression of High Crown in Millinery Exhibited at Guild Fashion Revue," *Women's Wear Daily*, March 9, 1933, p. 4.
64 "Lilly Daché Opens New 'Salon Jaune' with Reception and Fashion Promenade," *Women's Wear Daily*, February 13, 1933, p. 10.
65 Both in the Metropolitan Museum of Art's Costume Institute, accession numbers: 2009.300.1120 and 2009.300.1119.
66 While *Women's Wear Daily* articles routinely date the hats in Raton's collection to the late eighteenth century, those hats that Lilly Daché ultimately purchased from him and donated to the Metropolitan Museum of Art in 1974 have subsequently been dated by the museum to the nineteenth and twentieth centuries. This earlier dating by *WWD* seems to have been important since this was "before the European influence had a play; these are ideally suited to modern conception." Maude G. Moody, "18th Century African Craft, on Display in Charles Rattoon's [sic] Paris Studio, Expected to have Repercussions in Fashion World—Bead Embroidery Technique Especially Susceptible to Modern Adaptation," *Women's Wear Daily*, July 16, 1937, section 1. Thanks to Wendy Grossman for sharing the provenance information from the Daché bequest to the Metropolitan Museum with me.

67 Margaret Chase Harriman, "Hats Will Be Worn," *New Yorker*, April 4, 1942, p. 24.
68 "Daché Hats to go 'African' this Fall," *Women's Wear Daily*, September 10, 1937, p. 23.
69 Bullock's Wilshire advertisement, *Los Angeles Times*, August 9, 1937, A8.
70 "Exotic Designs from Alix and Schiaparelli," *Women's Wear Daily*, March 17, 1937, p. 1.
71 Emma McClendon, "Yves Saint Laurent and Exoticism," in *Yves Saint Laurent & Halston: Fashioning the 70s* (New York: The Fashion Institute of Technology, 2015), p. 103.
72 McClendon, "Yves Saint Laurent and Exoticism," p. 118.
73 There is much more to say about this show, and it is the subject of my ongoing research.
74 This occurs between 21:24 and 21:34 in: "MUGLER S/S RTW 1988," YouTube video, 46:34, posted by "Yukikoandthe," January 15, 2012, https://youtu.be/93l0oi1NbnU?list=PLdvjI6mkk-HxuYDBinjBYFk6gwisO-HA0.
75 The large black sombrero-style hats that Beyoncé wears throughout the video and on her tour is one example of attention being drawn to the question of who gets to look where. The hat allows her to deny viewers the pleasure of looking at her, and also allows her to freely survey others; this is particularly prominent in the song "6 inch," in which she is seen in a dark limo surveilling white men on the street as they try to hide from her gaze.
76 Tess, "Meet Julia Koerner, the designer who helped bring Black Panther's 3D printed costumes to life," *3Ders.org*, March 9, 2018: http://www.3ders.org/articles/20180309-meet-julia-koerner-the-designer-who-helped-bring-black-panthers-3d-printed-costumes-to-life.html
77 @f.bazin on Instagram, January 8, 2018 and February 14, 2017.

Adventure play in physical and virtual spaces

Gayle L. Goudy

In disorienting surroundings somewhat resembling an industrial ant farm, two restless kids and a grumpy dad absorb the labyrinth of slides and tunnels made of steel rebar and salvaged architectural remnants like a lantern that once adorned a stately St. Louis building or a bank vault door. Suddenly, the little girl disappears—dad can hear her calling from parts unknown far beneath him. He grabs his boy and jumps down a dark slide after her. With his adrenaline fired up, he reunites with her two stories below. This instant sparked dad's memory of being a kid on an adventure and the family spent the next three hours in that uninhibited mindset.[1]

The threat of real (or perceived) danger experienced by this family at the City Museum in St. Louis, Missouri, is the essence of "adventure play." The idea goes back to 1943, when landscape architect Carl Theodor Sørensen built a "junk playground" in Denmark following his observation of children enjoying play in construction sites. Though intended for children, adventure play spaces resemble spaces prohibited to them like junkyards with waste material, old cars, boxes, and timber.[2] Children have agency to transform adventure spaces with no set outcome; each play episode is unique.

In this chapter, I advocate for adventure play for children and chronicle how play spaces can take many forms, even if makers do not designate their space as an adventure play space. Video games can currently provide a psychological adventure play, and in the near future will provide fully immersive experiences as haptic technology develops.

Though adventure play has gained momentum in pedagogical and psychological fields, it began in the discourse of landscape architecture and has re-emerged in fields as diverse as fine art, sculpture, installation art, architecture, playground design, digital art, and video games. In this post-disciplinary discussion, the terms "maker" and "player" designate the designer, creator, sculptor, programmer, or artist and viewer, spectator, receiver, user, or co-creator (respectively, regardless of what the makers call themselves). This chapter will look at adventure play in physical play spaces made by Toshiko Horiuchi MacAdam and Bob Cassilly, digital play spaces such as *Windosill* and *Journey*, and manipulative objects by Rockwell Group. Playgrounds, including adventure play spaces, extend beyond the design canon because the progressive narrative of modern design has omitted play spaces. A reason for this omission may be that play spaces lack a disciplinary home emerging from landscape design, architecture, child psychology, early childhood pedagogy, art, and sculpture. Play spaces are not interdisciplinary or transdisciplinary because collaboration or theoretical insights are not necessarily part of their development.

The discussion of play spaces in the physical and virtual worlds are post-disciplinary since the organizational divisions of disciplines, as they have evolved in academia, and the definitions of genres do not serve us in understanding but create more artificial boundaries.

Physical adventure play spaces

Adventure playgrounds take many forms. The maker provides parameters of a mutable space and relinquishes control of the ultimate form to children (players) who experiment with the materials and every interaction is designed to be different. Ellen Sandseter, professor of psychology at Queen Maud University in Norway, points out that children naturally and intentionally seek risky play "to experience the thrill, joyful fear and the wonderful feeling of mastering something they wouldn't think they dared. In doing so, they find their own level of manageable risk, and progressively master more by seeking challenges suitable for their mastery level and courage."[3] In the United States, Richard Dattner designed several adventure play spaces in New York City in the 1960s and 1970s. Sesame Street featured one of Dattner's playgrounds in the 1970s and 1980s introduction, where children run toward the camera in what looks like a construction site. Like Sørensen's junkyard playground, Dattner's playgrounds had chaotic or anarchic elements in them that included tunnels, tree houses, dirt, sand, and water areas, and/or building materials such as palettes, blocks, or cardboard. Dattner said, "The next best thing to a playground that children design themselves is a playground designed by an adult but incorporating the possibility for children to create their own places within it."[4]

Adventure play spaces encourage children to experience autonomy and peer-cooperation without the intervention of adults. A core belief in adventure play is the idea that children should have the freedom to experience real risk to test their limits. Adventure play activist Lady Allen of Hurtwood said, "better to have a broken arm than a bruised spirit." However, this autonomous play outside constant adult supervision, along with the potential for real injury, is exactly what curtailed the growth of adventure play spaces in the United States as society grew more litigious in the 1980s.

Fear of litigation had changed play spaces in the United States by the 1990s into brightly colored, ultra-safe, plastic forts with cushioned rubber playground flooring beneath them.[5] ASTM Standards regulated critical fall heights, head-entrapment guidelines, and restrictions on the use of sand. Even Dattner's popular adventure playground in Central Park was blocked off in the 1990s after parents complained of not being able to see their children.[6] Illustrating this societal shift, a 1997 renovation took much of the adventure out of Dattner's Adventure Playground around the same time that the opening credits of Sesame Street replaced the construction-site-looking playground scenes with puppet characters and organized play, like baseball.[7]

Adventure play in physical spaces

Between 1993 and 2011, as a new generation of parents in the United States built protective bubbles around childhood, sculptor Bob Cassilly turned a derelict shoe factory in St. Louis, Missouri, into an elaborate adventure playground, though he never used the term.[8] After purchasing the building which covered an acre and a half of ground space, he rented space to artist friends and began collecting junk, including salvaged architectural remnants from demolished buildings. Affectionately, they called this "The Museum of Things that Could Kill You." To revitalize the neighborhood, the Danforth Foundation offered Cassilly and his wife Gail Soliwoda a $250,000 grant, and they registered as a non-profit children's museum with Soliwoda as the director.

Cassilly began to fill the enormous space with sculptures of animals, plaster versions of geological formations, forests, collages of architectural follies, and abandoned vehicles and airplanes (Figure 11.1). In one area of the museum above the caves on the first floor, a warren of rebar tunnels, slides made from sheets of metal or assembly-line rollers, and architectural remnants form a maze that extends five stories upwards (Figure 11.2). Exploring this dynamic play space feels like crawling through an elaborate steel hamster tunnel-maze or space station. Cassilly intended the museum to feel alive, breathing, and changing, so he used organic forms. Squares were too stable, Cassilly believed, but curves had energy, so dead ends and hard corners were avoided. Matt Philpott, former manager of the City Museum, describes the forms as moving around, diving into each other, appearing, disappearing, and reappearing "as if there were no one thing in control, but multiple principles competing against each other in almost a survival of the fittest."[9] The employees that Cassilly assembled at the museum joked that they were the City Museum Engineers: Creating the Impossible for the Insane.

Figure 11.1 Bob Cassilly, City Museum in St. Louis, Missouri, 1993–2011.

Figure 11.2 Bob Cassilly, City Museum in St. Louis, Missouri, 1993–2011.

Cassilly loved danger, fun, and fear, and thought that one intertwined with another. Like Lady Allen of Hurtwood, he believed that it was better to scrape your knee and develop confidence than to fabricate fears in your mind and never live. He would send his young daughter Daisy out onto scaffolding to see where she would stop or cry out to determine where handrails would go. Soliwoda said:

> Danger, for him, equaled challenge. It was something that would keep him from the mediocre, keep him alive. But he never wanted to subject others to real danger. For them, it was the illusion. He wanted them to get as close to it as they possibly could, and he took it to the farthest degree possible because he wanted people to feel the impact. He felt people had to get off their couches and away from their television screens and experience something real.[10]

This is related to the "Peltzman Effect," a risk compensation theory by economist Sam Peltzman who hypothesized that people tend to react to a safety regulation by increasing other risky behavior, which offsets the regulation.[11] When people feel safe, they are less cautious. Conversely, adventure play is safe because people feel unsafe and act more cautiously.

The requirements of running a nonprofit children's museum (fundraising and liability insurance) as well as some philosophical differences about the purpose of the museum eventually ended the non-profit children's museum and the couple's marriage. In 1997, Cassilly changed the status of the museum from non-profit to profit and began running an "anti-Children's Museum." Over the years, art expanded to fill the entire 762,000 square feet of the building with neither teachable moments nor signage or maps—typical in most children's museums—because they discourage exploration.

City Museum has few rules, but one that is enforced is that minors are accompanied by an adult. Richard Callow, a long-time friend of Cassilly who handled media for the City Museum, remarked that this rule brought a tension that Bob desired. The holes in the floor leading to tunnels and slides completely out of sight of their entrances could be reached faster by crawling than by walking, "to keep up with their kids, adults had to join them or lose them. That only bothered the adults."[12] Intuitively, Cassilly had embraced the idea of adventure play for his visitors, even if it was forced upon the adult visitors. The risk of injury was real and many visitors have left bruised and scraped. Frequent museum-goers advise wearing knee pads to everyone over twenty years of age. The City Museum has been sued twenty-six times, and Cassilly kept a mocking list of lawyers who had sued him in the museum lobby. His best-known infractions were building permit violations—how could he tell the city what he was going to build when his plans would only take shape as he worked? And yet, more than 700,000 people visit the City Museum each year. Many visitors who post online reviews of the museum report fear when separated from their children, bruises, and cries of lost children. At the same time, many of these visitors report that they return precisely because it is scary, intense, and a bit dangerous. While fear and danger in a dark cavernous place describes the play space in Bob Cassilly's Children's Museum, adventure play does not have to contain those elements to challenge and thrill the player's experience. Toshiko Horiuchi MacAdam's adventure playgrounds are bright and open, and the cries of children in this space are squeals of delight.

Toshiko Horiuchi MacAdam transitioned to play space designer after beginning her crocheted net sculptures as fine art installations in museums. In her art installations, she transformed spaces with knitted, large-scale, abstract geometrical shapes based on architectural forms, such as the Toshi Net at the Kaleideum Children's Museum in Winston-Salem, North Carolina (Figure 11.3) or the Takino Rainbow Nest in

Figure 11.3 Toshiko Horicuchi MacAdam, Toshi Nets Play exhibition, "Kaleidoscape," installed 2013.

the Takino Suzuran National Park in Hokkaido, Japan (Figure 11.4). MacAdam feels that Antonio Gaudí's forms are naturally connected to textiles, and his methods of sculpting using hanging chains or ropes bear a direct similarity to MacAdam's work (Figure 11.5). Gaudí would place a building's plan on the ceiling and suspend a chain or a rope from the plan to determine in three dimensions the volume, height,

Figure 11.4 Toshiko Horiuchi MacAdam with Interplay Design & Manufacturing, Inc., "Takino Rainbow Nest" in the Takino Suzuran National Park in Hokkaido, Japan, installed 2000.

Adventure play in physical and virtual spaces 177

Figure 11.5 Antoni Gaudí's inverted catenary arch model.

and curvature of the vaulting and the columns that supported them. MacAdam also drew inspiration from inlaid tile work, such as that covering the interior of the Shah Mosque at Isfahan (Figure 11.6), which compare readily to her knitted patterns when considering them in two dimensions. In her words, this tile work "forms part of the building's fabric and geometry [that] work together to create a space of fantastic beauty and spirituality."[13] Combining these elements, she transformed spaces with a knitted architecture, such as in the installation "Gothic Arches, Romanesque Church," 1976 (Figure 11.7).

MacAdam's art transitioned to a play space when two children asked her if they could swing in her installation *Multiple Hammock No. 1*. After nervously obliging these young patrons, who were unfamiliar with art gallery protocol, she watched how the work was suddenly imbued with an unanticipated new energy, "swinging and stretching with the weight of the small bodies, forming pouches and other unexpected transformations, and above all there were the sounds of the undisguised delight of children exploring new play space."[14] After this experience, the full-body interactivity became a greater priority to her than a visual experience. After this, she spent most weekends for the next three years visiting all the parks and playgrounds in central Tokyo with student collaborators.

MacAdams and her collaborators wrote to the national newspaper to express their concerns regarding this generation of children growing up in Tokyo who were often without siblings, living in cramped high-rise apartments, watching television, and only

Figure 11.6 Tile work in the entrance of the Shah Mosque, Isfahan, Iran, 1611–1629.

Figure 11.7 Toshiko Horiuchi MacAdam, "Gothic Arches, Romanesque Church," 1976. Collection of the Jean Lurcat Museum of Contemporary Tapestry, Angers, France.

playing in organized sports. She advocated for play spaces where children could use their bodies, challenge themselves, grow emotionally and imaginatively, develop social skills, learn to cooperate, and gain wisdom about life.[15] In so doing, she describes adventure play, and like Bob Cassilly, she does not use the term specifically.

In 1971, MacAdam intentionally created a play space that she donated to a kindergarten designed by architect Hatsue Yamada. For this new audience, she changed her color scheme from somber, monochromatic tones to bright rainbow colors and knitted with a twisted rope made of vinylon (PVA fiber) because nylon (her preferred material) was unaffordable to her at the time. In 1979, she worked with landscape architect Fumiaki Takano for a national park under construction in Okinawa, and soon she made "Unknown Pockets: A Gift / Knitted Wonder Space," which drew as many as 6,000 visitors in a single day. MacAdam's net play works were so appealing that in 1990, she and her husband, Charles MacAdam, established Interplay Design and Manufacturing, Inc. in Nova Scotia, Canada, to promote textile play environments commercially.[16]

She describes the nets as a womb, which imply a nurturing space of safety and comfort. However, her spaces intentionally encourage risk-taking; MacAdam believes that:

Children need to cope with risk.... [in] a challenging play environment, well designed so children challenge themselves but with many routes and options. There is no program of play. There are always alternatives. Each child plays at the level he or she is comfortable with.... Some groups of children come regularly to play on their own; their play is fantastic. They know what they are capable of and then stretch just a little further, becoming more and more adept. Some of their maneuvers are heart stopping to a bystander—but they know what they are doing. Often it is the parents who are the problem. They seem to have forgotten what it was like to be a child.[17]

For an adult to remember what it is like to play like a child is to connect to an intuitive self-confidence that allows the person to experiment within his or her innate limits of comfort rather than extrinsic fears or imposed limitations. Too often, adults limit their play (or that of their children) because of outside concerns such as the hundreds of ways a stunt could result in injury or embarrassment. Children play without these fears.

MacAdam's forms are deceptively complicated because nylon will continuously stretch over time (referred to as creep). One or more of the corners are tethered with ropes, which can be shortened to adjust the tension as necessary, compensating for creep and ensuring that the nets will clear the ground and nets below when they are weighted by children. Ideally, the units should approach a hyperbolic paraboloid shape (like a saddle), which makes them stronger and gives better tension throughout.[18] It is similar to Gaudi's catenary arch, but stretches dynamically in multiple directions.

To date, *Net of Woods* (2009) at the Hakone sculpture park in Sapporo, Japan, is MacAdams' most well-known work.[19] The large open-air pavilion designed by Takaharu

Figure 11.8 Nest of the Baya Weaver.

& Yui Tezuka of Tezuka Architects of Tokyo forms a frame from which the nets hang. Despite its shape being reminiscent of a primitive dwelling or beaver's mound, the stacked horizontal lintels of the outer pavilion frame were designed with the aid of structural analysis tools, CAD software, and numerically controlled milling equipment. However, the brightly colored nets that hang within were entirely knitted by hand. Concentric rings of color form around a hole large enough for a small person to crawl through. These rings join together forming a surface, like crocheted squares form a blanket. Players can bounce and perform daring flips on this surface or lay down and daydream. This area is contained within nets that stretch to the wooden dome, providing a safe boundary so children cannot fall from the edge of the surface. When a child enters one of the rings, she enters a semi-private netted pod that hangs from the surface toward the floor like nests of the Baya Weaver (Figure 11.8). From here, players can crawl to another pod or out of openings in the net to the floor of the wooden pavilion. Suspended from the net above, the player can hang or swing from one of the suspended balls or lounge on inflated seats covered with a knitted mesh in the form of a torus.

A structural engineer who admired the complexity of the work asked MacAdam how she had done the mathematical calculations; she responded, "I could not give him an answer; it was all in my head."[20] The weight, elasticity of the nylon material, and knit geometry form her parameters, but she lets intuition generate the shape of the nets as she knits them by hand. Because of this method, she cannot delegate the act of making to assistants and often knits the entire work alone during ten-hour days.

Adventure play in video games

Though the risk of real injury is non-existent in video games, adventure play is relevant because it carries the same sense of wonder, trial and error, and satisfaction in mastery in the physical space. The video games *Windosill* and *Journey* do not explain themselves or their goals, or even how to play with them. They invite experimentation and one player interaction leads to another interaction through curiosity, like child's play. These games have a minimalist approach to serve both aesthetic and functional purposes—less detail and animation mean faster processing time and better resolution on a smaller scale (such as on an iPhone screen).

In a virtual world, a maker must program gravity, material physics, or seismic events. Virtual worlds have no building codes, wildlife refuges, or NIMBYs ("Not In My Back Yard" neighborhood organizations bent on curtailing activities that might decrease future property values). Therefore, experimental forms should flourish. However, the majority of video game designers do not venture to create new worlds, but recreate our world instead—or a fantasy or historical version of it. Despite its status as an emerging field, the video game industry is remarkably conservative, catering to the same demographics that had access to program video games and the leisure time to play them in the 1950s and 1960s, that is, middle-to-upper class, well-educated, white males.[21] This demographic has favored outcome-based, first-person shooter games. Even among the non-violent games, most games are not exploratory, but outcome-driven (win or lose). However, as games have become readily available on multiple devices (smartphones, tablets, computers, television, and game consoles), the focus on game development for a perceived profitable demographic is ending.[22] A larger gaming audience playing on more platform types has created opportunities for the small game-makers to execute and find niche audiences for a wider variety of game types, such as narrative-driven, non-combative, exploration, or art games.

As with physical spaces, such as the City Museum and Net Play Works projects, adventure play in the video game experience is open and varies greatly with each play. Game developer Phil Fish describes the difference between the original 1986 version of *The Legend of Zelda* (adventure play) and more recent versions of *Zelda* (outcome-based play):

> The first Zelda just drops you into that world and it's a completely open, non-linear world. It's dangerous and it's hard and you have to learn from your mistakes and figure things out. There are these secrets, and these secrets are not obvious at all, which makes them secret and interesting. And then you play the latest *Zelda* and [it's like a] straight corridor ... just holding your hand the whole time. All the secrets have an arrow pointing at them. ... All the surprise and magic and danger and mystery is just gone completely because of an obsession with tutorials and making sure the player knows about everything.[23]

Most video games that include narratives do not use the interaction of the player with the game to tell the story. Action sequences and narrative sequences are separate; game play must stop for the narrative to be told in a more traditional cinematic way. Experiential games such as *Windosill* and *Journey* differ from these narrative games because they use the player interaction with the environment to tell the story. The play experience is the narrative adventure where the objective of the game is discovery, not objective-oriented (win or lose). These games have no points and you cannot die. They prioritize adventure play and interactivity while experiencing an engaging narrative.

Vecktorpark's *Windosill* (2009), a puzzle video where the player interacts with objects on a windowsill to move through eleven rooms, is a pioneer in the experiential subgenre of video games (Figure 11.9). *Windosill* maker Patrick Smith explained that young people are more willing to "just start touching things and playing around. People above a certain age will look for clues before they do anything."[24] Though the player interacts with *Windosill* through the computer, sound and the physical response of objects within the environment, like the reaction of a string that is pulled or the way that a toy car bounces away from a wall, give the game a tactile quality. The game has unexpected and humorous reactions to this interaction. The player can knock over letters, for instance, and a large arm comes out and puts them upright. A player may push a button to start a motor that causes dots to fly around like bugs. The unexpected and humorous response to the players' actions create the narrative contributing to the emotional experience of the game and structures this experience as adventure play.

ThatGameCompany advertises their game *Journey* as an interactive parable where the goal is to get to the mountain top, while you discover "who you are, what this place is, and what is your purpose. Travel and explore this ancient, mysterious world alone, or with a stranger you meet along the way. Soar above ruins and glide across sands as you discover the secrets of a forgotten civilization."[25] Unlike most of the games available in 2012, *Journey* aimed to make an emotional experience that fosters a feeling of connection, as Creative Director Jenova Chen recalled, "Either you are killing each other or killing something together. There was just a lack of connection between

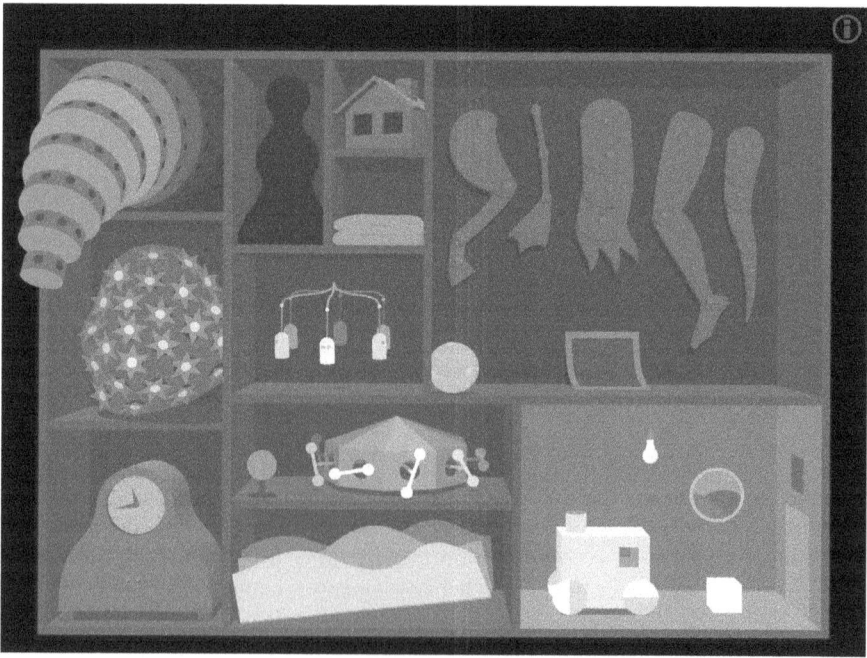

Figure 11.9 Patrick Smith, first room in Vectorpark's *Windosill* computer game, 2009.

Figure 11.10 ThatGameCompany, *Journey* computer game, 2012. Top: The landscape; Bottom: The character.

people."²⁶ The makers set *Journey* in a minimalist, pastel landscapes, including deserts, snow covered mountains, and ruins. Places throughout the world were reimagined in a minimalist aesthetic to be familiar yet unknown (Figure 11.10). The lonely landscapes help to focus the player on the avatar (called "the character" by makers) and strengthen the connection that player feels when the character travels with the stranger.

In a talk given at the Game Developers' Conference in 2013, art director Matt Nava explained that the evolution of "the character" began as a person with a face that would communicate only with eyes, and had arms, hands, and fingers. However, the team wanted the figure to be anonymous because, "we wanted people to play with each other no matter who they were. It was a subtractive process."²⁷ As the character developed, Nava removed everything that was not essential to game play. To this new minimalist character, Nava added a dynamic piece of cloth. The cloth adds to the experience of the world—it lifts up and trails behind as the character runs or glides down snow-covered slopes, flutters with the movement of the wind, swirls around the character's body when flying, and grows in length as the character gains wisdom and experience.

Although Nava refers to the avatar using masculine pronouns and calling him "guy" in his presentation, the final character is anonymous and gender neutral. The fact that Nava corrects himself during his presentation reveals the intention of creating an avatar which allows the player to play without preconceived ideas of gender and promotes the players empathy and ability to identify as the character.

Because *Journey* has no dialogue or text, the entire story unfolds through visuals accompanied by music with a similar emotional arc. The environmental color scheme evolves with the visual story as the character journeys through a desert with warm colors to a brightly colored desert with pink dunes and green skies, through a dark, misty underground passage to ultimately arrive on snowcapped mountains where the player finally sees blue sky. When the fog is farther away, the scene is clear and the mood happy. When the fog is near there is more danger.[28] The flying snakes and kites (or fish) add an ethereal element to the lonely landscape. In one of the scenes, the character meets a stranger. The player learns nothing about this stranger or the purpose of his or her presence, yet their presence presents the simple joy of being together playing together, if this is what the player chooses. If the character travels with the stranger, they will get a different experience than if they traveled alone.

Play and narrative in *Journey* create an experience of adventure play. Through the character, the player sand-surfs, soars, leaps, and floats. The player does not simply navigate through a predetermined experience; each repeated play offers different experiences. After the first completed game, your character comes back as the stranger and helps guide a new character through the world. Even the musical score of the game changes as the player makes choices. For instance, when you are with the stranger, the harp and the viola are added to the music and these instruments get louder in volume as the character and the stranger get closer to each other.[29] At another point in the game, the character might release a caged kite-animal. If you are playing alone, you will hear a flute solo and some percussion. If you are with the stranger, you will hear the harp and viola again. If you do not release the creature, you hear ambient sounds. Just like adventuring through the City Museum or climbing into a knitted net-pod, the structure of play in *Journey* is determined by the player. Though much of *Journey* has a tone of mystery and delight, there are aspects of fear and danger. The caves are dark with an ominous score and have dragons that will tear off part of your staff if you are spotted.

Mathew Dyason in *Game Score Fanfare* eloquently summarized the core idea behind *Journey* at the end of the game. After apotheosis, the player returns to play the game again with

> the knowledge of the game that you can bring to other people and help them through it. And that's the core idea behind *Journey*: To make your experience in life a blessing for other people. To bestow your knowledge onto others as a boon in order to help them through their own life. The purpose of your journey is that you can make other people's journeys easier, even if they are a complete stranger. And this is told through every aspect of the game: It's built into the gameplay, as travelling alongside someone else will refill both of your scarves' flying power. And even the art-style, as multiple play-throughs will grant you the white robes worn by your ancestors, thus making you the spiritual guide for others.[30]

In video gaming, the player's psychological connection with the avatar allows the player to experience the same emotional thrill and at times worrisome experiences that players can experience in physical spaces.

Today, adventure play is gaining momentum in child development fields because of the relationship between risk-taking and resilience. Some psychologists have correlated the decline of opportunities for children to play freely without adult control and in risky situations with an increase in childhood mental disorders, especially emotional disorders.[31] Yet as Susan Soloman, author of *American Playgrounds*, states "there is this sense that if you talk about [risky play], that is enough. There's this very real reluctance to get involved in anything that might at least potentially cause an injury."[32] For all the excitement players at the City Museum experience, it has true risk: falls resulted in two serious head injuries (an eighteen-month-old girl and a ten-year-old boy) and a woman lost two fingers.[33]

Current responses to adventure play that spur creativity without the liability include David Rockwell's *Imagination Playground* near the South Street Seaport in New York City, which eschews physical risk and puts creative risk back into childhood play. A key component of this playground is the giant foam blocks of various shapes, tubes, mats, wagons, and crates that can fit together or stack in an endless number of arrangements (Figure 11.11). In 2012, the National Building Museum opened PLAY WORK BUILD, a permanent exhibition designed in collaboration with Rockwell Group. Rockwell Group has marketed this a portable playground, and it has become part of play spaces in schools and museums across the United States.[34] Though these building toys foster creativity and cooperative play, creative risk lacks the sense of drama and elation found in adventure play spaces.

The next generation of games that use virtual reality with haptic experience to simulate the sense of touch, such as VRTouch, will create an experience much more like those on MacAdam's nets or Cassilly's City Museum, though with fewer bruises and lawsuits. Imagine the thrill of feeling the grit of sand beneath your feet as you sand-surf or the flapping of fabric as you soar on the back of a dragon as *Journey*'s character!

Figure 11.11 Rockwell Group (David Rockwell, designer), *Imagination Playground*, portable modular playground, 2011.

With this emerging technology, the video game environment will provide a space for adventure play where psychological risk merges with a tactile sense that can give the user/player the same arousal as adventure play with the physical and psychological benefits and no injury or litigation.

I advocate adventure play for children (and adults) because it allows players to test their limits in a context where they are comfortable, and in doing so gain confidence in their abilities (at whatever level they play). Adventure play spaces can take many forms even if the makers do not designate their space as an adventure play space. Video games can currently provide a psychological adventure play and as haptic technology develops, it will provide players with an immersive experience like those that can be experienced at the City Museum or in MacAdam's Net Play Works.

Notes

1. My family made this visit to the City Museum in July 2017.
2. After seeing Sørensen's "junk playground" in Endrup, Denmark, prominent English landscape architect and president of the World Organization for Early Childhood Education Margory Allen (Lady Allen of Hurtwood) promoted adventure playgrounds. Today, there are approximately a thousand adventure playgrounds (mostly in Europe and Japan). For the history of adventure playgrounds and the contradiction between free play and play as an instrument of social policy, see Roy Kozlovsky, "Adventure Playgrounds and Postwar Reconstruction," in *Designing Modern Childhoods: History, Space, and the Material Culture of Children*, edited by Marta Gutman and Ning de Coninck-Smith (New Brunswick: Rutgers University Press, 2008).
3. "Point Person: Our Q&A with Ellen Sandseter too-safe playgrounds," *Dallas News*, August 2001 (https://www.dallasnews.com/opinion/commentary/2011/08/05/point-person-our-qa-with-ellen-sandseter-too-safe-playgrounds)
4. Deborah Bishop, "Structured Play," *Dwell*, January 1, 2009. https://www.dwell.com/article/structured-play-8cd1a3a1, accessed February 20, 2018.
5. Rebecca Mead, "State of Play: How Tots Lots Became Places to Build Children's Brains" *The New Yorker*, 86(19) (July 5, 2010): 32.
6. Dattner's Adventure Playground in Central Park, New York City, was renovated in 2009. See Jeff Byles, "Adventure Central," *The Architect's Newspaper*, November 4, 2009, https://archpaper.com/2009/11/adventure-central/#.VnnFs8ArKi4, accessed December 12, 2017.
7. In the 1960s introduction, the entire fifty-two-second introduction is a montage of children play with one exception, a single shot of a seal at a zoo. The 1970s introduction devotes two seconds to a shot with Big Bird and a little girl. The 1980s introduction devotes twelve seconds to Big Bird. The 1990s introduction has a puppet character in every scene in the montage with a marked reduction in the scenes of children's play and no adventure playgrounds.
8. On May 21, 1972, while on his honeymoon with first wife Cecilia Davidson, Bob Cassilly wrestled the crazed Laszlo Toth (who vandalized Michelangelo's *Pieta* with a hammer) to the ground. See "Honeymoon Highlight—Punch for Pieta," *St. Louis Post-Dispatch*, August 11, 1972.
9. Jeannette Cooperman, "Deconstructing Bob Cassilly," *St. Louis Magazine*, January 25, 2012, https://www.stlmag.com/Deconstructing-Bob-Cassilly/ accessed August 3, 2017.

10 Ibid.
11 Sam Peltzman, Professor Emeritus from the University of Chicago has been writing about risk compensation since 1975 across industries. The Pelzman Effect is observed in automobile safety, sports safety equipment, unmanned aircraft, and shared spaces for automobiles and pedestrians without traffic lights.
12 Cooperman, "Deconstructing Bob Cassilly."
13 Vanessa Quirk, "Meet the Artist behind Those Amazing, Hand-Knitted Playgrounds," in *Archdaily*, November 28, 2012, http://www.archdaily.com/297941/meet-the-artist-behind-those-amazing-hand-knitted-playgrounds/, accessed on March 29, 2018.
14 Paige Johnson, "Playground Crochet by Toshiko Horiuchi" *Playscapes*, November 18, 2011, http://www.play-scapes.com/play-art-playgrounds-by-artists/playground-crochet-by-toshiko-horiuchi/, accessed March 29, 2018.
15 Quirk, "Meet the Artist behind Those Amazing, Hand-Knitted Playgrounds."
16 NetPlayWorks Website, http://netplayworks.com/NetPlayWorks/Home.html, accessed on March 29, 2018.
17 Quirk, "Meet the Artist behind Those Amazing, Hand-Knitted Playgrounds."
18 Elizabeth Cummins, "Art as Playspace: Interview with Toshiko & Charles MacAdam," in *How to Grow a Playspace: Development and Design* (ebook), ed. Katherine Masiulanis and Elizabeth Cummins (Abingdon, Oxon: Routledge, 2017), pp. 195–207.
19 Toshiko Horiuchi MacAdam with Interplay Design & Manufacturing, Inc. (design and fabrication), Norihde Imagawa, T.I.S. & Partners (structural engineering), Takaharu & Yui Tezuka (architects), Hakone Open Air Museum, Kanagawa, Japan, 2009.
20 Cummins, "Interview with Toshiko & Charles MacAdam."
21 Anna Anthropy, *Rise of the Videogame Zinesters: How Freaks, Normals, Amateurs, Artists, Dreamers, Dropouts, Queers, Housewives, and People Like You Are Taking Back an Art Form*, (New York: Seven Stories, 2012), pp. 5–6.
   In 2009, Rob Auten, who ran video-game production for 20th Century Fox, said, "Our industry is probably more risk-averse than Hollywood. It is extremely difficult to break the patterns of the establishment." See Joshuah Bearman, "Can D.I.Y Supplant the First-Person Shooter?" *The New York Times Magazine*, November 13, 2009: http://www.nytimes.com/2009/11/15/magazine/15videogames-t.html?pagewanted=all&_r=1&), accessed March 29, 2018.
22 In the United States, forty-nine percent of the adult population report playing video games. Men and women play games in equal numbers, though men are more than twice as likely to call themselves "gamers." About half of US adults report playing video games, and whites, blacks, and Hispanics are equally likely to report playing. See Monica Anderson, "Views on Gaming Differ by Race, Ethnicity," *Pew Research Center*, December 17, 2015; and Maeve Duggan, "Gaming and Gamers," *Pew Research Center: Internet and Technology*, December 15, 2015: http://www.pewinternet.org/2015/12/15/gaming-and-gamers/, accessed March 29, 2018.
23 Phil Fish made this statement in the context of comparing recent Japanese games with Western games at the Game Developer Conference in 2012, after insulting a Japanese game developer and saying "Japanese games just suck." The cultural aspect of his statement is not related to my argument. Quote from the documentary film *Indie Game: Life After*, directed by Lisane Pajot and James Swirsky (2016; Vancouver: BlinkWorks Media).
24 Kyle Vanhemert, "I Wish More Games were as Weird as This Guy's Interactive Alphabet," *Wired: Design*, February 12, 2015.

25 ThatGameCompany Development team: Kellee Santiago, Jenova Chen, Nicholas Clark, John Edwards, Martin Middleton, Robin Hunicke, Matt Nava, Bryan Singh, Aaron Jessie, John Nesky, Chris Bell, Ke Jiang, Rick Nelson, Michael Peddicord, Selijl Tanaka, Dallas Robinson, Austin Wintory, Steve Johnson, Aaron Grommesh (http://thatgamecompany.com/games/journey/).

   Journey was created in three years. See Dean Takahaski, "An Interview with Jenova Chen: How Journey's Creator Went Bankrupt and Won Game of the Year," *VentureBeat*, February 8, 2013 (https://venturebeat.com/2013/02/08/an-interview-with-jenova-chen-how-journeys-creator-went-bankrupt-and-won-game-of-the-year/).

26 "The Art of Journey—Hardcover Art Book Reveal," YouTube Video, 9:14 posted by "PlayStation," August 27, 2012, https://www.youtube.com/watch?v=RTTY7P8ukx4, accessed August 1, 2017.

27 Ibid.

28 Ibid.

29 See 04:32 in "The Story in Journey's Music" YouTube Video, 12:40 posted by Game Store Fanfare on July 6, 2017, https://www.youtube.com/watch?v=KeKnkaB0MBE, accessed March 1, 2018.

30 Ibid.

31 Peter Gray, "Risky Play: Why Children Love It and Need It," *Psychology Today*, April 7, 2014: https://www.psychologytoday.com/blog/freedom-learn/201404/risky-play-why-children-love-it-and-need-it, accessed March 29, 2018.

32 Susan G. Solomon, *American Playgrounds: Revitalizing Community Space* (Lebanon, NH: UPNE, 2005). See also John Tierney, "Can a Playground Be Too Safe?" *The New York Times*, July 18, 2011, http://www.nytimes.com/2011/07/19/science/19tierney.html?_r=0, accessed on March 29, 2018; and Nicholas Day, "Tear Down the Swing Sets: and the Plastic Forts. Here's How to Put the Play Back into Playgrounds" *Slate*, January 28, 2013, http://www.slate.com/articles/life/family/2013/01/loose_parts_are_having_a_moment_putting_the_play_back_in_playgrounds_with.html, accessed March 28, 2018.

33 Diane Toroian Keaggy, "Trial over City Museum Accident to Open Monday," *St. Louis Dispatch*, January 1, 2010, http://www.stltoday.com/news/trial-over-city-museum-accident-to-open-monday-fall-damaged/article_54c54f99-ec44-5819-ae1f-685cf91ff25b.html, accessed on March 28, 2018; and Conor Dougherty, "This Museum Exposes Kids to Thrills, Chills and Trial Lawyers," *The Wall Street Journal*, May 1, 2010: https://www.wsj.com/articles/SB10001424052702304159304575183463721620890, accessed on March 28, 2018.

34 Rockwell Group Website: http://www.rockwellgroup.com/projects/imagination-playground, accessed August 12, 2017.

The case of William Pahlmann: Challenging the canon of modern design

Marianne Eggler, Erica Morawski, and Sara Desvernine Reed

In an advertisement for Lord Calvert whiskey in 1949 (Figure 12.1), interior decorator William Pahlmann (1900–1987) sits in a well-appointed room in tones of beige with a bulldog at his feet and a tag line that reads, "For Men of Distinction...." The advertisement belongs to a series in which Lord Calvert featured various distinguished professional men, all smartly dressed and meant to evoke a sense of stateliness in their demeanors, thereby affording their product a similar air of sophistication. This image, along with the tagline, situates Pahlmann as a man of taste, but also affirms Pahlmann as an admired and accepted professional in the field of interior design. Already in 1948, *The Washington Daily News* described him as "one of America's most famous decorators." And, Pahlmann masterfully capitalized on a shifting cultural climate and burgeoning economy in the US during the postwar period to become a household name. However, despite this success, Pahlmann is excluded from the canon of "high" design history, and generally goes unmentioned in surveys of the modern interior.

Utilizing William Pahlmann's understudied papers at the Hagley Museum and Library Archive in Wilmington, Delaware, this chapter offers an alternative approach to teaching a design history survey or design studies course which uses William Pahlmann as a case study, broadening the canonical understanding of modernism at mid-century and underscoring its diverse, multifaceted nature during this period. We first look at Pahlmann's successful harnessing of multiple design fields, creating a mutually beneficial relationship between interior design and decoration, graphic design, and industrial design in order to provide a unified visual language for his clients while cultivating innovative branding methods and fostering design networks. We then present him as a representative of interior decorating, underscoring his unique vision—one in considerable contrast to the Museum of Modern Art's notion of "good design"—as he worked to professionalize interior decorating despite the fact that it was constructed as a lesser "other" to canonical, "high" modernism. We consider the bias against ornament and decoration and its relationship to gender and sexuality in the mid-twentieth century through a comparison between two popular New York restaurant interiors he worked on—the Four Seasons and the Forum of the Twelve Caesars. Finally, we look at Pahlmann's engagement with other cultures to enliven more mainstream modern décor, analyzing the interest in "international," "exotic" design themes and its ramifications. The

Figure 12.1 William C. Pahlmann pictured as Calvert whiskey's "Man of Distinction" in the Steinbach's living room at their home in Rye, New York (image used in Calvert whiskey advertisements), *c.* 1949.

case of William Pahlmann provides a productive way to enrich discussions of design (and architectural) history by critiquing formulations of "high" versus "low" design and the nature of taste, designers' engagement with other cultures, the roles that gender and sexuality have played in the construction of the canon, and the ways in which branding and media manipulation can be traced back to much earlier pioneers like Pahlmann.

William Pahlmann: The man and his brand

This section focuses on Pahlmann as a brand-maker, successfully marketing himself and his brand nationally and internationally during the postwar period. Between 1945 and 1960, United States' per capita income grew by thirty-five percent, and the number of people with discretionary income doubled during the 1950s. By 1960, over 75 percent of American families owned their own home.[1] Not only was homeownership on the rise, but an emphasis on the nuclear family was central to societal attitudes. A rise in homeownership and the commodification of the nuclear family aligned with an increased emphasis on domesticity and the professionalization of the field of interior design.[2] Pahlmann took advantage of the building boom to champion the field of interior design, along with his own burgeoning practice.

Design historian Grace Lees-Maffei identifies several factors that contributed to professionalization around the turn of the nineteenth century, including maturation of manufacturing industries and processes of industrialization, the rise of the US as a leading manufacturing nation, and the development of psychoanalysis and its influence on marketing and advertising.[3] Although these elements were present much earlier, the intense economic growth during the middle of the twentieth century further amplified the conditions for the professionalization of interior decoration and design during the postwar period. As president of the New York chapter of the American Institute of Decorators, Pahlmann helped to professionalize the field, and even agitated for changing the American Institute of Decorators to the American Institute of Designers, which was finally achieved in 1961. This seemingly simple nominal change had great significance in formalizing the field. And serving at the forefront of leading organizations allowed Pahlmann to demonstrate his expertise. However, it was his ability to exploit mass media that helped to catapult his career.

Design historian Penny Sparke describes the period after 1940 as one in which branding had become integral to all business practice, and Pahlmann successfully utilized his signature in his advertising and promotional materials, creating a unified brand. The personal signature, which had long been used by fashion designers such as Paul Poiret, implies a personal touch in an era of mass production and standardization.[4] One of Pahlmann's book plates includes an elaborate logo with the image of a fenced-in unicorn, his initials, and his full signature (Figure 12.2). The image is an allusion to the early Renaissance-era "The Unicorn in Captivity" from the Unicorn Tapestries (1495–1505), given by John D. Rockefeller, for the opening of The Cloisters in 1938.[5] By utilizing this classical allusion, Pahlmann situates himself as a pedigreed man possessing exceptional and sophisticated taste with a classical foundation.

Establishing himself as an arbiter of good taste was central to his brand. To that end, Pahlmann wrote several articles and even a well-received book of interior design (1955). His syndicated advice columns, including his thrice-weekly series "A Matter of Taste" (1962–1973), belong to a history of domestic advice dating back to the nineteenth century, and its emphasis on domesticity, with writers like Catherine Beecher and Elsie de Wolfe responding to a new socially mobile class of homeowners who no longer had servants. In *After Taste: Expanded Practice in Interior Design*, Penny Sparke discusses how greater disposable income, manufacturing capabilities, and greater social mobility created the need for taste-makers in the late nineteenth century.[6] Like de Wolfe's *The House in Good Taste* (1913), Pahlmann underscored taste as a marker of education, which also served to elevate the importance of an interior decorator in achieving a successful interior. While he advocated for good taste and functional interiors, he also

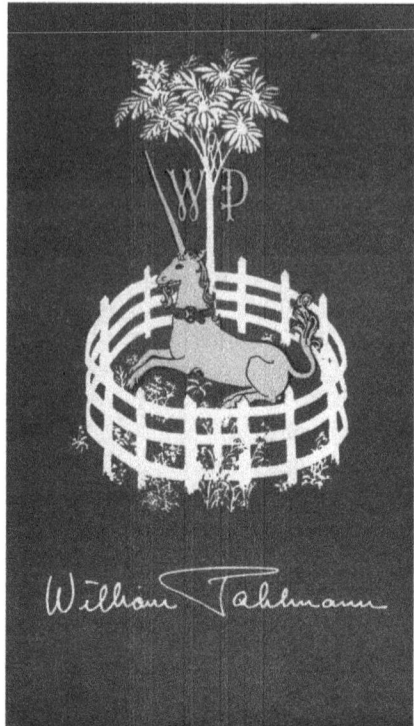

Figure 12.2 William Pahlmann book plate.

pushed for the need for a professional designer in creating a successful space. One of his articles, "It Takes Two Minds to Create One Perfect House," cites the value of using both an architect and an interior decorator, thereby aligning the two professions.[7]

Pahlmann's interiors were often featured in popular magazines because of their theatrical and dramatic qualities, stemming from his early career designing model rooms at Lord and Taylor, where he was head of interior décor. His background in merchandising helped him to understand the consumerist attitude and psychology for buying. He wrote, "good interior decorating is also good merchandising."[8] He created entire room arrangements for the department store, which was an innovative idea and contrasted dramatically with typical department store aisles at the time.[9] Instead of rows of furnishings by period, Pahlmann's model rooms acted as stage sets with a mixture of antiques and modernist forms, especially drawing from his recent travels.[10] Indeed, Pahlmann's eclectic curation of these model rooms was commended for exemplifying good taste, underscored in this quote from *Country Life* in 1936: "The mere listing of the different types and nationalities of furniture and accessories makes it evident that to create the impression of harmony which is the paramount feeling of the room, there must have been a presiding genius of extraordinary taste."[11] This understanding of the power of staging helped him to create interior vignettes for his subsequent promotional materials.

A supreme salesman, by mid-century, Pahlmann was indeed a celebrity. When he purchased a country home outside of New York City in Westchester County in 1955, news reports as far as Roanoke, Virginia, and Dayton, Ohio, featured the headline "Unique House Stuns Friends of Decorator."[12] Pahlmann entertained often in his Manhattan apartment and his new country home. When he completed the interior décor for his home in Bedford Village, which he called "Pahlmannia," he bussed in his friends and colleagues to mark the occasion. The home's interior was featured in several magazines, including one spread that showcased models wearing the fashions of the Canadian designer Arnold Sacco, in various rooms of his home.[13]

Pahlmann took advantage of the public's desire for experts and aptly filled the role by endorsing products for the home. One advertisement reads "William Pahlmann says Amtico Rubber Flooring is out of this world."[14] In addition to print endorsements, Pahlmann also appeared on television. This new medium was particularly suited to Pahlmann's demeanor; an aging bachelor who was charming and articulate, he created a particular persona that helped to elevate the design profession, giving it the gravitas lacking in the previous decades.[15] In the closing commercial for Ivory Soap for Lowell Thomas on CBS, the opening copy from Compton Advertising, Inc. reads, "A rising star in the field of interior design is Mr. William Pahlmann of NYC." And, it further states that Pahlmann recommends delicate oil paints for which ivory soap should be used to sponge walls.[16]

Pahlmann's network of friends and colleagues helped to shape his career and catapult him to fame. An understanding of this multifaceted network of writers, editors, designers, publicists, and advertisers helps to form a more accurate and expansive story about design at mid-century. Pahlmann's clients were often elite Manhattanites, and these commissions appeared in popular shelter magazines of the time.[17] In addition, Pahlmann also successfully networked with those within the magazine industry, including various magazine editors such as Elizabeth Gordon at *House Beautiful* and Betty Pepis, home editor for *The New York Times*. His relationship with Margaret Cousins, editor of *Good Housekeeping*, grew into a lifelong friendship, and Pahlmann designed her country house in Dobbs Ferry, New York, in 1951. Although she had a more limited budget than many of his other clients, he often cited her home as exemplary of a modern, informal, and flexible approach in keeping with the client's personality, and he featured it in print publications as well as his public lectures. Cousins, a respected writer, was also a sporadic ghost writer for Pahlmann's popular series "A Matter of Taste."[18]

Although Pahlmann successfully mastered his public persona and achieved great personal success through his carefully crafted brand, it was perhaps his ability to capture the sentiments of his era that made him most successful. In his acclaimed book *The Pahlmann Book of Interior Design* (1955), he states, "In our mechanized civilization, there is an increased yearning on the part of most people to create something for themselves."[19] Rather than a strict adherence to rules or a particular formula, he provides an overview of the principles of design, utilizing terms like "simplicity," "functionality," and "comfort" as guiding principles that in many ways mirrors Museum of Modern Art curator Edgar Kaufmann, Jr.'s description in "What Is Modern Design?" (1950).[20] The next section of this chapter delves more meaningfully into Pahlmann's design choices in relation to the modernist canon.

Parallel universes: Architecture, interior decorating, interior design, and the canon(s) of modernism, or, What happened to William Pahlmann?

A look at William Pahlmann's 1987 *New York Times* obituary is revealing in terms of the uneasy relationship that continues to exist between interior design and interior decoration. The headline: "William C. Pahlmann, Decorator Known for Eclectic Designs, Dies,"[21] specifically identifies Pahlmann as a "decorator" rather than a "designer." This specific terminology: "decorator" and "eclectic," signals a way of thinking—a modernist code of sorts—which positions Pahlmann in contrast to a canonical understanding of modern design as reductive, abstract, timeless, and even heroic.

The term "interior decorator" was first used in the United States in the early twentieth century, to describe practitioners who, as the advocacy group IDLNY (Interior Designers for Legislation in New York) has noted, generally lacked academic training, "... but the best of them had a combination of good taste, common senses [sic], and natural talent to interpret and address the issues, such as scale and proportion."[22] Elsie de Wolfe is recognized as the first professional interior decorator, and her influential 1913 publication *The House in Good Taste* is considered the first book on the subject. She was followed by Dorothy Draper, the first documented commercial interior decorator, establishing her design firm in 1923.[23] These pioneering female innovators defined the field from a specifically gendered perspective.

But as Joel Sanders convincingly argued in his 2002 essay "Curtain Wars: Architects, Decorators, and the Twentieth-Century Domestic Interior":

> While historians have described how decorating came to be considered a woman's pastime, they have yet to account for its emergence as a gay profession. One likely explanation is that interior design—like two allied design fields, fashion and theater—attracts a disproportionate number of gay men because gay men, already marginalized for their apparent femininity, are less reluctant to assume occupations that have traditionally been deemed feminine.[24]

Sanders examines the canonical view that situates architecture at the very top of the hierarchy and interior decorating (ephemeral, superficial, tainted by the whims of fashion, and saddled with its relationship to femininity and homosexuality) at the bottom. Like Philip Johnson and many other colleagues, William Pahlmann's "bachelor" persona was a discreet cover for a gay lifestyle during a period when the pressure for hetero-normative behavior was intense.[25]

But as the language of canonical, "high" modernism gained currency in the 1920s and 1930s, in particular as promoted by the Museum of Modern Art's 1932 influential "Modern Architecture, International Exhibition," decoration became increasingly taboo. The exhibition, curated by Philip Johnson and Henry-Russell Hitchcock, popularized a reductive, "less is more" approach to architecture and design, which, furthered by subsequent MoMA curators like Edgar Kaufmann, Jr., became the dominant aesthetic. With this development came an ever-more uneasy attitude toward the decorative, as evidenced in the change in name of the professional organization founded in 1931 as the Association of Interior Decorators (AID), which in 1936 became the American Institute of Interior Designers, taking its cue from the term used in the magazine *Interior Design and Decoration* in the 1930s. In 1975, the AID, together with the National Society of Interior Designers (NSID), was absorbed into the American Society of Interior Designers (ASID), today the leading professional organization for the field.[26]

Returning to Pahlmann's obituary, the *Times* obituary proclaimed that he "... was responsible for the theme and décor of the Forum of the Twelve Caesars Restaurant in Manhattan, as well as the Four Seasons, a celebrated late-modern masterpiece in Mies van der Rohe's Seagram Building (1958), said to be the costliest restaurant ever, when it opened in 1959,"[27] curiously not mentioning Philip Johnson, normally credited with the restaurant's famous design, at all. Even more remarkable is the juxtaposition of the two restaurants; the design of the Forum of the Twelve Caesars (Figure 12.3) was in highly questionable taste according to modernist orthodoxy, with a concept which came from a collection of portrait paintings of the Roman Caesars in Pahlmann's own collection. Its "authentic" Roman motifs created a unique if non-canonical *Gesamtkunstwerk* which included Fortuny fabric-covered walls, a pictorial wall mosaic, and waiters and busboys in appropriate costume. The restaurant was a huge hit.[28] For Pahlmann, God was in the details.

In fact, both restaurants were the productions of Restaurant Associates, managed by legendary restaurateur Joseph Baum, and Johnson and Pahlmann would seem to have been professional colleagues—albeit in parallel universes. By 1998, in Joe Baum's obituary, the *Times* gave Philip Johnson exclusive credit for the Four Season's design and repeated this assertion in a 2015 article lamenting the venerable restaurant's eventual demise.[29] What accounts for this lack of consistency over authorship, and why does it matter?

The fact is that the canon of architectural modernism, despite the best efforts of scholars over the last two decades, whose methodological approaches to the history of modern design are enriched by feminism, queer theory, postcolonial theory, and other critical analyses, continues to privilege architecture and interior design over interior decoration. This is to a great extent perpetuated by available design survey texts and their focus on the canonical figures. When the Four Seasons re-opened under a different name in 2017, a large photograph of a grimacing Philip Johnson was installed, facing cheekily into the women's bathroom. Johnson seems to get the last laugh, considering the fact that he is today a conspicuous part of the dominant narrative, situated at the pinnacle of the modernist canon (a canon which he, in the United States, to a great extent created), while Pahlmann's legacy is tenuous, present primarily in specialized texts on interior decoration.

This privileging of a master narrative in which Johnson, basking in the glow of Mies's genius, could nearly purge Pahlmann from the historical record suggests that a

Figure 12.3 Interior of the Forum of the Twelve Caesars restaurant, 1957.

great deal was at stake. Both Johnson and Pahlmann were arguing for their specific approach to "good design," and ultimately it became a matter of taste, with the Bauhaus/Mies/Le Corbusier-centric MoMA version of "high modernism" trumping a more eclectic, colorful, and one could say populist, approach like William Pahlmann's. Indeed, the fact that Johnson scorned Art Deco design as not truly modern, resulting in the absence of Art Deco design in MoMA's collection, underscores that bias.[30] That

Pahlmann chose those very words, "A Matter of Taste," for the title of his syndicated column suggests that he was well aware of the aesthetic battleground in which he was operating.

In the recent and exciting explosion of interest in the interior several critical texts have appeared which present revisionist approaches to the subject and provide a much-needed historiographic foundation for the field of interior design history and theory, particularly welcome for the purposes of pedagogy.[31] And yet, there is nary a mention of William Pahlmann in any of these revisionist studies, even though his was a household name in the mid-twentieth century as "one of America's most famous decorators."[32] What accounts for this continued slight? The bias against the decorator is evident in an examination of the scant literature on William Pahlmann. There is, in fact, an "alternate canon" of modern design history for specialized readers, which presents the history of design and decorating in a somewhat binary fashion.[33]

For example, Pahlmann is reduced to two brief passages in John Pile's *A History of Interior Design*, the second of which, introduced by the heading "Interior Decoration: The Reaction to Modernism" describes Pahlmann as one of several "versatile designers working in a variety of styles" whose "... floridly elaborate model rooms for the Lord and Taylor department store in New York became well known ...."[34] The first mention, relatively benign, states that the Four Seasons restaurant "was designed by Johnson in collaboration with the decorator William Pahlmann."[35] The idea that modern design was *the opposite of* "florid" or "elaborate" seems in line with established canon, and yet, if one considers one of Pahlmann's primary areas of inspiration, Surrealism, the importance of recognizing the existence of a wide variety of "modernisms" becomes critical.[36]

Even in this "alternate canon," however, Pahlmann's career is not given substantial attention, and these texts continue to perpetuate the sense of tension between "interior design" and "interior decoration" to a new generation of students. It is clear that Pahlmann deserves greater academic attention, as does his relationship with Philip Johnson, and although it is not chronicled in the canonical literature, some light is shed in the popular press. Influential food critic (and Four Seasons habitué) Mimi Sheraton, in an article celebrating the Four Seasons's fortieth birthday, describes Philip Johnson as a pragmatist and his relationship with Pahlmann as difficult.[37] She writes that Pahlmann was brought in by Joe Baum "much to Johnson's consternation." According to Sheraton, Johnson acknowledged: "'I was given the restaurants to oversee by Mies, and I only cared about the Grill. I hated Pahlmann's work, but I told him to do the big dining room. The pool was his idea and, I must say, a good one'" (idem). This anecdote seems to suggest that Johnson was scornful of interior decoration as being beneath his professional level (with perhaps a touch of jealous admiration there as well). But further complicating this discussion is an overlooked statement written by Johnson and Hitchcock decades before, in MoMA's seminal 1932 "International Style" show catalog. Surprisingly, they describe architect Mies van der Rohe as, among other things, "a decorator in the best sense."[38] While subsequent scholars have recognized the decorative qualities in Mies's interiors—his choice of richly patterned marble, his love of exuberantly striped, precious wood grain, and his use of sumptuous fabrics like velvet and silk (all designed, during Mies's Weimar period, in conjunction with Lilly

Reich),[39] these were not the aspects of "high modernism" that became codified in the canon. Further, if Mies was a "decorator in the best sense," does that make Pahlmann a *decorator in the worst sense*? Were Johnson and Hitchcock making a specific jab at the field of interior decorating in the International Style catalog? And what does the fact that Johnson himself, who enjoyed a long, if not uncontroversial, career, veered later in life from modernist orthodoxy into a postmodernism which challenged the very foundations of the "International Style" he had helped to popularize, add to this equation? The notion that the work of Mies van der Rohe was characterized by issues of the decorative is not often included in the normative, canonical presentation of modern architecture and design to students. And yet, this mention of "a decorator in the best sense" suggests that decoration—specifically *interior* decoration—was a point of contention, even at the Museum of Modern Art in 1932. William Pahlmann's success and his penchant for the decorative, along with his rampant historicism and eclectic borrowing from "exotic" cultures (the topic of the following section), were problematic in the construction of the "high" modernist canon, and yet he remained a powerful force to be reckoned with.

Enlivening modern interiors with the "Other"

In his practice of promoting an eclectic version of modernism, William Pahlmann turned to other cultures, specifically those constructed as more exotic. Memos, advertisements, exhibition catalogs, newspaper clippings, and *The Pahlmann Book of Interior Design*, reveal that Pahlmann engaged with what was considered exotic or international design as a way to enliven mainstream modern décor and used certain themes of the exotic other as the driving motif for room decoration. Pahlmann's love of eclecticism meant engagement with other cultures in design, which was not only welcome, but a fitting way for families to express their interests and tastes *vis-à-vis* the commodification of the nuclear family.[40] He used his position as an established and influential designer to promote the idea of the Other as a design source.

While Pahlmann encouraged the use of design from other cultures more broadly, his engagement with the Other was particularly focused on folk and/or indigenous aspects of Iberian and Ibero-American culture and the "Far East." This section looks at how Pahlmann capitalized on these other cultures, and how this functioned to reaffirm his cultural superiority as a designer who was well versed in global design, thanks to his extensive travels.

Pahlmann's engagement with the Other for design purposes began before the founding of William Pahlmann Associates. As a model room designer for Lord & Taylor department store, Pahlmann unveiled the "Pahlmann Peruvian" group of model rooms in November 1941, inspired by a five-week trip he took to South America (Figure 12.4). After returning, Pahlmann's declaration that, "South America is North America's newest design source," effectively reduced the entire southern hemisphere of the Americas to mere source material that exists for the purpose of providing designers in the US with inspiration.[41] By expressing this sentiment in the popular magazines of *House and Garden* and *House Beautiful*, Pahlmann, through his authority as interior

Figure 12.4 "Pahlmann Peruvian" model room designed by Pahlmann at Lord & Taylor, showing a modern interpretation of a Peruvian-inspired living room, promotional photograph, November 1941.

decorator, legitimized the adoption of elements of Ibero-American culture in the decoration of interiors for an audience that was, by and large, unversed in the particularities of this culture.

Through his travels to South America, Pahlmann located a number of visual elements to capture the essence of "Peruvian" and used these in his designs. He designed a line of fabrics and rugs for Schumacher & Company, and the prints depict such expected and essentializing iconography as Indian masks, Incan ruins, and colonial wrought ironwork. While the "Pahlmann Peruvian" rooms were didactic in how to decorate, the accompanying exhibitions that Pahlmann put together were meant to educate to an even deeper degree. Pahlmann curated and installed exhibits in nearby spaces featuring authentic Peruvian artifacts, such as clothing and decorative objects. Needless to say, this quasi-anthropological display comes freighted with a long tradition of representing the less civilized Other, and its location in a department store raises interesting questions about the intersection of educational display, commercialism, and consumption.[42]

Once working for his own firm, Pahlmann continued to use his international travels as source materials for his designs. His interest in Iberian culture spurred a six-week trip to Portugal to study folklore and customs in order to develop the "Pahlmann Portugal" line of Everglaze fabrics for the Cyrus Clark Company and to collect objects for use in design projects, which were highly publicized before and after the trip.[43] Although a trip to Europe often conjures images of Parisian fashion houses or styles of furniture named after any number of monarchs, Pahlmann focused on the folksy and historic aspects of the "Old World," presenting an image of Portuguese culture as rustic and quaint.[44] Different patterns were named after Portuguese cities and towns, at once intimating Pahlmann's conquest of these sites and suggesting place specificity to those who would incorporate these textiles into their interiors.

Pahlmann's interest in the folk and indigenous was not particularly unique at this time and warrants comparison to other more canonical mid-century designers. Textile designer Alexander Girard not only designed projects drawing on these sources, such as La Fonda del Sol Restaurant in New York (1960) and Braniff International Airways (1965), but amassed an extensive collection of folk art, which he ultimately donated to the Museum of International Folk Art in Santa Fe, New Mexico.[45] Perhaps even better known is the collection of folk art in Ray and Charles Eames's house in Los Angeles, knowledge of which was spread profusely through photographs of the interiors.[46]

Pahlmann continued to create Everglaze fabrics with his "Path of the Sun" line, which was the result of a two-month trip around the world that included visits to Japan, Hong Kong, India, and Lebanon (Figure 12.5). Like the "Pahlmann Portugal" line, his trip was publicized to the media beforehand as a means to build interest in the resulting designs.[47] Although the trip was around the world—it followed the path of the sun—the fabric line was designed around Asian motifs. An advertisement for the line notes Pahlmann's incorporation of the "simple, basic designs of the Far East," positioning Asian civilization as a more simplistic, less civilized Other.[48] The same ad admits the desire for exoticism by describing the fabric as conveying "a wanderlust for far-off places." Similar to his work with Ibero and Ibero-American sources, Pahlmann's Asian-inspired designs were based on essentializing iconography such as shoji screens, bamboo, rice paddy flowers, and Japanese characters. Interestingly, his othering of Asian culture is done without any reference to people. Rather than constructing the exotic Other through the representation of a person, these cultures and their societies are reduced to mere material objects in their textile representation, such as plants and man-made objects.

The "Path of the Sun" line was just one facet of a broad and sustained interest in Asian design on the part of Pahlmann. He relied upon Asian antiques to help create themes of the exotic other in interior spaces. One need not look much further than Pahlmann's own country home to see this approach in action. With its Moorish and Persian-inspired rooms, Pahlmann utilized his country home as publicity material to promote himself and his belief that Asian themes would be a lasting trend.[49] Here, it is useful to consider Pahlmann's engagement in orientalism, as defined by Edward Said as the acceptance in the West of the "basic distinction between East and West as the starting point for elaborate theories, epics, novels, social descriptions, and political accounts concerning the Orient, its people, customs, 'mind', destiny, and so on."[50] Through his deployment of Asian themes to create exotic and fantastical ambiances, Pahlmann offers a clear example of the way we can think of orientalism in design and in popular culture in the post-World War II period.[51]

William Pahlmann: Challenging the canon of modern design   201

Figure 12.5 Living room showing different patterns from the "Path of the Sun" line of Everglaze fabrics. A model room designed for Pahlmann Previews, exhibited at William Pahlmann and Associates studios, promotional photograph, Spring 1954.

In *The Pahlmann Book of Interior Design*, Pahlmann proposed the categories of modern, contemporary, and traditional, but each one was just a base upon which to display different cultural themes. Other cultures could be incorporated in any one of these categories in the form of textile patterns, furniture, artworks, and accessories. Pahlmann also includes visual examples of successful displaying techniques for one's collection of African masks, pre-Columbian artifacts, and Chinese pewter objects.[52] Besides displaying objects of the Other, Pahlmann also encouraged the repurposing of objects from foreign countries to meet the needs of the mid-century American. For example, in a room designed around a seventeenth-century Japanese screen, Pahlmann incorporated a traditional *hibachi* to serve as a nut bowl.[53] A functional object for cooking in Japanese culture, the *hibachi* is repurposed to serve as little more than a decorative touch, its Japanese aesthetic meant to enhance the overall theme of the room.

Pahlmann serves as a useful antidote to conceptions of mid-century design as homogenous and offers opportunity to investigate questions of individual expression through the use of the other in a period known for conformity and repression.[54] Despite the perceived universality of modernism at mid-century, Pahlmann shows us that mid-century design was not stripped of reference to unique cultures. His engagement with other cultures reinforced predominant conceptions of US exceptionalism during the Cold War, reinforcing a sense of US superiority through his emphasis on the folksy and regional aspects of Europe and Western superiority through the reification of constructs of an exotic non-Western Other. Pahlmann's designs offer an opportunity to explore the ways in which designers capitalize on other cultures. It raises questions about how design is informed by and reinforces unequal power relations between the designer/consumer and the other cultures, and how that reflects contemporaneous foreign relations and geopolitics.

Conclusion: When worlds collide—interior decoration as Modernism's Other

While the overarching truism that modern design is timeless, elemental, universal, and honest has long been deconstructed, a last taboo stubbornly remains, at least in terms of the ways in which design history is taught in the United States: interior decorating. This remains the case despite the best efforts of revisionist histories mentioned above. If interior decorating constitutes Modernism's Other—that side narrative for which, in an undergraduate design history survey, there is insufficient class time—then what is at stake when choosing, as many of us do, to focus on such material as Kaufmann, Jr.'s "Good Design" series (1950–1955)[55] and his well-known books *What Is Good Design?* (1950) or *What Is Modern Interior Design?* (1953), rather than, say William Pahlmann's bestselling *The Pahlmann Book of Interior Design* (1955)?

There is much to gain in constructively joining seemingly incompatible figures like Pahlmann, Johnson, and Mies in a course on the history of modern design;[56] a comparison of their respective debt to Neoclassicism, for example, or a study of the decorative in Modernism, are just two possible routes of inquiry. Not simply a matter of "high" versus "low," this approach offers the opportunity to elucidate the canon, to introduce alternate ones, and to understand their interdependence. Beyond issues of formal style, a comparative study of William Pahlmann in relation to the canonical figures in modern design history offers a variety of possibilities for constructive dialogue in the classroom. A study, for example, of Pahlmann's syndicated column in relation to readings from Kleinman, Merwood-Salisbury, and Weinthal's text *After*

Taste: Expanded Practice in Interior Design offers rich potential for canon-challenging discussions. Pahlmann's consummate use of media sources to further his artistic and commercial interests makes him a model for a study of contemporary branding.

William Pahlmann as case study offers the opportunity to explore how artistic figures negotiated their Otherness in an era of political, social, and cultural repression. Such an approach offers the opportunity to study the role of progressive ideals of tolerance and inclusion in modern society. However, the fact that Pahlmann also actively Othered non-Western cultures, and actively mined them for his own personal artistic inspiration, warrants close study, pointing as it does to the complexities inherent in Modernism and, indeed, its myriad forms.

Notes

1 Stephanie Coontz, *The Way We Never Were: American Families and the Nostalgia Trap* (New York: Basic Books, 1992), pp. 24–5.
2 Lizabeth Cohen, *A Consumer's Republic: The Politics of Mass Consumption in Postwar America* (New York: Alfred A. Knopf, 2003), p. 195.
3 Grace Lees-Maffei, "Introduction: Professionalization as a Focus in Interior Design History," *Journal of Design History*, 21(1) (Spring 2008): pp. 2–3.
4 Penny Sparke, *An Introduction to Design and Culture: 1900 to the Present*, 3rd edn. (New York: Routledge, 2013), p. 107. For a closer look at the use of the signature in fashion brands, see Nancy Troy, *Couture Culture: A Study in Modern Art and Fashion* (Boston: MIT Press, 2003).
5 James J. Rorimer, "New Acquisitions for the Cloisters," *The Metropolitan Museum of Art Bulletin*, 33(5), part 2 (May 1938): pp. 14–17, cover illustration.
6 Penny Sparke, "Taste and the Interior Designer," in *After Taste: Expanded Practice in Interior Design*, ed. Kent Kleinman, Joanna Merwood-Salisbury, and Lois Weinthal (New York: Princeton Architectural Press, 2012), p. 16.
7 Pahlmann seemed to be a great opportunist, taking advantage of the growing furniture industry by starting his own line for Hastings Square. And yet, he also responded to the popular do-it-yourself trend by advertising his own do-it-yourself designs.
8 Gina Marie Raimond, "'A Matter of Taste': The Interior Designer William C. Pahlmann and the Creation of an American Style in the Post-World War II Era," master's thesis, the Smithsonian Associates and the Corcoran College of Art + Design (2010), p. 36.
9 Ibid.
10 Beverly K. Grindstaff, "William Pahlmann and the Department Store Model Room, 1937–1942," in *Architectures of Display: Department Stores and Modern Retail*, ed. Anca I. Lasc, Patricia Lara-Betancourt, and Margaret Maile Petty (New York: Routledge, 2018), pp. 78–9.
11 Ibid., p. 82.
12 Syndicated columns appeared on October 10, 1957, in the *Cincinnati Enquirer*, and October 9, 1957, in the *Dayton Journal Herald*. Courtesy Hagley Archive.
13 *Milwaukee Journal*, December 29, 1957. Courtesy Hagley Archive.
14 *House Beautiful*, June 1951 and May 1951; *House and Garden*, May 1951. Courtesy Hagley Archive.
15 Pahlmann's public persona, gender, and sexuality will be discussed in greater detail in the following section of this chapter.

16 William Pahlmann Papers, Series II, Publicity Materials, 1935–1977, Hagley Museum and Library.
17 Ibid.
18 Raimond, p. 68.
19 Pahlmann, p. 2.
20 In Kaufmann, Jr.'s "What Is Modern Design?" he gives examples of four main traits of modern rooms: "comfort, quality, lightness and harmony." As the first section of this chapter attests, expanding on MoMA's Good Design series to include a discussion of Pahlmann's similar principles offers a more expansive and eclectic definition of "good design."
21 Albin Krebs, "William C. Pahlmann, Decorator Known for Eclectic Designs, Dies," *New York Times*, obituaries, November 11, 1987, n.p. http://www.nytimes.com/1987/11/11/obituaries/william-c-pahlmann-decorator-known-for-eclectic-designs-dies.html, accessed August 6, 2018.
22 https://www.idlny.org/history-of-interior-design/, accessed February 28, 2018.
23 Ibid.
24 Joel Sanders, "Curtain Wars: Architects, Decorators, and the Twentieth-Century Domestic Interior," *Harvard Design Magazine*, 16 (Spring/Summer 2002), n.p., http://www.harvarddesignmagazine.org/issues/16/curtain-wars, accessed August 6, 2017.
25 Pahlmann and his associate A. Jack Connor ("Jack"), a long-time colleague at the firm, also shared a more personal partnership; their relationship is indicated in the photographic record as well as in a 1989 interview, in which Conner explained: "He [Pahlmann] loved Mexican things. That's why we had a house in Mexico." Interview with Jack Connor by Gayle Gibson, December 6, 1989, 18. Collection Case File 2188, William Pahlmann Papers, Courtesy Hagley Archive.
26 https://www.idlny.org/history-of-interior-design/, accessed Feburary 28, 2018. In fact, Pahlmann himself preferred to be called an "interior designer" rather than an "interior decorator," so as not to be confused with, as he put it, "one of the little ladies who throw out a piece of chintz and never worry about the architectural background." "Viewpoints: Interview with William Pahlmann, F.A.I.D.," *Interior Design* (September 1972): 143–50, 150; cited in Raimond, p. 98f2.
27 Krebs, n.p.
28 Although the Forum closed in 1975 during New York's economic downturn, it is memorialized in an episode of the popular television series *Mad Men*. "The Suitcase," *Mad Men*: Season 4, Episode 7, AMC, New York City, September 5, 2010.
29 William Grimes, "Joseph Baum, American Dining's High Stylist, Dies at 78," *New York Times*, obituaries, October 6, 1998, n.p., http://www.nytimes.com/1998/10/06/us/joseph-baum-american-dining-s-high-stylist-dies-at-78.html, accessed August 6, 2017.
30 Encouraging in this regard was MoMA's 2017 exhibition "Frank Lloyd Wright at 150: Unpacking the Archive," in which the curators focus on Wright's ornament and the decorative quality of his oeuvre, suggesting that an unpacking of MoMA's historic biases is finally being done.
31 These include *Interior Design and Identity*, ed. Susie McKellar and Penny Sparke (Manchester: Manchester University Press, 2004); *Intimus: Interior Design Theory Reader*, ed. Mark Taylor and Julieanna Preston (Chichester: Wiley, 2006); *Designing the Modern Interior: From the Victorians to Today*, ed. Penny Sparke, Anne Massey, Trevor Keeble, and Brenda Martin (London: Bloomsbury 2009); *Toward a New Interior: An Anthology of Interior Design Theory*, ed. Lois Weinthal (New York: Princeton University Press, 2011); *The Domestic Space Reader*, ed. Chiara Briganti and

Kathy Mezei (Toronto: University of Toronto Press, 2012); and *After Taste: Expanded Practice in Interior Design*, ed. Kent Kleinman, Joanna Merwood-Salisbury, and Lois Weinthal (New York: Princeton University Press, 2012). Along with this efflorescence of critical texts was the founding of the Modern Interiors Research Centre at Kingston University (MIRC) in 2005.

32 *Washington Daily News*, 1938. Courtesy Hagley Archive.
33 Included here are survey texts like John Pile and Judith Gura's, *A History of Interior Design*, 4th edn. (Hoboken, NJ: Wiley, 2014); Jeannie Ireland's *History of Interior Design* (London: Fairchild Books, 2008); Stanley Abercrombie and Sherrill Whiton's *Interior Design and Decoration* (Upper Saddle River, NJ: Pearson, 2007); and others. While Ireland does devote a chapter section to "The Interior Designer" which includes Elsie de Wolfe, Dorothy Draper, and others, Pahlmann is absent. Pahlmann fares considerably better in Abercrombie and Whiton's survey; he is mentioned, albeit briefly, as one of a group of talented practitioners of a "new eclecticism" (p. 585) and receives double billing along with Johnson for the Four Seasons restaurant (p. 592). Pahlmann fares best in hagiographic books for a popular audience like *Legendary Decorators of the Twentieth Century* (1992) by decorator Mark Hampton and, of course, when he is authoring his own narrative; however, these are not scholarly and are rarely used in academia.
34 Pile and Gura, p. 391.
35 Ibid, p. 388.
36 Pahlmann was exposed to Surrealism in Europe when, after enrolling in 1927 at the New York School of Fine and Applied Arts (later, the Parsons School of Design) and studying design for two years, he left for Paris to study in their Paris Atelier. The absence of Surrealist interior design and decoration in Pile's book is thus particularly unfortunate. See "Biographical Note," William Pahlmann papers (Accession 2388), Hagley Museum and Library, Wilmington, DE 19807: http://findingaids.hagley.org/xtf/view?docId=ead/2388.xml.

In *Interior Design of the Twentieth Century* (1990), Anne Massey succeeds in communicating the rich diversity (and even the quirkiness) of the field, for example, in her examination of Surrealism's impact on interior design. She recognizes Pahlmann, describing his aesthetic as "baroque" while avoiding value-judgments. Massey points to the theatrical aspect of Pahlmann's oeuvre, and the evident tension between "modern" and "popular," "taste" and "camp" (a tension that Pahlmann appears to have gleefully and successfully exploited).

Joel Sanders discusses the concept of performing identity in relation to the gay decorator, who is often forced to "perform" one reality while, in private, living another. See Sanders, ibid. Pertinent to this discussion is the fact that Pahlmann was himself a professional performer as a young man; he supported his studies in New York by dancing in Broadway shows.
37 Mimi Sheraton, "Seasons in the Sun," *Vanity Fair*, August 1999, n.p. http://www.vanityfair.com/news/1999/08/four-seasons-199908, accessed August 6, 2017.
38 Philip Johnson and Henry-Russell Hitchcock, *Modern Architecture, International Exhibition* (New York: The Museum of Modern Art, 1932; reprinted 1969, Arno Press), p. 117.
39 On the decorative in Mies's work, see Marianne Eggler, "Divide and Conquer: Ludwig Mies van der Rohe and Lilly Reich's Fabric Partitions at the Tugendhat House," *Studies in the Decorative Arts*, XVI(2) (Spring/Summer 2009): 66–90. See also Robin Schuldenfrei, "Sober Ornament: Materiality and Luxury in German Modern

Architecture and Design," ed. Gülru Necipoğlu and Alina Payne, *Histories of Ornament: From Global to Local* (Princeton, NJ: Princeton University Press, 2016), pp. 334–45.

40 See previous section of this chapter, as well as Elaine Taylor May, *Homeword Bound: American Families in the Cold War Era* (New York: Basic Books, 1988), pp. 165–7; also "Decorating Means Good Merchandising: William Pahlmann, Lord & Taylor's, also feels mass produced furniture is better; Speaks to Boston Fashion Group," *Retailing*, December 2, 1940. Accession 2388, William Pahlmann and Associates Records, Series 8, Book 1, Hagley Museum and Library.

41 William Pahlmann, "South America—Modern Design Source," *House and Garden*, April 1947; "South America's Imprint," *House Beautiful*, September 1941. Accession 2388, William Pahlmann and Associates Records, Series 8, Book 2, Hagley Museum and Library.

42 For studies of issues surrounding exhibitions of the other, see, for example, Tony Bennett, *The Birth of the Museum: History, Theory, Politics* (New York: Routledge, 1994); Robert W. Rydell, *All the World's a Fair: Visions of Empire at American International Expositions, 1876-1916* (Chicago: University of Chicago Press, 1984). In addition, and relevant to Pahlmann's work in textile pattern design, see Ann Marguerite Tartsinis, *An American Style: Global Sources for New York Textile and Fashion Design, 1915–1928* (New York: Bard Graduate Center and Yale University Press, 2013).

43 William Pahlmann Associates wrote press releases to publicize his upcoming trip. William Pahlmann Associates, "Pahlmann Portugal," press release, June 26, 1952. Accession 2388, William Pahlmann and Associates Records, Series 8, Book 8, Hagley Museum and Library.

44 Everglaze fabrics, Cyrus Clark Company. "Pahlmann Portugal," advertisement, *c*. 1952. Accession 2388, William Pahlmann and Associates Records, Series 8, Book 8, Hagley Museum and Library.

45 Monica Obniski, "Selling Folk Art and Modern Design: Alexander Girard and Herman Miller's Textiles and Objects Shop (1961–1967)," *Journal of Design History*, 28(3) (April 2015): pp. 254–74.

46 On the Eames's use of folk art and exhibition in their home, see Pat Kirkham, *Charles and Ray Eames: Designers of the Twentieth Century* (Cambridge, MA, and London: MIT Press, 1995) and Colomina, *Domesticity at War*.

47 Raimond, p. 40.

48 Everglaze fabrics, Cyrus Clark Company. "Path of the Sun," advertisement, *c*. 1953. Accession 2388, William Pahlmann and Associates Records, Series 8, Book 9, Hagley Museum and Library.

49 Raimond, p. 36.

50 Edward W. Said, *Orientalism* (New York: Pantheon Books, 1978), pp. 2–3.

51 On Asia in the popular imagination in this period, see Christina Klein, *Cold War Orientalism: Asia in the Middlebrow Imagination, 1945–1961* (Berkeley and Los Angeles: University of California Press, 2003).

52 Pahlmann, pp. 134–5.

53 Pahlmann, p. 38.

54 Such books as Betty Friedan, *The Feminine Mystique* (1963); William H. Whyte, *The Organization Man* (1955); David Reisman, *The Lonely Crowd* (1950); and John Keats, *The Crack in the Picture Window* (1957) are great primary resources related to this topic.

55 For a critical analysis of Edgar Kaufmann, Jr.'s "What Is Good Design?" books, published by MoMA and, specifically, his *What Is Modern Interior Design?* (1953), see

Jennifer Tobias, *The Museum of Modern Art's What Is Modern? Series, 1938–1969*, doctoral dissertation, City University of New York Graduate Center, 2012.

56 Although outside the scope of this chapter, pertinent to this discussion is the artistic collaboration of German architect/design Lilly Reich with Mies van der Rohe's Weimar period interiors and the key role she played in their projects. Lilly Reich is another figure who has often been lost to the canon. On Reich's work, see Sonja Günther, *Lilly Reich 1885–1947: Innenarchitektin, Designerin, Austellungsgestalterin* (Stuttgart: Deutsche Verlags-Anstalt, 1988); and Matilda McQuaid, *Lilly Reich: Designer and Architect* (New York: The Museum of Modern Art, 1996). See also Esther da Costa Meyer, "Cruel Metonymies: Lilly Reich's Designs for the 1937 World's Fair," *New German Critique*, 76, Special Issue on Weimar Visual Culture (Winter, 1999): 161–89; and Eggler (2009).

"I was not a woman designer... I was a designer who happened to be a woman"

Russell Flinchum

MaryEllen Dohrs[1] stands out as the first woman hired by General Motors' Styling Division to move beyond the realm of automotive design to work as a professional industrial designer at a major firm, Sundberg-Ferar. The "model"[2] seated in the Le Sabre prototype that appears so frequently in publications on General Motors (GM) (Figure 13.1) is none other than Dohrs, who recalls that she was in fact photographed in the full-size wood and metal buck of the design before the completion of the fully functional automobile that would become Harley Earl's personal ride during the 1950s. Thus, her image is familiar to millions who have no idea of her identity, much less that she was employed at GM as a designer. There were no "Damsels of Design" to speak of in 1950–1952; this team of women designers would be recruited around the time of the completion of the GM Technical Center in Warren, Michigan, in 1956.[3] MaryEllen Dohrs was an exceptional figure for the time, and her cogent and insightful observations made to me over numerous conversations has driven my desire to examine her professional career, from her graduation from Pratt Institute with a degree in Industrial Design in 1950 (Figure 13.2) to the full realization of her goal of working as an industrial designer at Sundberg-Ferar, following two important years at the corporation she refers to occasionally as "Generous Motors."[4]

Design history and the history of technology remain somewhat preoccupied by "firsts" to their detriment. To frame the question properly, it is not "who was the first female automotive designer?" but rather "who was the first professionally trained woman to make a recognizable and significant contribution to the profession of automotive design?" It is within this framework that the importance of Dohrs to the design profession becomes clearer, whatever competitors she may have for this coveted title.[5]

In researching the career of Dohrs, it became clear that looking at her work solely in terms of what she achieved at GM between 1950 and 1952 was severely limited and was in itself unrepresentative of her greater contribution as an industrial designer where she worked within a major design firm, Sundberg-Ferar, and made key contributions there as well, a welcoming environment where her talents found even greater appreciation by her new bosses Carl Sundberg and Montgomery Ferar, as well as her new colleagues. But it was in fact Harley Earl, the first vice-president of design in a major American corporation, who gave Dohrs her first job upon graduation.

Figure 13.1 Contemporary publicity photograph of MaryEllen Dohrs seated in wood and metal buck full-scale model of the Le Sabre, 1951.

Dohrs found herself involved with special projects like the customized Cadillac Eldorado created for Hopalong Cassidy, near the peak of his fame at a time "when there wasn't much on television besides old cowboy movies and wrestling," as Dohrs recalled. In time, she had the responsibility of creating illustrations for the scrapbook that Earl kept for his personal friends in the Buhl family. Earl was not noted for lavish praise, but there were few designers who worked under him who doubted his visual sense, no matter how strange the pursuit of the final form might have been.[6] Earl did not draw to express ideas, he dictated changes to designers using full-scale tape "drawings" that could be easily altered in the occasionally indiscernible manner he directed ... to lower a line a quarter of an inch was not untypical. Thus, to be entrusted with such an intimate and demanding task with personal significance for "Mistearl" (as designer Strother MacMinn stated Earl's name was pronounced at GM among his contemporaries) would have been seen by Dohrs's colleagues in the interiors studio as not a particularly enviable job in the quest to realize their talents as automotive designers, but such approval from on high could hardly have escaped their notice as being exceptional, and in fact enviable, because it was not unheard of for Earl to have an employee dismissed the same day that he was particularly displeased with one of their efforts.

This is not a story about the capacities of a designer to find her place in the world as a wife and mother while maintaining a career.[7] I cannot, in this summary, adequately explore the startling discovery of her work in the world of military intelligence

"I was a designer who happened to be a woman" 211

Figure 13.2 MaryEllen Dohrs at display board, Interiors studio, General Motors, Detroit, 1950.

following the debacle of Francis Gary Powers' crash and survival (along with the components of his U-2 spy plane) while conducting aerial surveillance over the USSR. The US was "blind" in terms of such aerial spying until the launch of the first satellites capable of taking photographs from outer space in the early 1960s. When MaryEllen Green married geographer Dr. Fred E. Dohrs in 1955, she was also marrying a colonel in the military intelligence reserves with a superb cover as the head of his academic department—geographers must travel to compare notes and attend conferences. She helped identify a Soviet military and manufacturing installation from memory in a "double-blind" case in which she was never told what she was to identify; only to observe, while traveling through Siberia, the appearance of a structure she would see looking south from the train at a certain milepost. Upon her return to the United States, Dohrs was debriefed by being asked to draw the architectural features of the building from memory, allowing experts to identify the purpose of the facility. It is difficult to assess the impact of a single episode such as this in the scheme of the Cold War. It should be noted, however, as this may help establish the outlines of the involvement of the industrial design community with national defense beginning in World War II and continuing throughout the Cold War, an important narrative that is yet to be fully assembled. This episode is perhaps even more significant in the context of this chapter because it speaks volumes about her visual memory and ability to draw, showing a remarkable economy of line well documented in her book *Sketches of the Russian People* (1959) (Figure 13.3), and the book by Victor Herman and Fred E. Dohrs that she illustrated, *Realities: Might and Paradox in Soviet Russia* (1982).

Figure 13.3 MaryEllen Dohrs, *Water Wagon* (1958), from *Sketches of the Russian People* (Detroit: Garelick Gallery, 1959).

To speak with MaryEllen Dohrs today is to experience first-hand the "can do" attitude and work ethic of a generation that came to maturity during World War II. She is vibrant, thoughtful, and opinionated, and there is no puffery about her achievements. She still drives between Michigan and Florida, where she maintains residences. She was a few years younger than the American GIs who fought in Europe and Asia and who were her classmates at Pratt Institute between 1947 and 1950. Prior to graduation, Dohrs was extended an offer from General Motors that was arranged between none other than Earl and Alexander Kostellow, the legendary instructor at Pratt and head of the industrial design program. Pratt Institute was the most important school for industrial design on America's East Coast, and probably nationally prior to World War II, and was a significant source of automotive designers through the next two decades.

As a child, Dohrs was precocious; she recalled making a table well before she was six years old. "It was not a very good table," she has noted, but this gives a great insight into the volition and drive that characterized her career. The wood and nails for this project she scavenged from a construction site near her home. She became proficient in three-dimensional design early and was crafting model planes while still a child. In an interview with Marjorie Eddington, she described these years concisely:

> At age 6, I began building stuff—model airplanes, boats from kits. I also began processing film and printing pictures at that age. There was no TV, so I drew pictures in big newsprint "scrap books" for hours at a time. After [attending] Hollywood High School (I was born and raised in Los Angeles), I went to New York and Pratt Institute, hoping to go into Advertising. But I switched at the last moment to do all that I ever wanted ... to MAKE things! I graduated with a degree in Industrial Design, which is a combination of engineering, invention, convenience, comfort, and above all, beauty. It usually means making a "skin" for a product, which can be marketed successfully, used easily, and brings pleasure to the user. Then General Motors hired me to be the first woman in GM Styling.[8]

Dohrs recalled the following incident from much later in her career when she spoke at the eightieth anniversary for the firm Sundberg-Ferar in 2015.[9] While on a train trip to Poughkeepsie for IBM, she shared breakfast with her boss Carl Sundberg, who founded the firm with Montgomery Ferar in 1934 when both were fired on the same day and decided, in one of those quirks of the Great Depression with huge repercussions, to go into business for themselves.[10] In their conversation, Dohrs discovered that Sundberg had designed a plastic shaker cup for Ovaltine as his first industrial design job (there was a commercial tie-in with Little Orphan Annie which made this part of a national campaign). Dohrs was taken aback for a moment. One of those shaker cups "had been my most cherished childhood possession," Dohrs recalled. She remembered its beige plastic body and orange lid, and that it had to be used over the sink because it leaked. Sundberg laughed at her recollection and confessed that it had been his first effort on behalf of the new partnership, and it wasn't a very good design. This anecdote is worth examining. Dohrs was part of a new generation for whom designed objects, while still exceptional, were becoming part of the everyday environment. She found a point in common with a designer from the "bootstrap" generation of the late 1920s and 1930s. It certainly was no "passing of the baton" (Dohrs had no doubt that Sundberg and Ferar were her bosses), but it was a point of connection between a generation of designers who had created the profession of industrial design and the product of a sound education in the new profession that had been unavailable before the 1930s. Finally, the fact that a designed object, using plastic and a bright color, made an indelible impression on someone so young shows an incredible relation to three-dimensional form and appearances.[11]

Dohrs's father, John Lawrence Green, known in the automotive sales profession as "Larry," grew a career as a key importer of European cars beginning during the Great Depression. Eventually, he enjoyed the exclusive rights to market Austin, Renault, Peugeot, and Fiat automobiles nationally in the US. Dohrs, then six, recalled watching delivery of 1,100 Fiat Topolinos at San Pedro, California, probably the last shipment to reach the US from Mussolini's Italy. Green's journey into the marketing of European automobiles began in 1934 when he drove an Austin from British Columbia to Los Angeles, put it on public display, and promptly sold it. The postwar British Austin 8, a somewhat modest and economical vehicle, offered a distinct alternative to the ever-increasing size and bulk of American cars (for which partial credit or blame can be given to Harley Earl, who designed cars up to twenty-two feet long prior to the end of his reign at GM in 1958). Immediately following the war, the Austin 8 was one of the few automobiles that could be acquired new. Green felt that there was a considerable market for a car so different that it could appeal to the "lunatic fringe," as he characterized these potential customers many times to his daughter. He was particularly enamored of the luxury of the leather upholstery of the otherwise simple and tiny Austins. Automobiles, and their interiors, were part of his daughter's childhood education.

Growing up during World War II, Dohrs was an enthusiastic participant in the ethos of "use it up/wear it out/make it do/or do without." Historians have written a great deal about the accomplishments of this "Greatest Generation," to use journalist Tom Brokaw's phrase. Less explored has been the mobilization of the civilian populace of the United States and the impact on their psyche and work ethic. Out of the caldron of struggle, loss, and eventual victory taking place around the world, an independence of mind in terms of individual action was coupled with an ethos of the power of the US as "the Arsenal of Democracy," and the demonstrated power of group action. It is a longing for this unity of effort that seems to have become the touch point among political activists of many stripes, for that moment when the nation moved, with considerable difficulty, from isolationist complacency to that of an attitude of "we did it before/we can do it again," in the words of a popular song of the time. This work ethos aided Dohrs as the only female student in Pratt Institute's Industrial Design program. There were female students enrolled at Pratt before 1947, but Dohrs had found her way into one of the school's programs that was populated solely by male students. Alexander Kostellow, director of the program, would begin his class sessions with the greeting, "Good morning boys and *girl*" in his pronounced Persian accent. A contemporary photograph shows Kostellow lecturing to a crowded classroom where Dohrs's back is turned toward the camera, but it seems evident that he is addressing her (or looking at the photographer behind her) (Figure 13.4).

Figure 13.4 Alexander Kostellow addresses the Industrial Design class of 1950 at Pratt Institute; Dohrs's back is to the camera in the front row.

It was an enviable education with instruction from Rowena Reed Kostellow for studies in line and volume; Robert Kolli, who taught "glass and other manufacturing areas and shapes;" Ivan Rigby, the instructor for three-dimensional design; and Eva Zeisel, whose "Museumware" for the Museum of Modern Art had recently been produced.

Harley Earl was always in search of new talent, and even during the Depression was desperate for trained designers. Earl had decided that he needed a woman in the Interiors studio at GM; what prompted his decision seems to be known to Earl alone. Pratt had been a "go-to" source for educated new talent for years, and the contact between GM and Kostellow was frequent. The letter offering Dohrs a job at GM is dated May 8, 1950, and informs her she will be paid $275 per month, and inquires when she will be able to relocate. As Dohrs did not turn twenty-one until September of 1950 (the age of majority at the time), she could not begin working in the Interiors studio until then. She quietly worked on Interiors projects while clocking in with the employees in the secretarial pool and even joined their bowling team. But from the start, her work involved Interiors' projects, amid some secrecy. For a product of Los Angeles educated in Brooklyn, she adapted to Detroit readily.

Dohrs was not uncomfortable with an all-male environment, but initially found the atmosphere in the Interiors studio somewhat exclusionary. She recalled that "the girlie mags" would come out at the same time each month, and some of the employees would return to the studio with these publications and make purposefully audible comments on the relative attractiveness of the models. It is hard to imagine this as anything but alienating to a single twenty-one-year-old who was the only female present. With a sense of planning and wit that characterizes her nature, Dohrs went out one day and returned with a male body-building magazine, and began her own commentary on the "beefcake" displayed within. At this, the ice seemed to be broken and the head of the studio clapped her on the back and assured her "you're all right kid" (or something to that effect), and Dohrs found herself more fully integrated into the office's work. While there were "dream jobs" like the special-order Cadillac for Hopalong Cassidy, there was also plenty of routine work.[12] Interior fabrics may have been relatively plush for top of the line models for each division, but below that the quality fell off quickly to wool fabrics Dohrs described with some distaste as being akin to "mouse fur." Synthetic fibers had yet to make an impact, and when Nylon was introduced, it was discovered its durability came at the cost of wear to the driver's and passengers' clothes. It is in this context that the exceptional quality of her later work on the 1955 Packard Caribbean should be seen, for it was not until 1957 that a marked change in industry standards for interior finishes occurs. That was largely the province of Earl's new "Damsels of Design," whose work dominated GM's 1958 Motorama. Dohrs had moved on long before and was working with Sundberg-Ferar in 1953.

Dohrs had arrived. One secret of her success was her ability to accurately draw the human figures that populated the drawings depicting proposed new vehicles in various architectural settings. Many of her male contemporaries were excellent draftsmen but

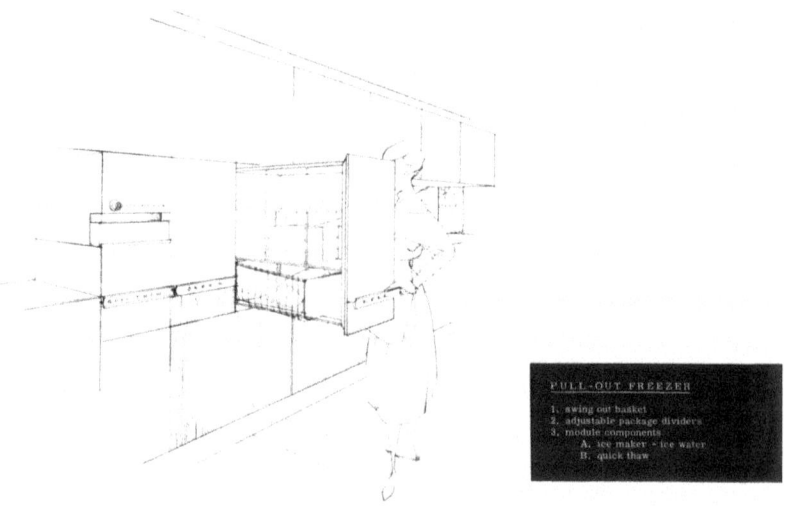

Figure 13.5 MaryEllen Dohrs's sketch of a proposed modular kitchen with female figure for Whirlpool, undated.

lacked her training and competence with the human figure. Once it was discovered that she had this facility, co-workers began to ask if she "could drop a few turkeys[13]" in a drawing they had done (in other words, she was asked to add human figures to provide scale and interest to these sketches while maintaining the perspective imposed by the creator: Figure 13.5). This built their confidence in Dohrs as a colleague, and her talents were rewarded with regular increases in pay.[14] To move from "Generous Motors" to Sundberg-Ferar, and to be compensated for being a true industrial designer, dealing with designs from children's tricycles to kitchen equipment and layouts, the full range of product design that had enticed her away from advertising to "making things," was Dohrs's personal achievement. She personally undertook work for major clients such as IBM and Samsonite (Figures 13.6, 13.7, and 13.8).

In addition to industrial design, Dohrs's familiarity with automotive design meant that she was responsible for bringing the Packard account to Sundberg-Ferar because she was a contemporary of Dick Teague while at GM, who now headed Styling for Packard. He contacted Dohrs personally; she referred him to the expansive Carl Sundberg, who sold Teague on a much broader consultation than interiors alone that resulted in changes to the exterior styling of the 1955 Packard line (Figure 13.9), as well as what Dohrs would characterize as her most enduring work, the interior of the Caribbean. She said, in summary, "of all the things I designed for Sundberg-Ferar,

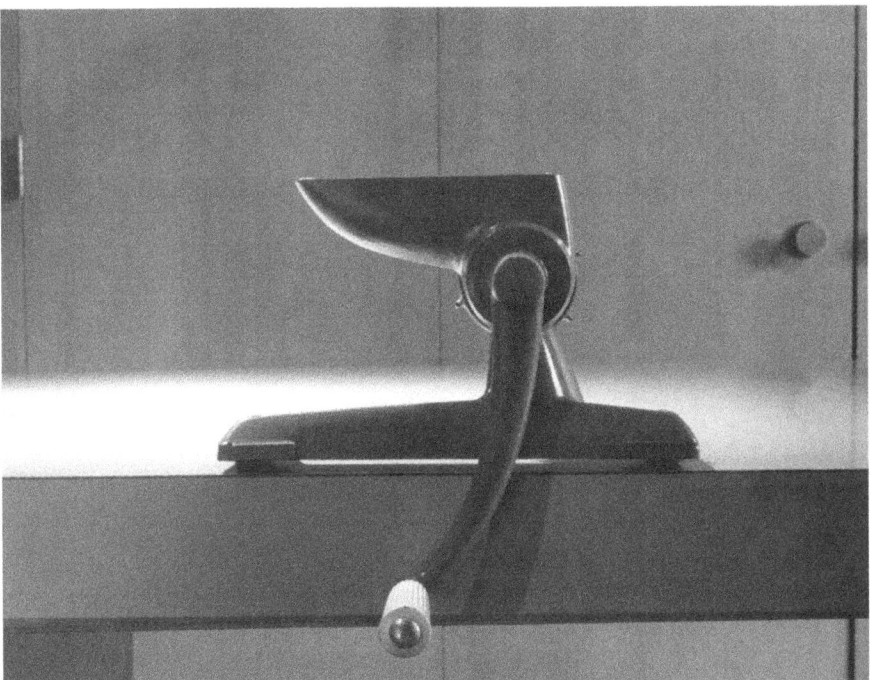

Figure 13.6 MaryEllen Dohrs's Food Mill for Landers, Frary Clark, designed while employed at Sundberg-Ferar, 1953–1956.

Figure 13.7 Advertisement for "Kid-Size" folding table and chairs designed by MaryEllen Dohrs and manufactured by Samsonite, a Sundberg-Ferar client.

this was exceptional." Dick Teague, best known to the public for his later work for American Motors, was fully confident of his own talent, but said of Dohrs's treatment of the Caribbean interior: "I wish I had done it myself." The back of the seat had a new profile and kicked in where it met the robe rail (Figure 13.10). This was more than choosing fabrics and finishes; this was the actual shaping of the interior components themselves.

Figure 13.8 MaryEllen Dohrs, "Medallion" luggage for Samsonite, undated.

The Caribbean has become a classic, and its popularity among historic vintage automobile collectors ensures that it will endure versus the more ephemeral products Dohrs designed in the age of planned obsolescence. It is a witness to her career in industrial design that she remains happy with after sixty-three years.

In the 1950s in the US, perhaps two dozen women were involved in automotive design who had an education in industrial design. Few went on to work as industrial designers as the Society of Industrial Designers then defined its membership (requiring designs to have been produced in three different areas), effectively eliminating most automotive designers, male or female (Figures 13.11 and 13.12). In this, she was exceptional. While industrial design firms like those headed by Henry Dreyfuss, Raymond Loewy, and Walter Dorwin Teague employed women in large numbers, few were designers (Dreyfuss's wife Doris Marks was his business partner; the first Mrs. Loewy, Jean Bienfait, remained a partner within the firm after their divorce, and her role in the construction of Loewy's career remains unexamined). It is possible that Dohrs's name change in 1955 has thrown some earlier researchers off the trail.[15]

Dohrs is a figure deserving of further research, and luckily has been interviewed by GM Archives and recorded informally by others.[16] She is certainly more than a precursor to the more celebrated "Damsels of Design." Her success proves that a woman

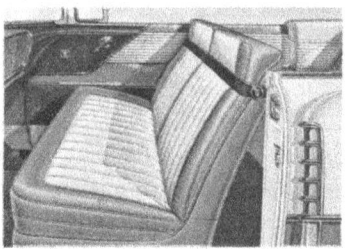

Figure 13.9 Advertisement for the 1955 Packard Caribbean, showing inset illustration with seating designed by Dohrs (the horizontal element at chest height is the "robe rail," dividing the seat into tripartite elements complementing the three-color interior and exterior color themes, and also providing hand-holds for passengers in the rear seats).

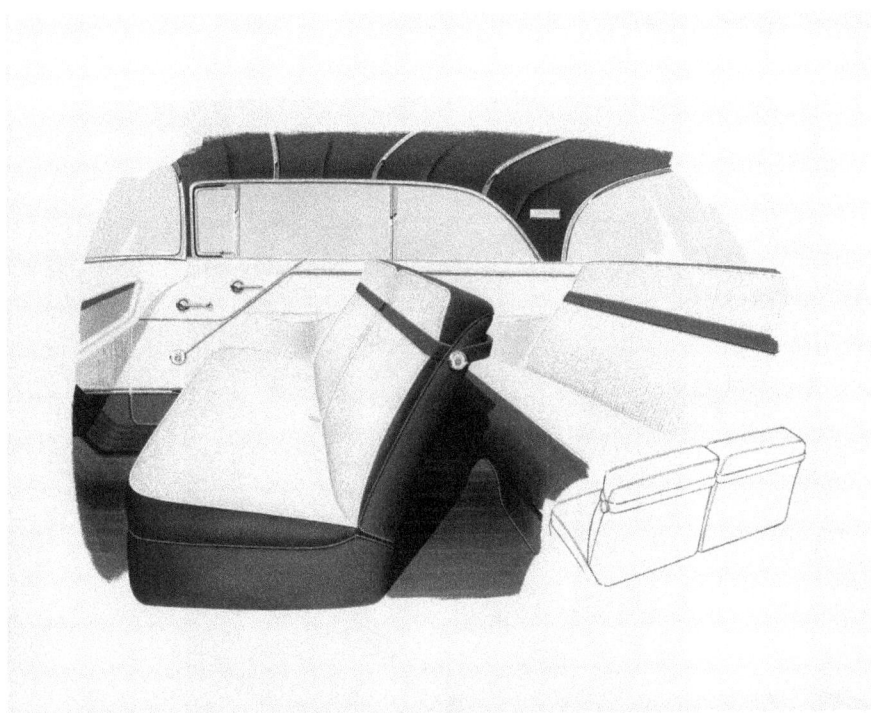

Figure 13.10 MaryEllen Dohrs, rendering of interior scheme for a 1955 Packard hardtop featuring her designs.

industrial designer was still exceptional in the post-World War II era, but not an impossibility.[17] Her exposure to the Soviet Union and her illustrations of life behind the Iron Curtain should not be viewed as a break with her career, even though 1963 brought an end to her industrial design work, because at the core, she was still working as a visual artist, and her drawing skills were such that they stand on their own as fine art. Today, working as a sculptor and teaching others to sculpt, she is pursuing her love of "making" still, and that making embraces her enthusiasm for creation. To be personally exposed to her appreciation for good design or artwork of any stripe is a lesson in seeing. Her accounts of her career are riveting for their incredible detail and recollection and insights into the personalities of those she worked with. While the Le Sabre was not painted to match her hair, as one source claimed (it was originally painted a copper color: Figure 13.13), this red herring is an appealing fiction as it captures an influential female designer at the dawn of her career, a thorough professional at the beginning of her post-Pratt education.

Figure 13.11 MaryEllen Dohrs, jukebox for Seeberg, designed while employed at Sundberg-Ferar, 1955.

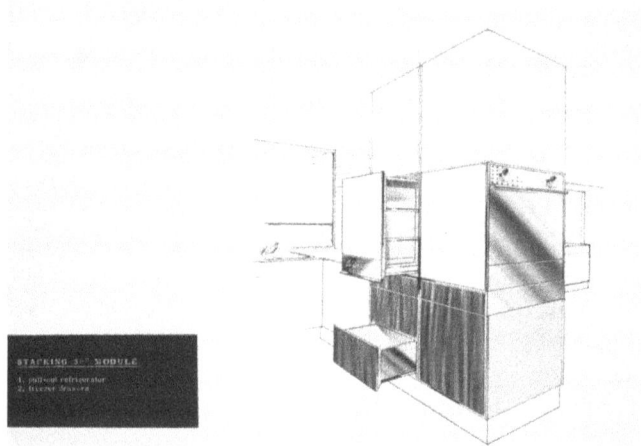

Figure 13.12 Mary Ellen Dohrs, sketch of a proposed modular kitchen showing color and finishes for Whirlpool.

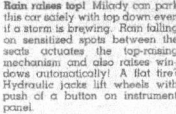

Figure 13.13 Harley Earl [top] and MaryEllen Dohrs [middle image] with the Le Sabre in its original copper finish. From *Cleveland Plain Dealer Magazine*, December 31, 1950, p. 11.

Notes

1. MaryEllen Green, born in Hollywood, California, on September 20, 1929, married Fred E. Dohrs, PhD, in 1955, and has referred to herself professionally as MaryEllen Dohrs since that date. Her name appears as MaryEllen Dohrs throughout this chapter.
2. Confirmation is found at the official General Motors website: https://www.gmheritagecenter.com/enthusiast-links/Enthusiasts/2015_August_Dohrs.html.
3. Constance Smith, another Pratt graduate with a career in automotive interior design at GM, recently published *Damsels in Design: Women Pioneers in the Automotive Industry, 1939–1959* (Atglen, PA: Schiffer Publishing, 2018). A great deal of new information is brought to light in her book, especially on Helene Anne Rother Ackerknecht (most often referred to as "Helene Rother" in contemporary accounts), an especially important "first" in the profession of automotive interior design (much of this evidence comes from Smith's collection). There are some internal inconsistencies between captions and text that bear keeping in mind, and while extensively researched, it is difficult to accept this account as factually definitive on the subject.
4. MaryEllen Dohrs, presentation at Burns Auditorium, NC State University College of Design, October 26, 2016 (https://vimeo.com/189181700) will provide the reader with Dohrs's own account of many of the anecdotes related in this chapter. A telephone conversation between Dohrs and the author on March 9, 2018, was conducted to verify factual contents of this chapter. Any errors of fact or interpretation lie with the author.
5. This is not to belittle the achievements of other women designers; we can hope for an assessment of the involvement of designers such as Helen Dryden at Studebaker, who goes unnoted in Smith's book. Helene Rother at GM, Betty Thatcher (later Oros) at Hudson were important pre-war figures, not to mention a contingent of women working with E. T. "Bob" Gregorie at Ford in the years prior to the war and immediately following; all the latter were gone by 1948, displaced by returning servicemen. Women would not play a role at Ford in this capacity again until the 1960s.
6. The best description of Earl's working process and its development over his thirty-year career with GM remains C. Edson Armi's *The Art of American Car Design: The Profession and Personalities* (University Park, PA: Pennsylvania State Press, 1988).
7. Dohrs took on these roles as well and worked part-time for Sundberg-Ferar from 1957 to 1963 after working full-time between 1953 and 1957. At this point, extensive foreign travel with her husband, whose specialty was the geography of the lands behind the Iron Curtain, made continuing as a practicing industrial designer untenable.
8. Eddington, Marjorie F., MaryEllen Dohrs, Artist: http://www.biblewise.com/living/guests/maryellen-dohrs.php
9. MaryEllen Dohrs, address at Sundberg-Ferar's eightieth anniversary celebration (MaryEllen also corrects host to confirm she worked at Sundberg-Ferar full-time from 1953 to 1957): https://www.youtube.com/watch?v=Aw5NvZaybx0
10. Per Dohrs, it was a perfect marriage of opposites: Sundberg was an unforgettable presence, a natural salesman who drank whiskey and smoked cigars freely. Ferar had trained as an architect and was reserved by nature, and luckily also understood finance.
11. Dohrs sculpts and teaches sculpture today in West Palm Beach, Florida; aiding her students in a quest to "learn to see," versus merely looking, remains a perpetual challenge in her dialogue with them.
12. Smith reproduces six important images of the Hopalong Cassidy Cadillac from the GM Archives on p. 46 of *Damsels in Design*. Dohrs was present at the event held on August 9, 1950, at Research "B" Building, 465 W. Milwaukee, Detroit. The unique

vehicle was on display at the Styling Section Auditorium on the 11th Floor, and "single children living at home" were invited to attend by Harley Earl.

13 The origin of this nomenclature remains undetermined. The jargon of automotive designers is notoriously exclusionary to those outside the field, perhaps of reflection of the very strict security that was part of Earl's system of locked studios for each division in Styling at GM; Cadillac, Buick, Pontiac, Oldsmobile, and Chevrolet designers did not "talk shop" with their counterparts in the other divisions, and non-disclosure agreements were the norm upon hiring.

14 Nevertheless, after some time in the Interiors studio, Dohrs compared take-home pay with a male co-worker at the same rank and found she made $72.00 to his $107. She philosophically viewed her time at GM as an unrivaled opportunity to continue her education, and advancement through a move to Sundberg-Ferar was not far away.

15 Dohrs stated in one email, "I go by MaryEllen Dohrs, not MaryEllen Green-Dohrs and not MaryEllen Green. You won't find my work (my sculpture) under MaryEllen Green. There's nothing there."

16 The acknowledgment of her contribution at General Motors is found at https://www.gmheritagecenter.com/enthusiast-links/Enthusiasts/2015_August_Dohrs.html. The author thanks Ms. Dohrs for providing a transcript of her interview with GM's archivist, as well as the bulk of the illustrations accompanying this chapter.

17 To demonstrate how forward and novel Industrial Design was as a profession at that time, Alfred Hitchcock introduced Eva-Marie Saint in the movie *North by Northwest* with the shocker, "I'm an industrial designer."

Epilogue

Beyond the canon—building the case for and cases for interdisciplinary design history

Stephanie E. Vasko

Introduction

As a formally trained chemist with little exposure to design history, attending the National Endowment for the Humanities "The Canon and Beyond: Teaching the History of Modern Design" Summer Teaching Institute in 2015 was pivotal in shifting the course of my research and giving me the confidence and tools to truly embrace becoming an interdisciplinary design history scholar. This experience crystallized for me that a "beyond the canon" approach to design history was one that put scholars from different disciplines in conversation with one another and with institutions (e.g., universities, colleges, archives, museums) to provide multi-, inter-, and trans-disciplinary perspectives. An interdisciplinary approach to design history is a way of getting beyond the canon that enables design history to create comprehensive narratives in conversation with other disciplines.[1]

In this epilogue, I call for an interdisciplinary approach to design history. I offer an example of how my own interdisciplinary background influences my work by introducing to two nascent, in-progress case studies of different technology companies in the twentieth and twenty-first centuries. These case studies bring perspectives from the disciplines of science, technology, engineering, and mathematics (STEM) together with other disciplines including, but not limited to, business history and philosophy. Finally, I conclude with ways that scholars can find support for their interdisciplinary scholarship.

Design history and interdisciplinarity

Design is a collaborative practice that occurs between designers, scientists, engineers, and other professionals. Moving to a fully interdisciplinary notion of design history serves as a smart, proactive move to begin capturing full and complete narratives of design. With examples ranging from Intel engineers and fashion designers working together to create wearable electronics to Nike's self-lacing shoes involving designers, engineers, and shoe archives, understanding the methods, processes, and ephemera used by a wide range of disciplines creates the conditions for a design history that captures the reality of current and future design processes.² Interdisciplinary approaches to design are also gaining ground in initiatives like the Leading Strand, "... a TED Residency-backed multidisciplinary initiative founded by Amanda Phingbodhipakkiya to bring the disparate worlds of design and science together to deepen our understanding of what's possible."³

Academic interdisciplinary design programs have also cropped up at a multitude of colleges and universities. Additionally, these programs have received attention from national funding agencies. In 2009, the National Science Foundation held a two-day workshop on interdisciplinary graduate education programs, whose conference proceedings contained suggestions on advancing interdisciplinary design activities, enhancing interdisciplinary design programs, and supporting interdisciplinary design research.⁴

This call for an interdisciplinary approach to design history is not new. In his introduction to the 2001 book *Graphic Design History*, Steven Heller argues: "While design historians must use cultural and political histories as backdrops, ultimately the stories they tell must be rooted in issues of design . . . ."⁵ Heller's view, which may be a reflection of the field at the time, seems to foreground the *design* in design history in place of the interdisciplinary story. But we see a shift in this thinking even as early as Fallan's introduction to *Design History: Understanding Theory and Method*, where he states that "design history today is no longer primarily a history of objects and their designers, but it is becoming more of a history of the translations, transcriptions, transactions, transpositions, and transformations that constitute the relationships among these things, people, and ideas."⁶

Echoing Fallan's sentiment, Townsend and Armstrong state in the introduction to the "Design and Academe" section of a 2017 issue of *Design and Culture* that "design research does not spring full-grown from the minds of academics; instead, the conditions, contexts, and values of our discipline, programs, and faculty, lead to a wide spectrum of investigations."⁷ The interdisciplinary envelope for design history gets pushed even further by Johanna Drucker's *Graphesis*, described by Harvard University Press as "an interdisciplinary study fusing digital humanities with media studies and graphic design history [whereby] Drucker outlines the principles by which visual formats organize meaningful content."⁸ Drucker's interdisciplinary work in this subfield of design history is therefore used as a *selling point* for its innovativeness.

Canonical design history journals have also gestured in the direction of accepting interdisciplinarity. The *Journal of Design History* has notably published a series of special issues over the years working on expanding notions of design history and including other fields in joint discussion with design history. For example, "Design Dispersed" was described by the editors as "... part of a rising tide of literature dedicated to design in the discipline of anthropology."⁹ Other journals, such as *Design and Culture*, publish articles that push design history "beyond the canon" by focusing on ephemera, perspectives, and methods (including interdisciplinary methods) not previously considered. Some of these articles and reviews are written by authors not considered "traditional" design history scholars.

New journals have also embraced interdisciplinary approaches to design history, most notably *She Ji*, which describes itself as "a peer-reviewed, trans-disciplinary design journal with a focus on economics and innovation, design process and design thinking." In explaining their scope, the *She Ji* website states, "Innovation requires integrating ideas, economics, and technology to create new knowledge at the intersection of different fields. *She Ji* provides a unique forum for such inquiry."[10]

The number of visible practitioners working at interdisciplinary intersections or in interdisciplinary collaborations within design history is still small, but growing. Prominent examples include Regina Lee Blaszczyk, whose University of Leeds faculty biography page states "Professor Blaszczyk likes to do things differently!" and highlights her vast array of experiences that have allowed her to author and edit such interdisciplinary volumes as *Imagining Consumers: Design and Innovation from Wedgwood to Corning* (2002), *Producing Fashion: Commerce, Culture, and Consumers* (2009), *The Color Revolution* (2012), and *Bright Modernity: Color, Commerce, and Consumer Culture* (2017).[11]

Our 2015 NEH Summer Institute also served as an incubator for several scholars whose research is inflected by a more interdisciplinary approach, including scholars bringing together topics and methods from architecture, fashion, American culture, non-Western history, graphic design, product design, and design practice, among other domains.

Building expertise and experience for creating interdisciplinary case studies

As mentioned above, I am interested in the history of technology and history of innovation as they entwine with design history during the twentieth and twenty-first centuries in the United States. In the vein of Dr. Blaszczyk, who brings business history in dialogue with the formal conceptions of design history, I seek to bring the history of technology and innovation, as well as scientific knowledge, into dialogue with design history. As I have previously argued in my work on fashion design and chemistry:

> Deciphering the intertwined histories of chemistry and fashion design requires an interdisciplinary approach... includ[ing] studying the archival records of synthetic fibers and their design applications, discussions between fiber producers and the fashion industry, advertisements to the public and to design-related industries, adjacent industries in the chemistry-design nexus such as the dye industry and the life cycle of synthetics and their impacts on the environment.[12]

While I have traced part of my evolution as a scholar elsewhere, here I would like to provide an expanded understanding. Completing a PhD in chemistry and nanotechnology equipped me with the facility to understand scientific concepts, jargon, and the types of ephemera associated with STEM research.[13] An interest in nanoethics and the ethics of emerging technologies in graduate school and during my first postdoctoral appointment led me to the Center for Nanotechnology in Society at Arizona State University's 2014 Winter School on Anticipatory Governance of Emerging Technologies, where I learned about responsible innovation and developed an interest in the history of innovation. My initial work on craft and STEM, as well as mentorship from scholars in the humanities, empowered me to apply for the 2015 NEH Summer Institute, which for me was an introduction to both canonical and non-canonical design history, as well as to archival research. It also exposed me to specific places where I could conduct archival research both as part of the program (e.g., Hagley Museum and Library) and as part of my free-time explorations of the resources at Drexel University (the NEH Summer Institute's host institution) and in Philadelphia, including the Chemical Heritage Foundation (now known as the "Science History Institute").

These experiences have formed the basis of two case studies I am currently pursuing that look at the advertisements of STEM-focused companies. The first case study focuses on a series of advertisements for the construction of a dye plant in Toms River, New Jersey, by Ciba. This case study has previously received attention through Dan Fagin's 2014 Pulitzer Prize-winning historical investigation *Toms River*.[14]

I received an exploratory research grant from the Hagley Museum and Library entitled "Weaving a History of Innovation: An Examination of Fiber Development and Responsible Innovation," which combined my scientific training, responsible innovation experience, and my exposure to archival research during the NEH Summer Institute. During a visit to the Hagley archives to explore primary resources related to this grant topic, I came across a series of advertisements for the construction of Ciba's Toms River plant in *American Fabrics* magazine, a former trade journal for the fashion industry. I had not previously seen these ads, nor were they included in *Toms River*, and so to deepen this historical case, I shifted my attention to the intersections of graphic design history (in the form of advertisements), trade journals, and the history of innovation. An introduction to this case study, including the rationale for using trade journal advertisements in design history, was published in the summer of 2017 in *Chemical & Engineering News*, the magazine for members of the American Chemical Society.[15]

Pushing this initial research forward requires bringing together multiple disciplines in constructing both the historical perspective of the advertisements and the analysis of their content and images. I am especially interested in putting their visual and textual content in dialogue with concepts of corporate social responsibility (CSR) and responsible innovation (RI), as well as with the evolution of types of advertisements. In order to unpack CSR and RI, I have needed to use the introduction to these topics gained at the ASU winter school to delve into the literature on the history of business and on the establishment of RI, including through the recently launched *Journal of Responsible Innovation*. From the geographical and historical perspectives of the project, I need to consider the history of chemical industries in New Jersey and the history of dye technology in general.

Examining the content of these advertisements requires expertise with methods such as content analysis and grounded theory. Initial explorations of the corpus built from the text of the advertisements has included using techniques from digital humanities (DH), including text-mining, word frequency, word correlation, and topic modeling.[16] The application of these DH techniques to design history also requires an exploration of their applications to the parameters of this case study, specifically that there is a small corpus derived from advertisements. In terms of the ethical implications of the graphic design of the advertisements and their content, bringing in notions of expanded STEM ethics, including the embedded ethical issues, and the philosophy of design can also potentially enhance the case study.[17]

When working at the intersection of design history and history of technology, it is also occasionally necessary to go on a "treasure hunt" to find pieces of ephemera that complete or enhance the story. Finding new ephemera in new places (specifically, online venues) has influenced scholarship in historical geography, studies of cultural and biographical texts, and even design history, as covered by several authors including the NEH Summer Institute's own Matthew Bird in both *Design and Culture* and in this volume.[18] The types of materials researchers may need to bring into dialogue also make the case for more interdisciplinarity. Working with these new materials may require bringing new scholarship on the types of ephemera or their interpretation into dialogue with a researcher's existing work.

The discussion of a collection of blended ephemera leads into my other case study, an in-progress effort focusing on the history of Intel's technological advancements and advertisement campaigns, with a focus on their Patrick Nagel-based graphic design campaigns and current (post-2010) campaigns.[19] My work on this Intel case study began when I found a picture of unknown provenance on Pinterest, and has expanded into an exploration of online artifacts and posts, museum collections, and oral histories. Comparing my two large case studies, Ciba is limited to advertisements in the form of print advertisements, while the Intel case study includes print, video, television, mobile, and live events. These additional formats require the consideration of literature and methods in new disciplines. Additionally, this exploration of how technological advances at Intel influenced (or were influenced by) advertisements allows me to bring my knowledge of semiconductor nanofabrication and advances in nanofabrication techniques into a dialogue with design history.

The combination of fields I use in these case studies is unique, and it is this unique, interdisciplinary perspective that not only allows me to tell two fascinating stories at the intersection of design history and the history of innovation, but also allows me to disseminate my works in progress to philosophy and chemistry departments and at new conferences, publish in non-traditional formats, and author manuscripts and book chapters, such as this one, for more traditional academic venues.

Enabling interdisciplinary scholarship in order to push design history beyond the canon

This section of my epilogue reflects my greatest hopes for the future of an interdisciplinary design history. For me, design history moves beyond the canon by exploring non-canonical places for publishing or talking about design history. For me, this movement has manifested through talking about design history when I teach electronic textiles workshops at makerspaces, writing both academic articles and articles that reach the general public rather than specialists (popular press writing, books written for the public, or publishing in professional association journals, and giving talks in departments outside of design history about design history topics).

Interdisciplinary centers have an extremely important role to play in helping to expand design beyond the canon. Institutions like Michigan State University's Center for Interdisciplinarity (C4I) can help faculty form research partnerships, receive encouragement and mentorship across the career spectrum, aid in grant preparation, and provide places for scholars to exchange ideas. The NEH Summer Institute was a great start to a conversation about design history outside of the canon. Hopefully, as centers like C4I evolve, partnerships between universities, museums, archives, businesses, practitioners, and funding agencies can grow and involve a wider audience in discussion, learning, and support, like those of us who attended the summer school received.

Language in recent NEH funding opportunities also indicates a shift towards interdisciplinarity. The "Humanities Connections Planning Grants" summary states, "Competitive applications will demonstrate ... that faculty and students will benefit from meaningful collaborations in teaching and learning across disciplines as a result of the project."[20] The "Research and Development" program "recognizes that finding solutions to complex problems often requires forming interdisciplinary project teams, bringing together participants with expertise in the humanities; in preservation; and in information, computer, and natural science."[21]

Online discussion forums also play a large part in supporting interdisciplinary design history scholarship. The Facebook group and listserv for our 2015 NEH Summer Institute has allowed me to continue to share resources, post questions, and receive peer mentoring from my fellow participants. The Design Studies Forum listserv is a low barrier to entry resource for finding out about special issues, opportunities, and conferences that might resonate with interdisciplinary scholars.

That is not to say that interdisciplinarity is not without its faults. For those in academia, the types of articles mentioned above can also be a source of tension when it comes to retention, promotion, and tenure, which is a much larger issue that is beyond the scope of this short chapter. There have been reports over the past few years about the costs of interdisciplinary scholarship, especially to junior faculty. However, it is my hope that as funding agencies place a greater focus on interdisciplinarity, as the number of interdisciplinary journals grows, and as academic programs listen to advice on interdisciplinary retention, promotion, and tenure, that these costs will diminish.[22] In the words of Meredith Davis, at the conclusion of her discussion of design research in "Tenure and Design Research: A Disappointingly Familiar Discussion," "it is time for schools and their measures for faculty performance to catch up."[23]

Conclusion

The NEH Summer Institute was an amazing celebration of diverse, interdisciplinary thought in design history, but our work cannot stop there. Interdisciplinary approaches to design history, such as those I pursue in my case studies, can create new and exciting ways to explore design history. Interdisciplinary approaches to design history also allow researchers to capture the interdisciplinary design processes happening in companies and universities. Therefore, scholars must continue advocating for interdisciplinary approaches through articles and projects, and the journals and institutions that support design history. Additionally, design historians must keep pace with the changing research world as well. While there are inherent risks in doing so, the ultimate rewards include a richer, more inclusive design history.

Notes

1. As I will use it in this piece, "interdisciplinary" is meant as a generic term for multidisciplinary, interdisciplinary, or transdisciplinary.
2. S. Lawson, "How Intel's Ayse Ildeniz Got Fashion Designers and Engineers To Play Nice," *Fast Company*, June 25, 2015: https://www.fastcompany.com/3047630/how-intels-ayse-ildeniz-took-got-fashion-designers-and-engineers-to-play-nic. S. Eden, "The Secret Lab Where Nike Invented the Power-Lacing Shoe of Our Dreams," *Wired*, October 2016: https://www.wired.com/2016/09/nike-self-lacing-design-hyperadapt/
3. The Leading Strand, "About," https://www.theleadingstrand.org/about-me-shift/#bio accessed on March 28, 2018.
4. T. W. Simpson, S. T. Hunter, C. Bryant-Arnold, M. Parkinson, R. R. Barton, D. Celento, and J. Messner, NSF Workshop, 2009, in San Diego, CA.
5. Heller quoted in Teal Triggs, "Designing Graphic Design History," *Journal of Design History*, 22(4) (2009): 329.
6. Kjetil Fallan, *Design History: Understanding Theory and Method* (London: Berg, 2010), p. viii.
7. S. Townsend, and H. Armstrong, "Introduction: The Value of Design in an Academic Context," *Design and Culture*, 9(1) (2017): 68.
8. Harvard University Press, "Graphesis," http://www.hup.harvard.edu/catalog.php?isbn=9780674724938, accessed on February 5, 2018.
9. P. Garvey and A. Drazin, "Design Dispersed: Design History, Design Practice and Anthropology," *Journal of Design History*, 29(1) (2016): 1–7.
10. *Shi Ji*, https://www.journals.elsevier.com/she-ji-the-journal-of-design-economics-and-innovation/, accessed March 28, 2018.
11. Dr. Blaszczyk was a visiting scholar for the NEH Summer Institute. "Regina Lee Blaszczyk," https://webcache.googleusercontent.com/search?q=cache:UhWWy31fWzkJ:https://www.leeds.ac.uk/arts/profile/20030/1153/regina_lee_blaszczyk+&cd=1&hl=en&ct=clnk&gl=us, accessed October 19, 2018.
12. S. E. Vasko, "Perspectives: The Intertwined Histories of Chemistry, Fashion, and Advertising," *Chemical & Engineering News*, August 7, 2017: 24–5.
13. Ibid.
14. Dan Fagin, *Toms River: A Story of Science and Salvation* (New York: Bantam, 2013).
15. Vasko, "Perspectives: The Intertwined Histories of Chemistry, Fashion, and Advertising."
16. Blending design history and digital humanities is also finding its way into the classroom, see K. Garza's talk abstract, "Design History Meets Digital History: A Classroom Experiment for the Texas Digital Humanities Conference 2015," which can be accessed at https://uta-ir.tdl.org/utair/bitstream/handle/10106/25692/Garza.jpg?sequence=1&isAllowed=y
17. E. Schienke, N. Tuana, D. A. Brown, K. J. Davis, K. Keller, and J. S. Shortle, "The Role of the National Science Foundation Broader Impacts Criterion in Enhancing

Research Ethics Pedagogy," *Social Epistemology*, 23 (2009): 317–26. N. Tuana, "Embedding Ethics in the Practices of Science: Bringing Humanities to the Sciences," *Synthese*, 190(11) (2013): 1955–73. Glenn Parsons, *The Philosophy of Design* (Cambridge: Polity, 2015).

18 D. DeLyser, R. Sheehan, and A. Curtis, "eBay and Research in Historical Geography," *Journal of Historical Geography*, 30 (2004): 764–82. K. D. Good, "From Scrapbook to Facebook: A History of Personal Media Assemblage and Archives," *New Media & Society*, 15(4) (2012): 557–73. M. Bird, "Design History Research in the Digital Age," *Design and Culture*, 6(2) (2014): 243–9.

19 S. E. Vasko, manuscript in process, 2018.

20 National Endowment for the Humanities, "Humanities Connections Planning Grants," https://www.neh.gov/grants/education/humanities-connections-planning-grants, accessed February 8, 2018.

21 National Endowment for the Humanities, "Research and Development," https://www.neh.gov/grants/preservation/research-and-development, accessed February 8, 2018.

22 J. T. Klein and H. J. Falk-Krzesinski, "Interdisciplinary and Collaborative Work: Framing Promotion and Tenure Practices and Policies," *Research Policy*, 46(6) (2017): 1055–61.

23 M. Davis, "Tenure and Design Research: A Disappointingly Familiar Discussion," *Design and Culture*, 8(1) (2016): 130.

Notes on the contributors

Nancy Bernardo is an award-winning designer whose design work has been recognized by the Society of Typographic Arts, PRINT Magazine, HOW Magazine, Design Observer, AIGA (American Institute of Graphic Artists), Designers and Books, Creative Quarterly, and AIGA Western New York. She is an Associate Professor of Graphic Design at Rochester Institute of Technology.

Matthew Bird brings his professional experience as a product and exhibition designer into the classroom at the Rhode Island School of Design (RISD), where he teaches design and design history. His knowledge of manufacturing techniques and materials informs his teaching and writing about design history. He also curates shows that introduce design to fine-art museums.

Maria Elena Buszek is Professor of Art History and President's Teaching Scholar at the University of Colorado Denver. Her publications include the books *Pin-Up Grrrls: Feminism, Sexuality, Popular Culture* (Duke University Press, 2006), *Extra/Ordinary: Craft and Contemporary Art* (Duke, 2011), and with Hilary Robinson she co-edited the collection of new writing *A Companion to Feminist Art* (Wiley, 2019). Dr. Buszek's current book project, *Art of Noise*, explores the ties between contemporary activist art and popular music.

Karen L. Carter is Professor of Art History at Kendall College of Art and Design, Ferris State University. Her research on nineteenth-century French posters has been published in *Le Magasin du XIXe siècle*, *Journal of Design History*, *Nineteenth-Century French Studies*, and *Yale French Studies* among others. She co-edited *Foreign Artists and Communities in Modern Paris, 1870–1914: Strangers in Paradise* with Susan Waller (Ashgate, 2015 and Routledge, 2017, paperback).

Marianne Eggler is an art and design historian and educator at the Fashion Institute of Technology and the Museum of Modern Art in New York. She received a BA from the University of Rochester and did her doctoral studies at the City University of New York Graduate Center, focusing on German modern architecture and design.

Russell Flinchum took BA and MA degrees at the University of North Carolina and his PhD in Art History at the Graduate School of the City University of New York in 1998. He has written *Henry Dreyfuss, Industrial Designer* (1997) and *American Design* (2008). He joined the faculty of North Carolina State University's College of Design as Associate Professor in December 2013.

Carma Gorman is Associate Professor in the School of Design and Creative Technologies at the University of Texas at Austin. Her recent writing focuses on how the USA's distinctive laws, regulations, and standards have shaped the national character of American industrial and graphic design.

Gayle L. Goudy, Instructor at the College of Charleston, earned her PhD in the History of Art and Architecture at the University of Oregon and a BFA in Industrial Design from the University of Kansas. She researches the human–machine integration (digital technologies) in art, architecture, and education.

Brockett Horne is a writer, designer, and educator. She teaches Graphic Design at Maryland Institute College of Art and Northeastern University and is Co-Director of the People's Graphic Design Archive.

Jennifer Kaufmann-Buhler is an Associate Professor of Design History at Purdue University in West Lafayette, Indiana. She earned her MA in the History of Design from the RCA/V&A and her PhD from the University of Wisconsin. She is the author of the book *Open Plan: A Design History of the American Office* (Bloomsbury, 2021).

Yelena McLane is a faculty member in the Department of Interior Architecture and Design at Florida State University. Her current research focuses on Soviet design history and technical aesthetics after World War II, exhibition design, and the intersection of spatial configurations and social uses in historic and contemporary architectural settings.

Erica Morawski is Assistant Professor of Design History at Pratt Institute. She received her doctorate from the University of Illinois-Chicago. Her work considers how design mediates relationships between state and populace through approaches that give agency to under-represented voices and expand the canon. Her work currently focuses on the Hispanic Caribbean.

Victoria Rose Pass is an Associate Professor of Design and Art History at the Maryland Institute College of Art. She co-edited the volume *Women's Magazines in Print and New Media* with Noliwe Rooks and Ayana Weekley (Routledge, 2016) which included her essay "Encountering Africa in Vogue: Irving Penn's African Essays." Her essay "Racial Masquerades in the Magazines: Defining White Femininity Between the Wars" was published in the *Journal of Modern Periodical Studies* in 2020. She received her PhD in Visual and Cultural Studies from the University of Rochester.

David Raizman (1951–2021) was Distinguished University Professor Emeritus in the Westphal College of Media Arts and Design at Drexel University in Philadelphia, PA. Dr. Raizman was the author of *History of Modern Design* (Laurence King and Pearson Publishing, 2nd edn. 2010) and *Reading Graphic Design History: Image, Text, and Context* (Bloomsbury, 2021).

Sara Desvernine Reed, PhD, is an adjunct professor in the Department of Interior Design at Virginia Commonwealth University in Richmond, VA, where she teaches undergraduate- and graduate-level courses in the history and theory of interior environments.

Stephanie E. Vasko received her PhD in Chemistry and Nanotechnology from the University of Washington. She is currently a Senior UX Researcher for MESH Research at Michigan State University. Her research interests include the intersections of sound production, archival work, performance, and augmented reality.

Christopher S. Wilson, PhD, teaches architecture and design history at Ringling College of Art and Design, Sarasota, Florida. Dr. Wilson has earned three different degrees on three different continents: B. Arch, Temple University, USA; Master of Arts, Architectural Association, London, England; and PhD, Middle East Technical University, Ankara, Turkey.

Emily Wolf is an adjunct lecturer in Historic Preservation at Boston Architectural College. A graduate of the University of Chicago and the University of Pennsylvania School of Design, she formerly served as the Boston Landmarks Commission's Architectural Historian. Her current research focuses on intersections between architectural history and heritage conservation.

Index

Numbers in *italics* indicate illustrations

Acme Attractions 99
adventure play 171–2
   in physical spaces 172–80, 185
   in video games 180–6
advertisement. *See also* branding
   dye plant, Toms River 230–1
   Futurama lipstick *117*
   home modernization 50–1, 52, *53*, 54–5, 57–62
   Intel 231
   print ads 115–18
   racial stereotypes 129–30, *135*, *138*, 139–40
   Scotch tape dispenser *118*
   Soviet Union 19–20, *24*
   TV ads 114
   William Pahlmann 189, *190*, 193, 200
aesthetics
   Afro-futuristic aesthetic 163–5
   architecture 57, 78
   Mangbetu women 151–2
   radios 22
affordability 119
affordances 44–5
"Affording Meaning" (Almquist and Lupton) 44–5
Africa 154, 157, 162. *See also* La Croisière Noire (The Black Crossing)
African-American artists 163–5
African-American culture 131
African-Americans 129–30, 138. *See also* Baker, Josephine
Afro-futuristic aesthetic 163–5
After Taste: Expanded Practice in Interior Design (Sparke) 191
Agnès 155–6, 158–60
Albertine, Viv 87–8, 94–5, 97
Almquist, Julka 44–5
amateurs 113–14

"Ambassadeurs" poster (Lévy) *138*
American Society of Interior Designers (ASID) 195
Ancient Egypt 149, 150, 152
Anglomania 105
appropriation. *See also* Mangbetu coiffeur
   African culture 130, 131, 134–5, 137
   Black Lives Matter 139
   detournement 90
   Native Americans 140
   punk 89, 97
architectural tourism 84
architecture 194, 195. *See also* commercial architecture; modern architecture
   aesthetics 78
Armstrong's Idea House *50*
Art Deco 134, 152–4, 158, 196
Asian design 200, 202
Association of Interior Decorators (AID) 195
auction house websites 113
Aunt Jemima 129–30, 137, 139
Austin 8 214
automotive design
   General Motors (GM) 209–10, 216
   Packard Caribbean 217–19, *220*

Baker, Josephine 132–7, 150, 156, *157*, 159, *164*
Baum, Joseph 195
Baya Weaver nest *180*
Beaufort Market 99
Best magazine *106*
"Better Homes Contest" (*Better Homes & Gardens* magazine) 52, 54
Better Homes in America 52
Better Housing News Flashes (FHA) 54, 57–8, 61

Beyoncé 163, 164, 170 n. 75
bias 1–2, 8–9
Black Crossing, The (La Croisière Noire) 145, 147–9, 150
   film 145, 148, 150, *153*, 156, 159–60
Black Panther, The (film) 163, 165
Blaszczyk, Regina Lee 6, 229
bondage 100
bondage suit 95–6, 98
bondage trousers 97
"boss key" feature 40
Bowie, David 89
brand identity 129–30, 145, 154–5
branding
   Agnès 148
   Daché, Lilly 161
   Soviet Union 32
   William Pahlmann 190–4, 203
British Library, *Punk 1976–78* exhibition 87, *88*
building types and styles 81
business 9–10

canon 1–2
Caribbean. *See* Packard Caribbean
caricatures 143 n. 33
cars. *See* automotive design; Citroën
Carter, Ruth E. 165
Cassilly, Bob 172–5
Celotex Corporation 62–3
Center for Interdisciplinarity (C4I), Michigan State University 232
"Charles R. Runkin Building" 74–5
chemistry 229
Cherry, Neneh 99, *101*
children 172, 175, 177, 179
Citroën 145, 147, 148, 154
City Museum 173–5, 184
Clash, The 93, 101–2, 102–5, *106*
CLOTHES CLOTHES CLOTHES (Albertine) 87–8
Colin, Paul
   La Revue nègre 134, *135*
   Le Tumulte noir 134, *136*
Colonial Williamsburg 63
colonialism 130, 137, 147
commercial architecture 78–9
computer games. *See* video games
computers 40

Congo. *See also* Mangbetu coiffeur; Mangbetu people; Mangbetu women
consumerism 17
consumers 5
control 36, 43–4
Coon, Caroline 87, 89, 94, 96–7, 103, *104*
cosmetics 155
cost 119
Cousins, Margaret 193
Creem magazine 89
Crowd, The (film) 35
cultural appropriation. *See* appropriation
cultural goods, Soviet Union 17–18
   and cultured masses 18–20
   and design 20–1
   end of 30–2
   kul'ttovary store *18*
   musical instruments 26–7
   photography 25–6
   radios 22–3, *24*
   record players 23–5
   sports equipment 27–9
   toys 29, *30*
cultured masses 18–20
"Curtain Wars" (Sanders) 194
Curtis, Williams J. R. 73
cyberloafing 40

Daché, Lilly 161
danse sauvage (savage dance) 133, 134
Dattner, Richard 172
de Wolfe, Elsie 194
Design and Culture (journal) 228
design history
   canonical approach 1–2
   definitions of good design 122–3
   diversity 3, 10–11
   interdisciplinarity 11–12, 227–33
   role of 3–4
designers 7–8. *See also individual designers*
   as corporate ethnographers 36–7
detournement 90–1
digital resources 111–12
   amateurs 113–14
   combined use 120–2
   images 112–13
   online inflation calculators 119
   patent searches 119–20

print advertisement 115–18
video 114
diversity 3, 10–11, 45–6, 131
DIY ethos 98–9
DIY movement 56, 63
Dog Day Afternoon, A (film) 73
Dohrs, MaryEllen 209–21
    childhood 213, 214
    education 214–15
    Food Mill for Landers *217*
    General Motors (GM) 209–10, 215–17
    interior scheme for Packard *221*
    jukebox for Seeberg *222*
    "Kid-Size" folding table and chairs for Samsonite *218*
    Le Sabre 209, *210*, *223*
    "Medallion" luggage for Samsonite *219*
    military intelligence 210–12
    Packard Caribbean *220*
    sketch of modular kitchen *216*, *222*
    Sundberg-Ferar 209, 213–14, 217–19
    Water Wagon, 1958 *212*
"Don's Boss Page" 40, *41*
Douglas, Aaron 152, 154–5, 163
Draper, Dorothy 194
Dunand, Jean 158, 169 n. 56
Dundes, Alan 39
Dyason, Mathew 184

Earl, Harley 209–10, 214, 215, *223*
eBay 113–14, 120
education 30
Elliott-Said, Marianne Joan. *See* Styrene, Poly
environmental justice 2–3
ethno-eroticism 133, 134, 149–50, 151, 155, 162
ethnographic imagery 147–51
    aesthetic appeal 151–2
    as brand identity 154–5
    stylization 152–4
exoticism 200

fabrics 200
Fallan, Kjetil 228
fashion 11. *See also* punk fashion
    Lemonade (film) 164
    racial othering 155–61

fashion design 229
fashion intermediaries 6
Federal Housing Administration (FHA) 54, 57–8
feminism 93, 96–7, 100
Field Museum, Chicago 150, 167 n. 27
film 114, 148, 150
    Black Panther, The 163, 165
    Crowd, The (film) 35
    Dog Day Afternoon, A 73
    La Croisière Noire 145, 148, 150, *153*, 156, 159–60
    Lemonade 163, 164–5, 170 n. 75
    racial stereotypes 134–5, 150
    Taxi Driver 73–4
Fish, Phil 181
Fitch, James Marston 49, 63
Flickr 113
folk art 198, 200
Food Mill (Dohrs) *217*
Forum of the Twelve Caesars Restaurant 195, *196*
Four Seasons restaurant 195, 197
France 133–4, 135, 137, 147
Frith, Simon 89
Futurama lipstick 114–17
futuristic aesthetic 163–5

Game Score Fanfare (Dyason) 184
gaming. *See* video games
Garner, James 71–2
Gaudí, Antonio 176
    inverted catenary arch model *177*
gay culture. *See* queer culture
gender 130. *See also* women
General Motors (GM) 209–10, 215–17
Girard, Alexander 200
globalization 139
Goldman, Vivienne 99, *101*
good design 122–3, 196
Google 119
Google Images 112, 120
Granny Takes a Trip 90
graphic design 130–1
    racial stereotypes 134–40
Graphic Design: A New History (Eskilson) 130
Green, John Lawrence 214

Haardt, George-Maris 145, 148, 149, 150
hairstyles. *See* Mangbetu coiffeur
Harper's Bazaar 159
hats 155–6, *157*, 158, 159–61
    Lemonade 170 n. 75
Hebdige, Dick 89
high modernism 196
historic preservation 50, 51, 57, 61–4
History of Interior Design, A (Pile) 197
Hoffman, Malvina 150–1
"Home Improvement Pictorial, The" (Celotex Corporation) 62–3
home modernization 49–51
    government programs 54
    market for 52–4, 54–6
    mediated modernism 57–61
    as preservation 61–4
Home Modernization Bureau 52
homebuyers 61
homeownership 51–2, 56, 191
Horne, Brockett
    notebook sketch *2*
    visual presentation of the book *4*
"house of tomorrow" 58, *59*
Housing Home and Finance Agency 61

identity 8–9
image-first browsing 112–13, 120
images. *See* ethnographic imagery
Imagination Playground (Rockwell) 185
Imagining Consumers (Blaszczyk) 6
inclusion 124
income 191
industrial design 214–15, 217–19. *See also* product design
inflation calculators 119
Intel 231
interdisciplinarity 11–12, 227–9
    case studies 230–1
    future 231–2
interior decorating 194–8, 202–3
interior design 191, 192, 195
intermediaries 6–7
internet 111–12, 139. *See also* digital resources
internet usage 40–2

Japan 176–80
Japanese culture 202

Jarman, Derek 93
jazz 157–8, 169 n. 52
jewelry 158
Jim Crow Laws 131, 132
Jim Crow Museum 137–9
Johanna Drucker 228
Johnson, Philip 195–6, 197, 198
Jordan (née Pamela Rooke) 93–4, 95–6
Journal of Design History 228
Journey (video game) 180–1, 182–4
jukebox for Seeberg (Dohrs) *222*

"Kaleidoscape" (MacAdam) *175*
Keck, George Fred 58
Kendall College of Art and Design (KCAD) 130–1
"Kid-Size" folding table and chairs (Dohrs) *218*
King Mob group 90–1
knitted spaces 175–80
Kostellow, Alexander 214, *215*
Ku Klux Klan 132
kul'ttovary 17–18
    and cultured masses 18–20
    and design 20–1
    end of 30–2
    kul'ttovary store *18*
    musical instruments 26–7
    photography 25–6
    radios 22–3, *24*
    record players 23–5
    sports equipment 27–9
    toys 29, *30*

La Croisière Noire (The Black Crossing) 145, 147–9, 150
    film 145, 148, 150, *153*, 156, 159–60
La Revue nègre 132–4, *135*
Laktionov, Aleksandr 31
Le Sabre 209, *210*, *223*
Le Tumulte noir (Colin) 134, *136*
Legend of Zelda, The (video game) 181
Lemke, Sieglinde 133–4
Lemonade (film) 163, 164–5, 170 n. 75
Lenin, Vladimir 18, 22
Les Jolly Koon'ess poster (Lévy) *138*
Levine, Alison Murray 148
Lévy, Emil 137
    "Ambassadeurs" poster *138*

Lichtman, Sarah 130
Linder Sterling 97
lipstick 114–17
litigation 172, 175
London 89–90
Los Angeles 72, 73, 74, 78, 81
"Loves/Hates T-shirt 91–2, 93
Lunarcharskiy, Anatoliy 20
Lupton, Julia 44–5

MacAdam, Toshiko Horiuchi 175–80
MacDonald, Freda Josephine. *See* Baker, Josephine
managerial control 36
Manchester 90, 97
Mangbetu artists 155
Mangbetu coiffeur 148–9, 152, 154–5
  African-American artists 163–5
  European designers 162–3
  hats inspired by 155–6, *157*, 158, 159–61
Mangbetu people 145, 148–9
Mangbetu women 147, 149, 150–1, 156, 162. *See also* Nobosodru
McLaren, Malcolm 90, 91–3, 98–9, 100
"Medallion" luggage (Dohrs) *219*
mediated modernism 57–61
Megg's History of Graphic Design (Megg and Purvis) 130
Michigan State University 232
Michon, Alex 97, 100–1, 102–5
  Best magazine *106*
Microsoft Windows 40
military intelligence 210–12
misuse 38–44
  versus use 44–6
modern architecture 72–8
  multiple modernisms 84
  vernacular modernism 78–83
modern design 122–3
modernism 10
  mediated 57–61
  multiple modernisms 84
  vernacular 78–83, 84
modernization of homes 49–51
  government programs 54
  market for 52–4, 54–6
  mediated modernism 57–61
  as preservation 61–4
Montgomery Ward plumbing catalogue *55*

Moving to a New Apartment (Laktionov) 31–2
Mugler, Thierry 162–3
Muller-Munk, Peter 119–20, 153
Multiple Hammock No. 1 (MacAdam) *177*
multiple modernisms 84
museum collections 112
museums. *See* City Museum
music 25, 90, 157–8
musical education 27
musical instruments 26–7

National Endowment of the Humanities (NEH) Summer Institute 1, 232–3
National Geographic 148, 150
National Historic Preservation Act 1966 63
"National Home Improvement Year" 56
National Housing Act 1934 54
National Science Foundation 228
Nefertiti 152
nest of Baya Weavers *180*
Net of Woods (MacAdam) 179–80
New York 73–4
Nobosodru 145, *146*, 149, 150
  aesthetic appeal 151–2, 156, 158, 161–2, 163
  appropriation 165
  as brand identity 154–5
  stylization 152–4
non-work 35, 38–42. *See also* sabotage

Obama, Barack 138
office design 35, 36–8, 45
office technologies 38
  alternative uses 44–6
  misuse 38–43
"Oh Bondage! Up Yours! (Poly Styrene) 99, 100
Olympic Games 29
online inflation calculators 119
online patent searches 119–20
online resources. *See* digital resources
open plan offices 36, 37
Opportunity Magazine 152
organizational control 36, 43–4
organizational misbehavior 35, 38–43
organizational power structures 37–8

othering
  in fashion 155–61
  Mangbetu people 145, 147, 149, 150, 151
  in modernism 202–3
  William Pahlmann 198–202

Packard Caribbean 217–19, *220*
Pagter, Carl 39
"Pahlmann Peruvian" model rooms 198–9
Pahlmann, William 189
  as brand-maker 190–4
  versus the canon 202–3
  interior decorating 194–8
  other cultures 198–202
  Surrealism 197, 205 n. 36
Paris 133, 135, 137
patents 21, 119–20, 120–1, 122
  lipstick case *116*
"Path of the Sun" fabrics 200, *201*
Pavlish, Don 40
Peltzman Effect 174
personal computers 40
personal hygiene 19–20
personal signatures 191
photocopiers 39–40
photography 25–6
  La Croisière Noire (The Black Crossing) 145, *146*, 147, 150
physical play 172–80, 185
Pile, John 36–7, 197
Pinterest 113
PLAY WORK BUILD 185
playgrounds 171–2, 185. *See also* adventure play
pop boutiques 90
pornography 42
Portugal 200
"Post-Modern Architecture" 73
Pratt Institute 214–15
preservation. *See* historic preservation
price 119
primitivism 130, 141 n. 11, 145–7, 148, 151
print advertisement 115–18
Processed World 42–3
product design. *See also* industrial design
  definitions of good design 122–3
  Soviet Union 17–18, 20–1
propaganda 17, 22, 25, 27, 138
public health 19–20

punk
  definitions 89
  feminism 96–7
  origins 89–90
  women 87, 88, 93, 94, 96, 102–3
Punk (magazine) 89
Punk 1976–78 exhibition 87, *88*
Punk: Chaos to Couture 105
punk fashion 88–90
  Alex Michon 102–5, *106*
  Poly Styrene 99–100
  Westwood and McLaren 90–6, 97–9, 100
punk rock 89
purchase price 119

queer culture 89–90

race 99, 130, 131
"Races of Man" exhibition, Field Museum, Chicago 150, 167 n. 27
racial stereotypes 129–31, 150. *See also* ethnographic imagery; Nobosodru; othering; primitivism
  contemporary advertisement 139, 140
  Jim Crow Museum 137–9
  La Revue nègre 132–4, *135*
  Le Tumulte noir (Colin) 136
racism 156
radios 22–3, *24*
Ratton, Charles 161, 169 n. 66
record players 23–5
Reed, Lou 89
Reinecke, Jean Otis 120–1, *122*
restaurants 195, *196*, 197
Revlon lipstick 114–17
Rhodes, Bernard 91–2, 93, 101–2
Robertson's Jam Company 129
Rockford Files, The 71–2
  modern architecture 72–8
  multiple modernisms 84
  vernacular modernism 78–83
Rockwell, David 185
Rooke, Pamela. *See* Jordan (née Pamela Rooke)
Rosen, Jeff 151
"Runkin Building" 74–5
Russia 17. *See also* Soviet Union

sabotage 42–3
Saint Laurent, Yves 162
Sanders, Joel 194
"Santa Monica County Building" 75, *76*
Savage, Jon 93, 94, 97, 103, 105
savage dance (*danse sauvage*) 133, 134
Schildkrout, Enid 147, 149, 155, 156, 168 n. 42
school supplies 30
Scotch tape dispenser 115, *118*, 120–2, 122–3
sculptures 150–1, 155
Seditionaries 93
segregationism 131, 132
SEX (shop) 91, 93
Sex Pistols 89, 93, 94
SEX T-shirt 91–2, 93
sexuality. *See* ethno-eroticism
Shaginyan, Marietta 23
Shah Mosque, Ishfahan 177, *178*
Shaw, Greg 89
She Ji 228–9
Sheraton, Mimi 197
signatures 191
Simonon, Paul 102, 103
Siouxsie Sioux 90
Situationist International (SI) movement 90–1
skull elongation 148, 149, 150, 151, 152, 156
social justice 2–3
social media 112
Soliwoda, Gail 173, 174
South America 198–9
Soviet Union
    cultural goods 17–18, 20–1, 30–2
    cultured masses 18–20
    kul'ttovary store *18*
    musical instruments 26–7
    patent system 21
    photography 25–6
    radios 22–3, *24*
    record players 23–5
    sports equipment 27–9
    toys 29, *30*
Sparke, Penny 191
Specht, George 145, 152, 153, 154
sports equipment 27–9
stereotypes 143 n. 33. *See also* racial stereotypes

streamlining 154
Strummer, Joe 102, 105, *106*
Styrene, Poly 99–100
Sundberg, Carl 209, 213, 217
Sundberg-Ferar 209, 213–14, 217–19
Surrealism 197, 205 n. 36
surveillance 36

Taking of Pelham One Two Three, The 73
"Takino Rainbow Nest" (MacAdam) *176*
tape dispensers 115, *118*, 120–2, 122–3
taste 191
Taxi Driver 73–4
Teague, Dick 217, 218
technology 148. *See also* video games
television 22, 114, 193. *See also Rockford Files, The*
textile spaces 175–80
tile work 177, *178*
time theft 35. *See also* non-work
"Tits T-shirt" 94–5
Toms River 230–1
Too Fast To Live Too Young To Die 90, 91. *See also* SEX (shop)
Toshi Net (MacAdam) *175*
tourism, architectural 84
Townsend, S. and Armstrong, H. 228
toys 29, *30*
turbans 155–6, *157*, 158, 159–61
typewriters 38, 39–40

"Uncle Tom" 130
use 44–6. *See also* misuse
user-generated content 113–14
users 5, 45–6

van der Rohe, Mies 197–8
vernacular modernism 78–83, 84
Victor, Sally 161
video 114
video games 180–6, *181*, 187 n. 22
Vogue 158, *159*

Waring blender 119–20
Water Wagon (Dohrs, 1958) *212*
web resources. *See* digital resources
Weimar Republic inspirations 89–90

Westwood, Vivienne 90, 91, 93–4, 98–9, 100
    bondage suit 95–6, 98
    bondage trousers 97
    feminism 93, 97
    SEX T-shirt 91–2, 93
    "Tits T-shirt" 94–5
What Is Modern Design? (Kaufmann) 122–3
Windosill (video game) 180–1, 182
With Heritage So Rich 63

women. *See also individual women*
    Mangbetu women 147, 149, 150–1, 156, 162
    in punk 87, 88, 93, 94, 96, 102–3
work. *See* non-work
work ethic 214

Yost, L. Morgan, modernization scheme 60
YouTube 114

Zelda (video game) 181

www.ingramcontent.com/pod-product-compliance
Ingram Content Group UK Ltd.
Pitfield, Milton Keynes, MK11 3LW, UK
UKHW021905220326
469204UK00008B/203